African American Manumissions of Washington County, Maryland

Marsha Lynne Fuller, CGRS

HERITAGE BOOKS
2019

HERITAGE BOOKS
AN IMPRINT OF HERITAGE BOOKS, INC.

Books, CDs, and more—Worldwide

For our listing of thousands of titles see our website
at
www.HeritageBooks.com

Published 2019 by
HERITAGE BOOKS, INC.
Publishing Division
5810 Ruatan Street
Berwyn Heights, Md. 20740

Copyright © 1997 Marsha Lynne Fuller, CGRS

Heritage Books by the author:
African American Manumissions of Washington County, Maryland
Family Bible Records in the Washington County Free Library, Hagerstown, Maryland
Naturalizations of Washington County, Maryland, Prior to 1880
*St. Mary's Catholic Church Records:
1818–1900, Hagerstown, Washington County, Maryland*

All rights reserved. No part of this book may be reproduced or transmitted in any form or by any means, electronic or mechanical, including photocopying, recording or by any information storage and retrieval system without written permission from the author, except for the inclusion of brief quotations in a review.

International Standard Book Number
Paperbound: 978-1-58549-716-4

This book is dedicated to my brother,

Mark Guthrie Fuller

"a man for all seasons"

Acknowledgments

My grateful thanks to the following people who helped to make this book possible:

Douglas G. Bast, Boonsboro, Maryland

Marguerite Ann Doleman, author of *We the Blacks of Washington County*, Hagerstown, Maryland

John Frye, Director, Western Maryland Room, Washington County Free Library

Rick L. Hemphill, Administrative Officer/Deputy Clerk of the Circuit Court of Washington County, Maryland

Kristin L. Higgins-Chilcote, Washington County Public Schoolteacher, and Master's Degree Candidate in History at   Shippensburg University

Patricia Nowell Holland, Sharpsburg, Maryland

Wendell Joice, Ph.D., Washington, DC

Robb Jones and Lucinda McDonald Jones, Rohrersville, Maryland

Table of Contents

Freeing Slaves: Clues to the Past

How to Use This Book

Key to Symbols, Definitions and Abbreviations

Appendix

    A - Magistrate's Guide and Manumission Laws

    B - Emancipation Proclamation

    C - The Constitution of the United States

    D - African American Populations

    E - Excerpts from the Family Bible of Nathaniel Nesbitt

    F - Diary and Letter of Otho Nesbitt

    G - Original Slave Documents

    H - Civil War Documents

    I - Newspaper Articles

    J - Washington County Court Documents

Washington County Manumission Book A

Washington County Manumission Book B

Index

This original slave auction block, which sat near the Washington County Courthouse, is now on the property of Bruce and Kathleen Hynes at 821 The Terrace, Hagerstown, Maryland. There is a plaque on the block which reads "Gen. Andrew Jackson and Henry Clay spoke from this slave block in Hagerstown during 1830."

Photograph by Marsha L. Fuller

Freeing Slaves: Clues to the Past

he concept of slavery is so deplorable to any thinking person that it assaults the mind: tearing husband from wife; mother from child; brother from brother. The very idea is beyond belief! The stories I have read while researching this book fill me with sadness, and have brought tears to my eyes on more than one occasion.

However, on the following pages, you will find the starting points of new lives for these people brought to a country against their will. They worked hard and they survived. These are stories of hope, rebirth and new life. I hope that everyone will treasure them.

<u>Manumission Papers</u>
Acquiring one's manumission papers must have been a time of almost unbelievable excitement in the life of an African American in the nineteenth century. To finally be free ... to be able to call one's life one's own...to live where one wanted...to legally marry whom one chose...the thrills of a lifetime!

Freed men and women needed to carry their manumission documents at all times. The reason for these documents was to prove that the carrier of them was, indeed, a free person. A physical description was included in the document so the person could prove that it belonged to him or her - that it had not been stolen from someone else. As a professional genealogist, I know what a joy that finding these descriptions can be to present-day descendants who cherish the word pictures of their ancestors.

After languishing for over a century in the basement of the Washington County Courthouse, it seems only fitting that the records of these people should be brought to light -

African American Manumissions

their voices should be heard - the legacy of their memory should be passed down to their descendants.

There are many fascinating vignettes within the following pages: a free African American who fought in the Revolutionary War; speakers of the German language; players of musical instruments; professional iron workers; and steerers of canal boats on the C & O Canal. This is real life, just as it was lived so many years ago.

I hope that this book proves useful to everyone. If you do find a mistake in this book, please notify me by writing to the publisher; I will not be offended. I know well that no work is perfect. My only wish is to make this as correct and complete a record as possible of the African American manumissions of Washington County. Your help will make future editions more accurate and will assist others who are doing similar research.

Mood of the Times

The men and women who freed their slaves were among the prominent members of Washington County business and society: people such as Frisby Tilghman, William Gabby, William Fitzhugh, and William Price were Presidential Electors; Zacharias Clagett was a State Senator; John T. Mason, Daniel Heister and Samuel Ringgold Congressmen; and Nathaniel Rochester a member of the House of Delegates, the Sheriff and the first postmaster of Hagerstown.

The area of Ringgold in northern Washington County was named for Samuel Ringgold's family, and the village of Tilghmanton in the southern part of the county for Frisby Tilghman's family. A point of interest is that Rochester left Hagerstown in 1810 and went north to become the founder of the city of Rochester, New York.

of Washington County, Maryland

There were several ways to manumit a slave: through a manumission; through a Deed of Manumission; and through a Certificate of Freedom as part of a last will and testament. Here are some examples of the latter two:

Washington County Land Record K 674
At the request of Negro Ceasar the following Certificate was recorded the 17. day of January 1798. I hereby Certify that Cesar a black Man so called the Bearer was slave to Thomas May of the State of Delaware Iron Master who by will, recorded in the Records at new Castle Granted him full Liberty and Freedom to take effect on the sixteenth day of February in the year of our Lord one thousand seven hundred and ninety five - which time being now fully compleat & ended as by the said Will is declared the Extracts whereof is lodged amongst the papers of the Pennsylvania Incorporated Society for promoting the abolition of slavery etc. Thomas Harris Secty to acting Committe of Abolition Society, Philad. 3 m. 23. 1795.

Washington County Land Record K 705
At the request of Negro Bob Negro Milly & Negro Patty Manumission the following Deed was recorded the 13th Day of February 1798.
Washington County State of Maryland know all men by thease [sic] Presents that I Thomas Prather of the said County Believing it to be unjust to hold any of the Human spieceies [sic] in Slavery Do hereby for myself my hieres [sic] Executors administrators or assigns Manumit Set free and forever Relinquish all title or Claime to one Negroe boy Named Bob after he Shall arrive to the age of Twenty four years likewise two Negroe girls Children Named Milly and Patty after they Shall arrive to the age of Twenty years Agreeable to an act of Assembly in Such Cases made and Provided In testimony hereof I have hereunto Set my hand and affix my seal this thirteenth day of February Seventeen hundred and Ninety Eight.

African American Manumissions

Thomas Prather Seal, Witness: J. Schnebly, Land Recordsumm[?], JordHary[?]

The Civil War

The movement toward the freeing of slaves in America was fueled by the growing influence of religious beliefs that man was a divine creature and, as such, could not be subjugated to the will of others.

Organized in December 1833 at Philadelphia, the American Anti-Slavery Society (abolitionists) grew to more than one thousand societies in America by 1838, with almost 250,000 members. [See newspaper excerpts in Appendix I]

By two decades later, anti-slavery feelings had risen to a feverish pitch. "On a quiet Sunday, October 16, 1859, John Brown, an abolitionist, who laid plans at his farm located in Pleasant Valley [in Washington County] raided the placid town of Harpers Ferry, at the scenic confluence of the Potomac and Shenandoah Rivers. Brown and his followers seized the Federal Armory. The episode electrified the nation. The possibility of slave uprising horrified and terrified the South. In the North, the hanging of John Brown in December placed his name first on the list abolitionary martyrs. The time had come when the South knew that her existence as a slave-holding territory depended on separation from an anti-slavery union. The Civil War ensued." - *The First Two Centuries of the Washington County Courthouse*, The Commissioners of Washington County, 1974, Hagerstown, Maryland [See map for location of Pleasant Valley, and the index for a list of manumitted slaves from there. See Appendix H for public announcement of hanging.]

The Battle of Antietam at Sharpsburg, in Washington County, on September 17, 1862, was a defining moment of the Civil War. It was the bloodiest single day of battle of

of Washington County, Maryland

the war, with over 23,000 soldiers lying dead or wounded at day's end. This event changed the entire course of the war; from then on, the Union was in a winning position.

During the first year of the War Between the States, great pressure had been put on President Abraham Lincoln to declare freedom for the slaves in those states which had seceded from the Union. The Union victory at the Battle of Antietam gave him the opportunity he needed. President Lincoln issued a preliminary version of the Emancipation Proclamation on September 22, 1862. It stated that, after January, 1, 1863, slaves in areas still fighting against the Union would be free. Issuance of the Emancipation Proclamation paved the way for European countries to provide aid and support to the North because Europe did not believe in slavery and would not support the South in its pro-slavery stance.

Underground Railroad
There is speculation that the Underground Railroad went through Washington County. It is likely that it did but, unfortunately, I could find no proof of this. It may be that it was unnecessary to house anyone here overnight because the slaves could be hidden in Virginia and brought north across this tiny six-mile-wide strip of Maryland into Pennsylvania before dawn broke on the horizon.

African Americans in Washington County
Nathan Williams, his parents and siblings, born slaves, were purchased by a Quaker woman from Washington County who freed them in 1826. Quakers did not believe in slavery; many of them bought slaves so that they could free them. Williams became the owner of the well-known Fort Frederick where his own grandmother had taken refuge during the Pontiac uprising. He farmed the land until his death in 1884. His wife and children continued to run it until 1911. A picture of him can be seen on the cover

African American Manumissions

of the January 1990 issue of the "Maryland Cracker Barrel" magazine.

James W. C. Pennington was a minister and civil rights worker. Born and raised in Washington County, he lived from 1809 until 1870.

Henry O. Wagoner was born in Hagerstown on February 27, 1812. He was a civil rights activist and correspondent for Frederick Douglass' newspaper. He later moved West to become the first African American deputy sheriff of Arapaho County, Colorado.

Lass Long, born into slavery, lived his entire life at Hancock. He remembered plucking chickens to feed officers of the Union Army during the Civil War.

Joseph Moxley was also born a slave in Hancock. He was later freed and subsequently enlisted in the Civil War. He fought at the Battle of the Wilderness in 1864. He was a Musician First Class, in the United States Colored Troops, and a member of Moxley's Number One Brigade Band. - *Roster of Civil War Soldiers from Washington County, Maryland*, Roger Keller, 1993, Genealogical Publishing Co., Baltimore.

Slaves at Work in Washington County

Colonel John Blackford was the owner of a ferry service which ran from Washington County across the Potomac River to Shepherdstown, West Virginia. In his journals of 1839, he talks about his slaves who managed and ran the ferry. They seem to have had a great deal of responsibility and needed very little supervision. [Photocopies of journals are in the Western Maryland Room, Washington County Free Library.]

John Brien and John McPherson owned Catoctin Iron Works in Frederick County, and Antietam Iron Works

of Washington County, Maryland

which was situated about three miles below Sharpsburg at Mouth of Antietam. John Brien's grandson was later named John McPherson Brien, in honor of his partner. References to slaves who worked in the iron industry at Antietam Iron Works are seen in Entries # A9a, A10a, A35a, A38a, A38b.

The following account of the Antietam Iron Works is from *A History of Washington County, Maryland*, Thomas J.C. Williams, 1906, John M. Runk & L.R. Titsworth

"The old Nail Factory at Antietam Iron Works, owned at the time by John McPherson Brien, was burned on the 25th of April 1841. It was rebuilt, increased in size and in successful operation in two months. These works situated about three hundred yards from the junction of the Antietam and the Potomac, gave employment in 1811 to two hundred white laborers and sixty slaves. To these slaves Mr. Brien was a remarkably kind master and it was said that their clothing, food and general condition of happiness were superior to those enjoyed by any free negroes." p. 247

Further information on the Antietam Iron Works comes from *The Iron Industry in Western Maryland*, Michael D. Thompson, 1976, West Virginia University, Morgantown, West Virginia

"Slaves employed permanently at the Catoctin Furnace [in Frederick County] were few in number when compared to the slave population at the Antietam Iron Works. Of course, this would not rule out the use of large numbers of freed slaves and other blacks, especially in the cutting of large quantities of timber needed for charcoaling. The census and personal property assessment records portray a mixed picture of these slave holdings. By 1830, it appeared that Brien and McPherson had as many as 20 male slaves of mature age who could have been employed at the Catoctin Iron Works. This figure dropped off considerably in 1835 and again in 1841. Those few who remained may have been either highly skilled artisans or house slaves. None of these slaves appears to have been transferred to the subsequent furnace owner, Peregrine Fitzhugh." p. 85

"After the death of John McPherson in 1833, John McPherson Brien purchased his grandfather's part ownership in the Antietam Iron Works...The Antietam Iron Works, at the time of John McPherson's death, was a considerable establishment, ranking with some of the largest industrial plants in the United States at that time." p. 87

"The Antietam Iron Works in 1840 was valued at $80,000 and employed 250 persons. By 1830, the iron works owned 45 slaves, of which 28 males and females were of a working age. This number had grown in 1840 to 53, of which 35 could be considered in their prime work age.

"Both Scharf and Williams, in their histories of Washington County, pointed out that John McPherson Brien was a kind master. However, the reality of the iron works' financial difficulties must have made slave life bleaker than it normally would have been. A clue to slave dissatisfaction with the life at the iron works was supplied by John McPherson Brien in a letter to Jonathan Meredith of Baltimore.

"There is a good deal of dissatisfaction among the negroes...many of them came to me and expressed their unwillingness to remain with me, to my great ___[?], for I have always treated them most kindly, this is indeed gross ingratitude; what would you have me to do with those who have shown such ungratification. It would be circus loss to me if they leave this place for Pennsylvania." p. 90

<u>of Washington County, Maryland</u>

"This letter [from John McPherson Brien to Jonathan Meredith, June 12, 1848, Meredith Papers, Maryland Historical Society, and Washington County Land Record Book, YY 281 and 403-404] was written after the iron works had ceased operation and the free workers discharged. The slaves were no doubt hungry at times, and when they did eat, it was a fare of bacon and bread and little else." Footnote on p. 91

There is a reference in the journals of Dr. Augustin A. Biggs, Sharpsburg, Maryland, to the account of "John McP. Brien" for "April 10, 1849 - Treated Luke, dispensed pills". The bill was $1.00. [Journals are in the Western Maryland Room, Washington County Free Library.]

In the manumission documents, some slaves are listed as working at "Jacques Furnace." This reference is to Green Spring Furnace which was owned by the Jacques family. References to slaves who worked at Green Spring Furnace are seen in Entries # A13a, A50b, A51a. [See map for location near Clear Spring.]

Slave Block

In *We the Blacks of Washington County*, 1976, Washington County Bicentenniel Committee, Marguerite Doleman states that "There was an old slave block where auctions were held, located on Jonathan Street where the side entrance to the Hamilton Hotel now stands. The block has since been moved." It is now in the front yard of the house formerly owned by the Hamilton family, very near to where I grew up. This property was originally known as Oak Hill Farm. The location is further corroborated by John Frye, Director of the Western Maryland Room, Washington County Free Library, who says that he was always told that this slave block was moved from the courthouse to somewhere in the north end of Hagerstown.

African American Manumissions

It is said that there is an original slave block on the main street of Sharpsburg in the southern part of the county. Some feel that this is more likely a carriage step-up; townspeople and local historians are undecided. John Frye agrees with the carriage step-up theory because, traditionally, there was only one slave block in a county, located near the courthouse.

Washington County, Maryland

Washington County, formed out of Frederick County in 1776, sits on the crossroads of two major travel routes, the National Road (present-day U.S. Rt. 40) which ran east-west, and the route from Pennsylvania to the Shenandoah Valley in Virginia which ran north-south.

Hagerstown, the county seat, was originally named for the founder, Johnathan Hager's, wife, Elizabeth. On January 26, 1814, the Maryland Legislature passed an act "to alter and change the name of Elizabeth Town, in Washington County, to Hager's Town, and to incorporate the same." This is why you will find early references to Elizabeth Town in the manumission documents. A few decades later, the name evolved into the present-day Hagerstown.

The first courthouse for Washington County sat in the public square of Hagerstown. This courthouse stood until the early 1800's when it was decided that it was time to build a new one. Two slaveowners who manumitted their slaves, Samuel Ringgold and William Gabby, were among the commissioners appointed by the Maryland General Assembly to select and purchase a lot for the new courthouse. At this time, Ringgold was also serving as a Congressman in Washington, DC. It was there, no doubt, that Ringgold met the famous architect of the White House, Benjamin Henry Latrobe, who was subsequently commissioned to draw up the plans for the new courthouse in Hagerstown.

of Washington County, Maryland

This building was used until a fire destroyed it on the night of December 5, 1871. Luckily, the manumission books, along with many other records, were stored in the fire vault and were thus saved. These records were then temporarily stored in the attics of townspeople's homes until the completion of the third courthouse in 1873.

One of the books which survived, an old county assessment book, drawn up in 1803, shows that Hagerstown residents owned 151 slaves. [Microfilm of book is available at the Western Maryland Room.]

Elie Williams was the first Clerk of the Court, serving from 1777 until 1800. He was the brother of Revolutionary War General Otho Holland Williams, who founded Williamsport. Elie's son, Otho Holland Williams, II, was the second Clerk from 1800 until 1845. The third Clerk of the Court, Isaac Nesbitt, took over at the beginning of 1845 and continued until 1865.

The town of Williamsport, in southern Washington County, was founded in 1787 and named for General Otho Holland Williams, an officer on the staff of General George Washington. General Williams initially proposed to George Washington that Williamsport become the national capital,[1] but the plan had to be abandoned when it was discovered that the Potomac River was not navigable for sea vessels at this point. Though Williamsport did not become the national capital, it prospered through another project backed by George Washington - the Potomac Co. and, later, by its successor, the Chesapeake and Ohio Canal Co. The Canal was begun in 1828 and completely finished in 1850 from Georgetown to Cumberland. "For nearly one hundred years, until 1924, the canal brought progress and prosperity, recognition and importance to the little historic community of Williamsport - almost the nation's capital."

[1] Letter from Otho Holland Williams to George Washington, dated November 1, 1790.

African American Manumissions
How to Use This Book

All records in this book were typed from the original manumission documents located in the Washington County Courthouse. I have made an exact transcript of the records - nothing has been changed, including the punctuation and the spelling. There is, however, one deviation from this policy: superscript letters have been written as "Mrs." instead of "M$^{rs.}$"; and "3^d day of May" has been written as the more familiar "3rd day of May".

There is a lot of poor spelling, especially in the early records, and an odd use of capitalization in many words. Capital letters frequently looked alike - L and S and T are very hard to tell apart. In addition, you'll note that a person's name was sometimes spelled differently within the same record.

When Isaac Nesbitt took over as Clerk of the Court in 1845, he (or another clerk) started writing the manumitted person's name in the margin of the page. You can see the change on page 51 in the original book. Sometimes this spelling was different from the name as written within the record. If this was the case, I so noted it in brackets [ ] at the end of the entry.

The manumission documents are in two books at the courthouse. Book A has only the letter "A." written on the cover. It is comprised of 108 written pages followed by blank pages. The entries are from August 1806 to February 1834. It has a leather spine and a cardboard cover. In the fashion of those days, the book was turned over and upside down and was used as if it were a separate book to record the stray horses of the county and entitled on the reverse side, "Maryland. Washington County, A Record of Strays Commencing August 20th 1777 and Ending ____?, Elie Williams Cl of the County 1778 J. Russoll, Elie Williams Clk E.W. Williams Clk".

of Washington County, Maryland

Book B has only the letter "B." written on the cover. It has the same type of leather spine and cardboard cover as Book A. It is comprised of 179 written pages which are followed by blank pages. An index, referred to below, was written in the midst of these blank pages. The entries in this book are from April 1834 to Dec 1862 ending, no doubt, due to the Emancipation Proclamation taking effect on January 1, 1863. This book was also used on the reverse side to record twenty pages of stray horses.

As mentioned, there is an original index in the middle of Book B which has all the names of manumitted persons from Books A and B, listed in alphabetical order. Although I created my own index for this book, I did refer to this original index to cross-check the spelling of slaves' names in cases where the handwriting in the original record was indecipherable. Where the spelling of a free person was difficult to decipher, I cross-checked it with the Washington County Land Records.

The Index I created at the back of this book uses entry numbers instead of page numbers. I did it this way because of all the times I've had to scan an entire page instead of being able to go right to the name I want. Please note that Book A has pages which are numbered 1 - 108 and Book B also has pages which are numbered 1 - 179. These entries are differentiated by use of the capital letter "A" or "B" at the beginning of the entry number. The numbers for each entry correspond to the page numbers in the original manumission books. For example: if there were three entries on page 18 in Book A, they would be listed as A18a, A18b and A18c.

Also in the Index, I listed children both by their first names and by the last names of their mother (or father, if listed). At times, it was unclear as to whether a child was using the last name of the mother, be it her maiden name

African American Manumissions

or married name, so I thought it best to index by mother's maiden name, mother's married name, and by child's first name in those cases. Example: the same child is indexed as "Niles, Mary", "Lake, Mary", and "Mary."

Key to Definitions and Abbreviations

____? - the handwriting is indecipherable

[?] - means I was unsure of the spelling in the original document

/ - the word could be either one. Ex: "four/five" means the word could be a four or a five

[ ] - encloses my comments; not part of the original document

[crossed out - ""] - The words enclosed in quotes are words which were crossed out by the Clerk, probably as being a mistake on his part.

Bile - a boil

Bright mulatto - very light skinned

Dec. - deceased

Edw. - Edward

Elie - Eli

Elizabeth Town - first name for Hagerstown

Felon - an inflamed sore or swelling under or near the fingernail or toenail

Good countenance - appears to be a respectable member of society

Hagers Town - first spelling of Hagerstown

Indentured Servitude - service to another person for a specified period of time: this could happen as punishment for a crime, payment of ship passage or a debt; or as training to learn a new trade

Kings evil - a whipping

Mulatto - being of mixed blood, i.e., having one African American parent and one Caucasian parent

Test / In Test - In testimony; or giving one's word

Towit - therefore

Wm. - William

Slave Rental Paper, Western Maryland Room, Washington County Free Library

E.

DEED OF MANUMISSION AND RELEASE OF SERVICE.

Whereas my slave Andrew A. Jackson, has enlisted in the service of the United States: now in consideration thereof, I, Elias Snively, of Washington county, State of Maryland, do hereby, in consideration of said enlistment, manumit, set free, and release the above-named Andrew A. Jackson, from all service due me; his freedom to commence from the Thirtieth Sept. 1863, the date of his enlistment as aforesaid in the Fourth Regiment of Colored Troops, in the service of the United States.

Witness my hand and seal, this Third day of May, 1864.

Elias Snively [SEAL]

Witness:
John Ranels
Jn Leeth

Washington County.
State of Maryland May 3, 1864.

Before me appeared this day Elias Snively and acknowledged the above Deed of Manumission and Release of Service to be his free act and deed.

Jn Leeth, J.P.

Deed of Manumission, Collection of Doug Bast, Boonsboro, Maryland

of Washington County, Maryland

Appendix A

MAGISTRATE'S GUIDE
Lewis and Sutton
CITIZEN'S COUNSELLOR;
Being a digested Abstract of those Laws of the State of Maryland most necessary to be known, and most useful in common transactions of life.
INTERSPERSED WITH A VARIETY OF PRACTICAL FORMS AND PRECEDENTS;
FOR THE USE OF JUSTICES OF THE PEACE AND OTHERS.
by John B. Colvin, Frederick-Town, Md., 1805

MANUMISSION.

Slaves not exceeding forty-five years of age, and who are of sound body and mind, and are capable of labor sufficient to maintain themselves, may be manumitted by last will and testament, provided the same is no prejudice to creditors. 1796, c. 67, s. 13

Persons possessed of slaves of the same age, etc. may manumit them by writing under hand and seal, evidenced by two good and sufficient witnesses at least. ibid. s 29

Form of a Deed of Manumission.

To all whom it may concern, be it known, that I, A.B., of _____ county, in the state of Maryland, for divers good causes and considerations me thereunto moving, as also in further consideration of _____ current money, to me in hand paid, have released from slavery, liberated, manumitted and set free, my negro man named _____ _____, being of the age of _____ years, and able to work and gain a sufficient livelihood and maintenance, and him the said negro man, named _____, I do declare to be henceforth free, manumitted and discharged, from all manner of servitude or service to me, my executors or administrators, forever.

In testimony whereof I have hereunto set my hand, and affixed my seal, this _____ day of _____, in the year of our Lord _____.

                          A. B.   Seal.

Signed, sealed and delivered,
in the presence of
C. D.   E. F.

African American Manumissions

"Received, on the day of the date within mentioned, the sum of _____ current money, it being the full consideration money, within mentioned.

A. B.   Seal

(The foregoing deed must be acknowledged before a justice of the peace of the county where the master resides, and the justice must endorse on the back thereof the time of the acknowledegment and the party making the same, and it must be recorded within the records of that county within six months after the date of manumission. 1796, c. 67, s. 29.)

Form of the Acknowledgement
_____ County, To Wit:

On this _____ day of _____, personally appears A. B. party to the within instrument of writing, before me the subscriber, a justice of the peace of the state of Maryland for the said county, and acknowledges the same to be his act and deed for the purposes within mentioned, and the negro man within named to be henceforth manumitted and discharged from all services to him, or to any claiming under him, and to be free and manumitted, according to the act of Assembly in such cases made and provided.

Acknowledged before   J. S.

- *These excerpts were taken from a book printed in 1805 for the use of attorneys. It is now in the Western Maryland Room, Washington County Free Library, Hagerstown, Maryland.*

Manumission Laws of Maryland

Chapter 67. An Act relating to Negroes, and to repeal the acts of assembly therein mentioned.

Section 13. *And be it enacted,* That from and after the passage of this act, it shall and may be lawful for any person or persons, capable in law to make a valid will and testament, to grant freedom to, and effect the manumission of, any slave or slaves belonging to such person or persons, by his, her or their last will and testament, and such manumission of any slave or slaves may be made to take effect at the death of the testator or testators, or at such other periods as may be limited in such last will and testament; provided always, that no manumission hereafter to be made by last will and testament shall be effectual to give freedom to any slave or slaves, if the same shall be in prejudice of creditors, nor unless the said slave or slaves shall be under the age of forty-five years, and able to work and gain a sufficient maintenance and livelihood at the time the freedom given shall commence.

By 1809, ch. 171, persons manumitting slaves, to take effect at the expiration of years, or upon contingencies, may determine the condition of the issue, born during the time of service. If they omit to do so, their condition to be that of slaves.

Section 18. *And be it enacted,* That in all cases where certificates from a clerk of any court, or from any judge or magistrate, have heretofore been granted, or may hereafter be granted, to free negroes or mulattoes, if such negro or mulatto shall hereafter give or sell such certificate to any slave, by which means such slave may be enabled to abscond from the service of his master or owner, and personate the grantee of such certificate, it shall and may be lawful for the master or owner of such slave to have remedy against such free negro in any court of law in this state, and the court before whom such free negro may be tried, shall have full power and authority, upon conviction by the verdict of a jury, or upon confession or otherwise, to fine such free negro or mulatto a sum not exceeding three hundred dollars, in the discretion of the court, one-half to the use of the master or owner of such absconding slave, the other half to the county school, in case there by any, if no such school, to the use of the county; and in case the said fine shall not be paid, or secured to be paid, within thirty days, then and in such case, the said court may abjudge such free negro to be sold, at public vendue, for such a term as the said court may deem just and proper, not exceeding seven years, and the money arising from such sale shall be paid to the person or persons whose slave shall have absconded by means of such certificate.

Section 19. *And be it enacted,* That any person or persons, who shall hereafter be convicted of giving a pass to any slave, or person held to service, or shall be found to assist, by advice, donation or loan, or otherwise, the transporting of any slave, or

African American Manumissions

any person held to service, from this state, or by any other unlawful means depriving a master or owner of the service of his slave, or person held to service, for every such offence the party aggrieved shall recover damages in an action on the case against such offender or offenders, and such offender or offenders also shall be liable, upon indictment and conviction upon verdict, confession or otherwise, in this state, in any county court where such offence shall happen, be fined a sum not exceeding two hundred dollars, at the discretion of the court, one-half to the use of the master or owner of such slave, the other half to the county school, in case there be any, if no such school, to the use of the county.

Section 29. *And be it enacted,* That where any person or persons possessed of any slave or slaves within this state, who are or shall be of healthy constitutions, and sound in mind and body, capable by labour to procure to him or them sufficient food and raiment, with other requisite necessaries of life, and not exceeding forty five years of age, and such person or persons possessing such slave or slaves as aforesaid, and being willing and desirous to set free or manumit such slave or slaves, may, by writing under his, her or their hand and seal, evidenced by two good and sufficient witnesses at least, grant to such slave or slaves his, her or their freedom; and that any deed or writing, whereby freedom shall be given or granted to any such slave, which shall be intended to take place in future, shall be good to all intents, constructions and purposes whatsoever, from the time that such freedom or manumission is intended to commence by the said deed or writing, so that such deed and writing be not in prejudice of creditors, and that such slave, at the time such freedom or manumission shall take place or commence, be not above the age aforesaid, and be able to work, and gain a sufficient livelihood and maintenance, according to the true intent and meaning of this act; which instrument of writing shall be acknowledged before one justice of the peace of the county wherein the person or persons granting such freedom shall reside, which justice shall endorse on the back of such instrument the time of the acknowledgment, and the party making the same, which he or they, or the parties concerned, shall cause to be entered among the records of the county court where the person or persons granting such freedom shall reside, within six months after the date of such instrument of writing;

and the clerk of the respective county courts within this state shall, immediately upon the receipt of such instrument, endorse the time of his receiving the same, and shall well and truly enrol such deed or instrument in a good and sufficient book, in folio, to be regularly alphabeted in the names of both parties, and to remain in the custody of the said clerk for the time being among the records of the respective county courts; and that the said clerk shall, on the back of every such instrument, in a full legible hand, make an endorsement of such enrolment, and also of the folio of the book in which the same shall be enrolled, and to such endorsement set his hand, the person or persons requiring such entry paying the usual and legal fees for the same.

Section 30. And be it enacted, That a copy of such record, duly attested under the seal of such office, shall at all times hereafter be deemed, to all intents and purposes, good evidence to prove such freedom.

1860 Manumissions Laws of Maryland

Article 66. Free Negroes. Manumission.

42. No slave shall henceforth be manumitted by deed or by last will and testament, nor shall the fact of a negro's going at large and acting as free, or not being claimed by an owner, be considered as evidence of the execution heretofore of any deed or will manumitting the party, or as a ground for presuming freedom; *Provided*, that this section shall not apply to such negroes as may have been heretofore manumitted by deed or by the last will and testament of a deceased person to become free at a period which has not arrived, and who are now in service as slaves for a term of years.

43. Any free negro above the age of eighteen years may go before the Circuit Court for the county in which such free negro has resided for three years next preceding such application, or before the Superior Court of Baltimore city if such negro has resided in said city, and after a full examination in open court, by said court, so as to ascertain whether force, fraud, imposition or undue persuasion has been used to induce such application, and upon being perfectly satisfied by such examination, and by any other evidence which the said court may think it proper to inquire, that such application has not been

African American Manumissions

induced by force, fraud, imposition or undue persuasion, the said court may permit such negro to select a master or mistress and become a slave for life to such master or mistress, and shall cause such order to be recorded in perpetual proof of the fact. If such negro shall be a female, her children, if any, under five years of age, shall be included in such order and become slaves, and those above five shall be bound out.
- *From Maryland State Law Library*

The Constitution of the State of Maryland Reported and Adopted by the Convention of Delegates Assembled at the City of Annapolis, April 27th, 1864, and Submitted to and Ratified by the People on the 12th and 13th Days of October, 1864. With Marginal Notes and References to Acts of the General Assembly and Decisions of the Court of Appeals, and an Appendix and Index,
by Edward Otis Hinkley, Esq. of the Baltimore Bar
Annapolis, 1865

Constitution of Maryland, Adopted in Convention, Which Assembled at the City of Annapolis, on the Twenty-seventh Day of April, Eighteen Hundred and Sixty-four, and Adjourned on the Sixth Day of September, Eighteen Hundred and Sixty-four.

Declaration of Rights.

Article 24. That hereafter, in this State, there shall be neither slavery nor involuntary servitude, except in punishment of crime, where of the party shall have been duly convicted; and all persons held to service or labor as slaves, are hereby declared free.

Article 3. Section 36. The General Assembly shall pass no law, nor make any appropriation to compensate the masters or claimants of slaves emancipated from servitude by the adoption of this Constitution.

- *This excerpt was taken from a book printed in 1865. It is now in the Western Maryland Room, Washington County Free Library, Hagerstown, Maryland.*

Public Sale.

WILL be sold at public sale, On Thursday the 26th of October, at the late residence of George Mish, dec'd, about 2 miles from Clear-Spring and about 5 from Williams-Port—

All the Personal Estate of said deceased, consisting of

Horses, Cows, Sheep and Hogs; 1 negro Man, 1 Boy & 2 GIRLS—Wagons, Ploughs & Horse Gears—Wheat, Rye and Oats, in the straw and by the bushel—Hay in the mows and stacks—Corn on the stock—a large quantity of Flax and Hemp Linen—a great variety of Farming Utensils—Household and Kitchen Furniture—with a great variety of other articles too numerous to particularize. Sale to commence at 9 o'clock A. M. on said day, and continue from day to day, until all is sold, when due attendance and a reasonable credit will be given, by   MARY MISH, Adm'x.
September 21.   47—ts.

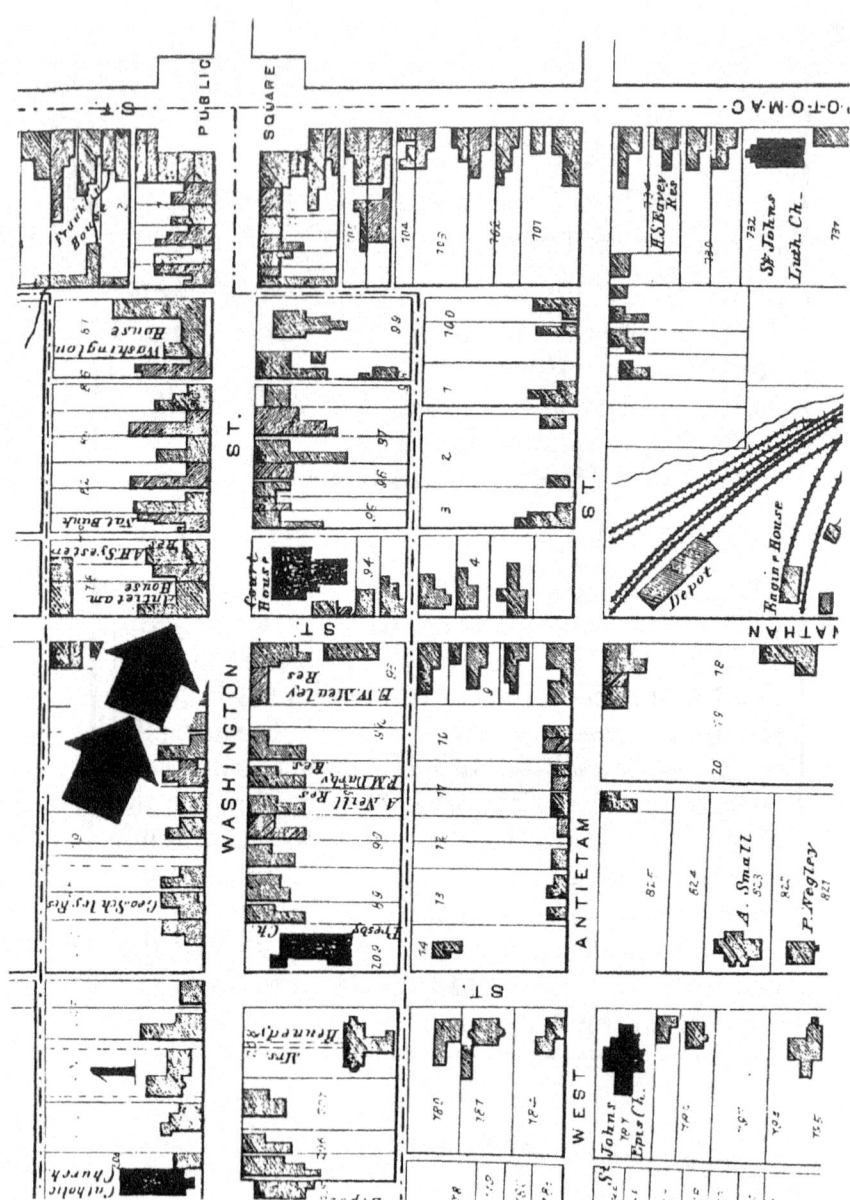

Original Location of Slave Block in Hagerstown

Appendix B

Emancipation Proclamation

By the President of the United State of America:

A Proclamation.

Whereas on the 22nd day of September, A.D. 1862, a proclamation was issued by the President of the United States, containing, among other things, the following, to wit:

That on the 1st day of January, A.D. 1863, all persons held as slaves within any State or designated part of a State the people whereof shall then be in rebellion against the United States shall be then, thenceforward, and forever free; and the executive government of the United States, including the military and naval authority thereof, will recognize and maintain the freedom of such persons and will do no act or acts to repress such persons, or any of them, in any efforts they may make for their actual freedom.

That the executive will on the 1st day of January aforesaid, by proclamation, designate the States and parts of States, if any, in which the people thereof, respectively, shall then be in rebellion against the United States; and the fact that any State or the people thereof shall on that day be in good faith represented in the Congress of the United States by members chosen thereto at elections wherein a majority of the qualified voters of such States shall have participated shall, in the absence of strong countervailing testimony, be deemed conclusive evidence that such State and the people thereof are not then in rebellion against the United States.

Now, therefore, I, Abraham Lincoln, President of the United States, by virtue of the power in me vested as Commander-in-Chief of the Army and Navy of the United States in time of actual armed rebellion against the authority and government of the United States, and as a fit and necessary war measure for suppressing said rebellion, do, on this 1st day of January, A.D. 1863, and in accordance with my purpose so to do, publicly proclaimed for the full period of one hundred days from the first day above mentioned, order and designate as the States and parts of States wherein the people thereof, respectively, are this day in rebellion against the United States the following, to wit:

Arkansas, Texas, Louisiana (except the parishes of St. Bernard, Plaquemines, Jefferson, St. John, St. Charles, St. James, Ascension, Assumption, Terrebonne, Lafourche, St. Mary, St. Martin, and Orleans, including the city of New Orleans), Mississippi, Alabama, Florida, Georgia, South Carolina, North Carolina, and Virginia (except the forty-eight counties designated as West Virginia, and also the counties of Berkeley, Accomac, Northampton, Elizabeth City, York, Princess Anne, and Norfolk, including the cities of Norfolk and Portsmouth), and which excepted parts are for the present left precisely as if this proclamation were not issued.

And by the virtue of the power and for the purpose aforesaid, I do order and declare that all persons held as slaves within said designated States and parts of States are, and henceforward shall be, free; and that the Executive Government of the United States, including the military and naval authorities thereof, will recognize and maintain the freedom of said persons.

And I hereby enjoin upon the people so declared to be free to abstain from all violence, unless in necessary self-defense; and I recommend to them that, in all cases when allowed, they labor faithfully for reasonable wages.

And I further declare and make known that such persons of suitable condition will be received into the armed service of the United States to garrison forts, positions, stations, and other places, and to man vessels of all sorts in said service.

And upon this act, sincerely believed to be an act of justice, warranted by the Constitution upon military necessity, I invoke the considerate judgment of mankind and the gracious favor of Almighty God.

Appendix C

The Constitution of the United States
Article Thirteen
Section 1. Neither slavery nor involuntary servitude, except as a punishment for crime whereof the party shall have been duly convicted, shall exist within the United States, or any place subject to their jurisdiction.

of Washington County, Maryland

Article Fourteen
Section 1. All persons born or naturalized in the United States, and subject to the jurisdiction thereof, are citizens of the United States and of the State wherein they reside. No State shall make or enforce any law which shall abridge the privileges or immunities of citizens of the United States; nor shall any State deprive any person of life, liberty, or property, without due process of law; nor deny to any person within its jurisdiction the equal protection of the laws.
Section 4. ...But neither the United States nor any State shall assume or pay any debt or obligation incurred in aid of insurrection or rebellion against the United States, or any claim for the loss or emancipation of any slave;...

Article Fifteen
Section 1. The right of citizens of the United States to vote shall not be denied or abridged by the United States or by any State on account of race, color, or previous condition of servitude.

Appendix D

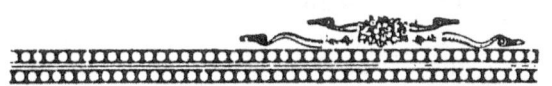

African American Population in the United States

1830	Free White		Slaves		Free Coloured	
	M	F	M	F	M	F
MD	147,325	143,777	53,429	49,449	24,920	28,922
US	5,353,739	5,167,290	1,014,345	996,284	153,495	165,962

-*The Hagerstown Mail; Torchlight & Public Advertiser, 1830-1831.*

1860	White Males 18-45 yrs.	Free Col. Males 18-45 yrs.	Slave Males 18-45 yrs.
MD	102,715	15,149	16,108

- *The War of the Rebellion* (Washington: GPO, 1899) III, III, p. 44.

African American Population in Washington County

Year	Total	Free	Slave	% Population
1790	15,822	64	1,286	8.5
1800	18,650	342	2,220	13.7
1810	18,730	483	2,656	16.8
1820	23,075	627	3,201	16.6

African American Manumissions

Year	Total	Free	Slave	% Population
1830	25,268	1,082	2,909	15.8
1840	28,850	1,580	2,546	14.3
1850	30,848	1,828	2,090	12.7
1860	31,417	1,677	1,435	9.9
1870	34,712	2,838	0	8.2
1880	38,561	3,066	0	8.0

- *Figures from Matthew Humphrey, librarian at Maryland Correctional Institution, Hagerstown, Maryland.*

Free African Americans in Washington County in 1830

Name	Gender	Age Group	Number in Household
Washington County			
Francis Chesley	m	55-100	8
John Thomas	m	24-36	4
Sarah Butler	f	36-55	7
Hez (?) Clemens	m	36-55	6
Patty Peters	f	55-100	6
Lucinda Blake	f	55-100	10
Juliet Brook	f	24-36	2
Jane Butler	f	24-36	5
James McQuade	m	10-24	7
Part of Hagerstown			
Tom Russell	m	36-55	2
Nancy Snowden	f	24-36	6
Elie Kelley	f	24-36	6
Negro Phillis	m	55-100	2
Walter Davis	m	24-36	2
Rebecca Chase	f	24-36	3
Darky Brock	m	24-36	5
Letts Williamson	m	36-55	9
Rebecca Dorsey	f	10-24	2
Nancy Bond	f	36-55	5
Elizabeth Henry	f	55-100	6
Jim Scott	m	24-36	5
Chs. Brison	m	36-55	5

of Washington County, Maryland

Name	Gender	Age Group	Number in Household
Henrietta Cain	f	36-55	1
Hamilton Stewart	m	36-55	5
Chs. Butler	m	36-55	6
F. Stansburry	m	55-100	5
Seaman Duffin	m	36-55	6
Jacob Diggs	m	36-55	8
Ruben Johnston	m	36-55	4
Thomas Harry	m	55-100	6
Jane McCoy	f	24-36	9
Jeffry Booth	m	55-100	7
David Booth	m	36-55	2

Western Division of Hagerstown

Name	Gender	Age Group	Number in Household
Wm. Burrell	m	36-55	7
Thos. Tilghman	?	24-36	3
Catherine Creek	f	55-100	5
Jno. Cook Neg.	m	36-55	4
Tom Henry	m	36-55	8
Jane Fox	f	36-55	4
Maria Butler	?	10-24	2
James Cranford	?	24-36	6
Neg. Susan	f	55-100	6
Sopy Monk	f	36-55	3
Neg. McHenry	m	36-55	4
Jess Ryan	m	55-100	7
Geo. Handy	m	55-100	2
James Brown	m	55-100	4
Negro Jim	?	55-100	16
Ned Dorsey	?	36-55	2
Lewis Gruber	m	36-55	3
David Handy	?	55-100	7
Polly Swans	f	24-36	6
Ben Snowden	m	36-55	3
Wm. Cook	m	55-100	2
Polly Dorsey	f	24-36	7
Eliza Russell	f	55-100	2
Neg. Richardson	m	55-100	3
Joseph Taylor	m	55-100	2
Jno. Hemsley	m	55-100	2
Chs. Butler	m	36-55	6

African American Manumissions

Name	Gender	Age Group	Number in Household
Seaman Duffin	m	36-55	6
Frank Standsberry	m	55-100	4
Jacob Diggs	m	36-55	8
Tom Harry	m	36-55	6
Saml. Nemmy?	m	24-36	5
Neg. Shorter	m	55-100	2

District 1

Name	Gender	Age Group	Number in Household
Negro Beall	m	36-55	4
Polly Brown	f	24-36	6
Lewis Howard	m	36-55	6
Mich. Homes	m	36-55	3
Job Moats	m	36-55	5
Negro Stinebaugh	m	24-36	5
Jerry Swearingin?	m	36-55	2
Danl. Ilis	m	36-55	6
Charles Lear	m	36-55	5
Benj. Bell	m	36-55	7
James Wright	m	55-100	5
Thos. Kuhn	m	55-100	8
Zack Patterson	m	55-100	4
B. Barker	f	36-55	5
Thos. Duckett	m	55-100	12
James Bose	m	55-100	3
Guy Pinkney	m	55-100	4
Mary Howel	f	36-55	1
Aquila Yarrow	m	36-55	2
Chales Adams	m	36-55	3
Wm. Callman	m	36-55	6
Negro Patterson	m	55-100	5
Negro Let	m	24-36	7
Benj. Luckett	m	36-55	9
Chas. Adley	m	36-55	7
James Adley	m	55-100	3
James Douglass	m	24-36	5
Nancy Garner	?	24-36	3

District 2

Name	Gender	Age Group	Number in Household
Hanson Jones	m	24-36	4
Perry Riley	m	36-55	4

of Washington County, Maryland

Name	Gender	Age Group	Number in Household
Caroline Coats	f	55-100	5
Wm. Burrell	m	24-36	1
Chs. Gates	m	36-55	6
Chs. Briscoe	m	10-24	9
Benj. Gates	m	24-36	6
Caesar Monte	m	24-36	5
Adam Timus	m	55-100	3
H. Williams	m	24-36	6
Richd. Briscoe	m	24-36	6
Benj. St. Clare	m	55-100	2
Sally Pearce	f	100 etc.	9
Nace Casper	m	55-100	4
Sarah Diggs	f	36-55	8
James Handy	m	36-55	6
Polly Brown	f	36-55	6

District 3
Name	Gender	Age Group	Number in Household
Polly Hurdle	f	36-55	5
Thos. Butler	m	55-100	2
John Bourke	?	55-100	3
Thos. Brown	?	55-100	1
Rachael Briscoe	f	55-100	4
Tobias Miller	m	36-55	8
Peter Richerdson	m	36-55	4

District 4
Name	Gender	Age Group	Number in Household
Osborn Pie	m	36-55	10
Jno. Truman	m	36-55	7
Cato Smith	m	10-24	10
David Hatton	m	36-55	7
Catherine Long	?	55-100	7
Charles Rideout	m	24-36	7
Esther Sharp	f	100 etc.	1
Saul Stoops	m	36-55	8
George Williams	m	36-55	9
Harry Groce	m	55-100	2
James Groce	m	36-55	5
Saml. Lake	m	36-55	9
Thos. Watts	m	55-100	8
John Greer	m	24-36	6

African American Manumissions

Name	Gender	Age Group	Number in Household
Brook Seburn	m	36-55	8
Rebecca Watts	f	100 etc.	4
Jeremiah Cook	m	36-55	1
Saml. Miller	m	36-55	7
Tos. Sanders	m	36-55	7
Jacob Burrs	m	36-55	7
Saml. Williams	m	36-55	19
Henry Stephens	m	55-100	2
Richd. Miles	m	36-55	3
Saml. Miller	m	36-55	6
Jno. Gates	m	36-55	9
John Wallace	m	36-55	5
James Young	m	36-55	1
Levin Groce	m	24-36	3
M. Truman	m	36-55	10
Wm. Brown	m	24-36	7
Jno. Harris	?	24-36	5

District 5

Name	Gender	Age Group	Number in Household
Negro Phil	m	36-55	3
Phil Silleby	m	55-100	2

District 6

Name	Gender	Age Group	Number in Household
Jetson Key	m	55-100	11
Thos. Galaman	m	24-36	8
E. Calaman	m	24-36	10
Frank Matthews	m	24-36	10
Geo. Washington	m	55-100	10
Elie Butler	f	24-36	5
Jesse Gwinn	m	36-55	6
Edwd. Stewart	m	55-100	5
Bazill Taylor	m	55-100	4
Jno. Lee	m	55-100	10
Chs. Herbert	m	55-100	4
Sally Chase	f	55-100	6
Negro Chase	m	24-36	6

District 7

Name	Gender	Age Group	Number in Household
Negro Jerry	m	55-100	2
Sophia James	f	24-36	5

Mr. Catharine Facey To Joseph P. Mong, Col'r. Dr.

1845.
June 4. To amount of County Tax } $ 66
on $ 360   at 22 cts. per $100,

1845.
June 4. To amount of State Tax } $ 75
on $ 300   at 25 cts. per $100,

Plate exceeding $50,
G. and S. Watches,

I will be at the Hotel of Dissuel in Leesburg on the Nov 23 = 24th Sep where I expect you to pay your tax without fail. If you fail to pay at the above named time and place, I will proceed to collect according to law.

JOSEPH P. MONG, Collector.

$360

Acres of Land,

House and Lot,
No. of Slaves under 14 years,
No. of Males from 14 to 45 y's.
No. of Males over 45,
No. of Females from 14 to 36,
No. of Females over 36,
General description of stock in trade:
Bank stock,
Private securities,
Live stock,
Furniture,
Gold and silver watches,
Other Property,

Washington County Tax Paper, Copy in Collection of Marguerite Doleman

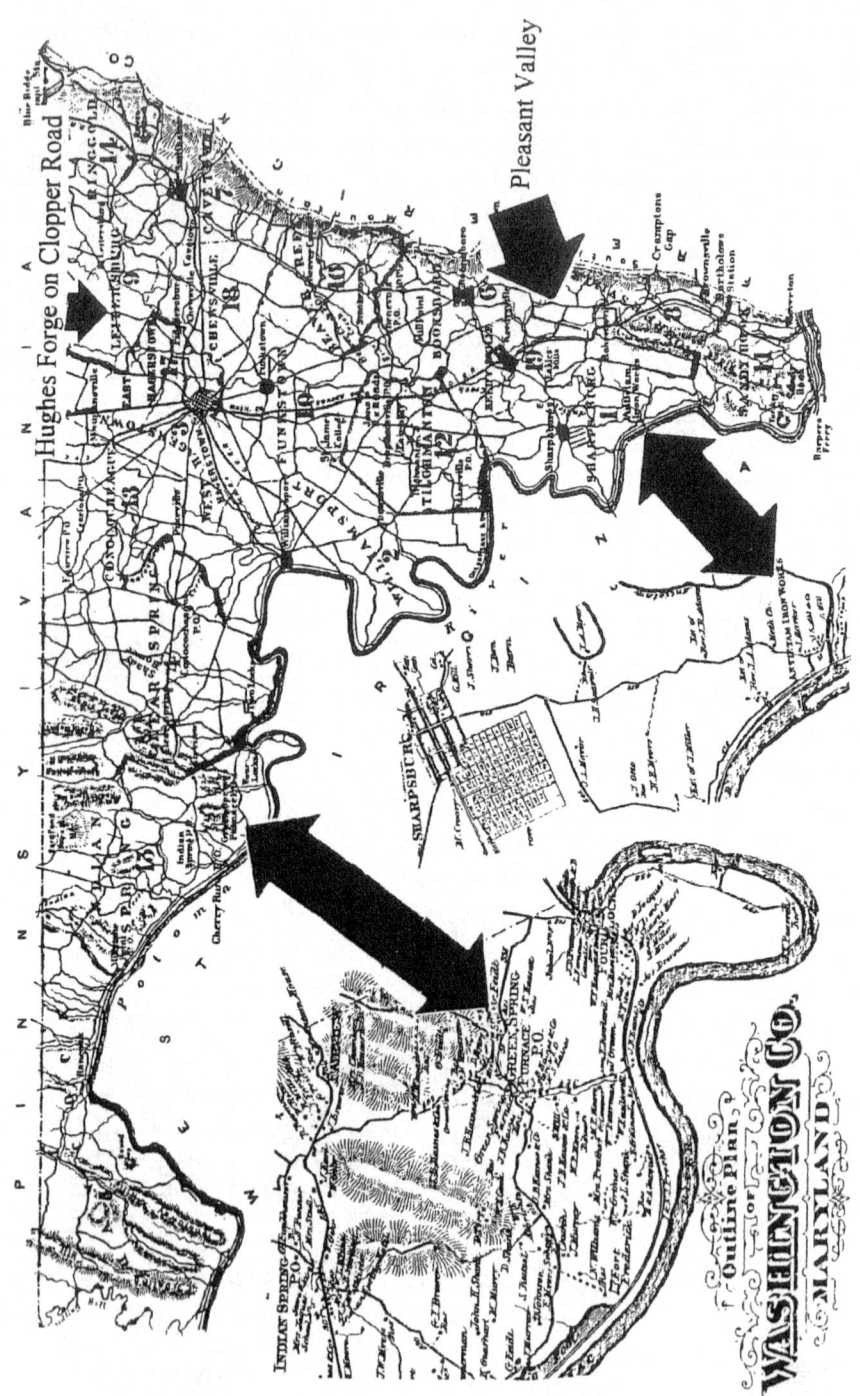

of Washington County, Maryland

Name	Gender	Age Group	Number in Household
Sucky Dunmore	f	36-55	4
Joseph Green	m	36-55	7
Robert Harding	m	24-36	4
Saml. Keyser	m	24-36	2
Nace Kelley	m	24-36	4

Key
f = female   Neg. = Negro   m = male

African Americans in the United States

	Free	Total
1790	59,557	757,881
1830	319,000	N/A
1860	488,000	N/A

- *Free Negro Heads of Families in the United States in 1830*, Carter G. Woodson, Ph.D., 1925, The Association for the Study of Negro Life and History, Inc., Washington, DC [Book in Western Maryland Room, Washington County Free Library.]

African American Census of Washington County for 1860 and 1870

1860 Town	People	Born in MD	Own Property
Sharpsburg	212	212	11
Williamsport	230	230	13
Hagerstown	494	482	31
Clear Spring	285	283	4
Hancock	70	68	3
Boonsboro	82	82	4
Cavetown	30	30	2
Rohreresville	15	15	3
Leitersburg	21	21	0
Funkstown	73	73	4
Sandy Hook	90	84	6
Tilghmanton	58	58	1
TOTAL	1684	1658	84

African American Manumissions

1870 Town	People	Born in MD	Own Property
Sharpsburg	178	164	6
Williamsport	373	267	10
Hagerstown	878	785	66
Clear Spring	338	269	17
Hancock	252	189	6
Boonsboro	114	111	5
Cavetown	22	22	1
Rohrersville	43	42	2
Leitersburg	14	11	0
Funkstown	102	87	5
Sandy Hook	146	89	2
Tilghmanton	90	84	2
Wilsons	79	77	5
Ringgold	0	0	0
Indian Springs	61	34	3
Beaver Creek	133	132	2
Antietam	3	3	0
TOTAL	2826	664	132

- *Data compiled by Marguerite Doleman, Hagerstown, Maryland*

.|.|.|.|.|.|.|.|.|.|.|.|.|.|.|.|.|.|. **Appendix E**

From the *Holy Bible* of Nathaniel Nesbitt of Clear Spring, Maryland, published by Selby, Kimber, and Sharpless.

Negro Sam was born Feb. 1814
Morris was born about 1819
Nance was born July 1816   Died July 1891
Git was born March 1822
Nance married Charles Gillis. Children:
    Sarah Ann Gillis   born May 31, 1836
    Mary Margarest Gillis   born August 31, 1839
    Eli Gillis   born November 30, 1842
                                   died June 9, 1865
    Francis Cornelia Gillis   born June 5, 1845
    William Gillis   born August 25, 1847
                                   died February 20, 1848

of Washington County, Maryland

Thomas Henry Gillis	born March 17, 1849
	died April 22, 1860
Charles Gillis	born May 11, 1853
Mary Ann Elizabeth Gillis	born October 2, 1855
Ellen Serenah Gillis	born February 6, 1861
Allis Verge Gillis	born [blank]
	died May 7, 1855

Git married a Dorrace. Children:

Harriet Shorter Dorrace	born August 29, 1841
Joseph Dorrace	born October 3, 1844
	died April 1855
George T. Dorrace	born July 25, 1846
John Adams Dorrace	born March 4, 1848
Isaiah Dorrace	born October 27, 1849
Charles Albian Dorrace	born October 25, 1854
	died April 1855
Mary E. Dorrace	born March 24, 1843
	died April 1855

- *The Bible was in the possession of Mrs. Florence Frantz on October 21, 1975. This excerpt was taken from a typewritten copy owned by Marguerite Doleman, Hagerstown, Maryland in December 1997.*

Appendix F

Excerpts from the Diary of Otho Nesbitt of Clear Spring, Maryland

April 29, 1842 - Paid to James Dorrance for one small coffin (Nance's child)
February 25, 1847 - Paid for Morris and Ely $6.00 for Schooling
April 30, 1847 - Paid Mulain $1.75 for schooling for Morris
September 13, 1850 - Morris Taken very sick today. Had coctor.
March 27, 1851 - Paid to James Dorrance [furniture maker and undertaker] $4.00 for walnut bedstead for Morris.
April 5, 1851 - Paid to James Dorrence for two walnut steps and 11 ft. walnut planking to finish rooms
June 17, 1851 - Circus to be in Town on the 30th, gave all The Negroes money to go

African American Manumissions

October 17, 1851 - Swept down the old house left with a view to have steps go up and four rooms petitioned off for Morris, Ely, and Joe. Made windows and put washboard around.

January 30, 1852 - Black woman preached in the old Academy, said to be a Bethelite or Protestant Methodist. She was born a slave on the Eastern Shore of Md. Went to hear her. She did very well.

February 7, 1853 - Ely and Joe commenced going to school to Mathias Truman's daughter in ClearSpring

May 24, 1853 - Mat Truman's daughter for teaching Ely and Joe

May 24, 1853 - Eli sick - had doctor

March 21, 1855 - Git had a little boy buried today, about 1 yr. old

April 2, 1855 - Git buried another of her little children today, a little girl about 2. Swollen stomach, Joe, her oldest boy is sick in the same way. Dr. Jones is tending them.

April 2, 1855 - To James Dorrance for little coffin $3.00

May 8, 1855 - To James Dorrance for Joe's coffin $3.00. Joe died today. He was within 3 mo. of being 11 years old. A very likely, fine, smart boy. The lower part of his bowels seemed to be afflicted. No medicine would help him and no food would nourish him.

July 6, 1855 - Joe was buried today about 3 o'clock. He never appeared to be in much pain but just pined away until he became a mere skeleton with dropsy in his feet. His belly was always swollen. Perhaps he is in a better country. Whether his disease was natural or whether it originated from a cold or from putrid air, is probably hard to tell.

December 16, 1855 - Father gave Virginia Miller, Sarah Ann Gillis by instrument of writing attested to by two witnesses and a squire that she was not to be sold out of the state of Maryland and that she and her offspring were to be free at the age of 24.

December 30, 1855 - Today by instrument of writing gave me Morris, Nance, and her family. Jonothan got Git and her family. Margaret, 15, is to be free at age 24.

October 11, 1856 - Kate Dodd was here today and cut out 2 shirts for Morris, 2 for Eli, and two for Tom, 2 for Charles, 2 undershirts for Morris, 2 for Francis, 1 lining and calico dress for Nance and 1 palmetto yellow for Francis.

March 15, 1857 - Nance has a young son. River Prathers black woman is caring for her.

January 5, 1858 - Morris in jail in Berkely Springs.

of Washington County, Maryland

March 18, 1858 - Nance buried her youngest daughter today. Dr. Firy attended her.

November 2, 1860 - Morris' mother from W.Va. here today. Quite a good looking old darkey.

July 27, 1862 - Music teacher here today from Baltimore, teaching piano. also teaches a day school in the little negro church about which there was a great fuss last night. The old side Methodist negroes and the Bethelite negroes both claiming it or rather the African Episcopal Methodist.

September 9, 1862 - Free negroes taken by the army.

September 10, 1862 - I sent Morris and Eli to the mountains to hide.

January 23, 1863 - Smallpox in town in the Francis [Frantz] family.

January 29, 1863 - I had Eli, Francis, Charles, Mary A., Elizabeth and another little one vacinated today.

June 17, 1863 - I sent the rest of the blacks and the horses to the mountain to save from the Rebels.

June 4, 1864 - Miss Kate Ridgley here nearly all day teaching the Negroes.

July 24, 1864 - Rebels took Mary Jane and her mother

July 24, 1864 - The Rebels came into town. Eli and Charles went to the mountain with some of my horses to hide. The Rebels ran off all my horses. Took my fine bull. Drove off all my cattle. Took my saddle bags, pants and hats. The Union Army had taken my finest horse and spring wagon. The Rebels ran.

October 30, 1864 - The Negroes had a meeting today for the first time in their new log church towards the Big Spring.

November 1, 1864 - The Negroes all set free in Maryland without compensation to their owners.

November 2, 1864 - Told the Negroes today that I had nothing more to do with them. It was now near winter and they had no and I said they would have to shift for themselves. They had no house, no home, and probably could get no work this time of year and if they cared to work on as they had been doing till Spring they might do so that I couldn't pay a whole family of Negroes to cook a little vituals for me after all that I had lost to both Armies. They said it was so and they would work on until Spring as they had been.

February 25, 1865 - Rebels propose to put 200,000 Negroes in the field.

African American Manumissions

February 26, 1865 - Frances came back from Harrisburg today. Eli still very sick.

June 8, 1865 - Eli died this morning.

June 10, 1865 - Eli was buried today. Aged 22 years, 5 mo., and 22 days.

October 8, 1865 - Nance, Ben, and Frances Gillis all came home today.

December 22, 1865 - Frances Gillis left for Harrisburg. Her father took her as far as Hagerstown in my sleigh.

January 22, 1867 - Ben Gillis came home from Harrisburg today. He says that Morris is very sick, probably consumption and wouldn't live until Spring. Says he is nothing but skin and bones and looks like death. He is sorry he ever left and would have liked to come back. (June 18, 1864 Morris ran away today persuaded no doubt by his old rip Sidny) Morris has done nothing for a year. Ben says that Morris's son is getting $11 a month in a livery stable and they give Morris something to eat.

June 8, 1867 - Frances Gillis very sick.

October 3, 1868 - Nance quite sick. Has to stop work because of her age. Ben sick. Nothing but skin and bones.

October 14, 1868 - Ben gillis died today.

October 27, 1868 - Nance, Frances and Sal Gillis all moved today into my little house in ClearSpring. Nance cooked my vituals for many a long year, but she has probably left the old kitchen forever. Mary, Liz, Ellen and Charles come back often.

1871 - Paid John Sosy 25 cents for getting Jeff to go to school

May 14, 1872 - Nance Gillis will work all summer. Mary Jane Truman helping. Also Suse Sofhes and Cloe. Nance does all the bossing.

September 14, 1872 - Old Nance here today making peach preserves. Likes to come when she is able to make a little money. Came last week and baked me six loaves of bread.

December 15, 1873 - Betsy Truman buried today.

April 1874 - Paid Charlie Sosy in full for taking Jeff Nesbitt to school every day

January 1, 1875 - Election in ClearSpring today. Dave Flory elected Burgess and Sam Cautions, colored, elected one of the commissioners.

January 1, 1876 - I went to the Negro Concert tonight in the old Academy. Quite good.

✠ ✠ ✠ ✠ ✠ ✠

of Washington County, Maryland

- The diary of Otho Nesbitt was owned by Mrs. Florence Frantz in October 1975. The excerpts here were taken from a typewritten copy which was in the possession of Marguerite Doleman in December 1997.

Letter to Otho Nesbitt of Clear Spring, Maryland

Mr. Nesbitt received this letter stating that his slave, Morris, was jailed for not having a pass:

Berkeley Springs, VA   Dec 26th 1858

Mr. Nesbit Dear Sir there is a Mullato man confined in this Jail who sais he belongs to you he sais he left home on yesterday morning 25th for the purpose of going to Mr. Grafflins to see his mother. he was stoped on his way and brought to this Town and having no pass the Justice before __[?] home he was examined. Commited him to Jail - he is about 5 feet 9 or ten inches high has on a cap and drab ___ Coat his pants are corded and drab brown coat he is a bright Mulatto and seems to be about __[?] or 45 years of age you will have to appear here and prove him before he can be Released   I do not know what you will hav to pay for his apprehension but if you lived in this state you would have to pay 10 percent on his value nothing more only he wishes you to come as soon as posible as he dont like this boarding house
With Respect Yours
Wm. Armstrong, I.M.C.

Excerpts from the Diary of Otho Nesbitt of Clear Spring, Maryland Regarding this Letter

Editor's Note: Mr. Nesbitt wrote each day's entry as one long sentence. I have added punctuation to this excerpt in order to make it readable.

So I thought he was only going to Hancock it didn't matter much whether he had a pass or not. He started on Chrismas day Saturday Morning, on Monday he didn't come back. Monday evening I received two letters stating Morris was in jail at Bath Berkly Springs [Berkeley Springs, West Virginia]. One I believe from the Jailer or the Man who committed and one from Grafton at Sir John's Run about 6 Miles up the River on the Virginia Shore where his Mother lives. The latter stating he was

African American Manumissions

in Jail and the former that I would have to pay the one tenth part of his value to get him out. What was to be done? Monday evening at dusk and Lona Nesbitt to be Married Tuesday evening 1/2 past 7 O'clock to leave him there we couldn't enjoy the parties and if we went could we get back in time? We come to the conclusion to try it.

We got Casly's Spring Waggon and Charley the Horse I got of Lesher not knowing wheather he would go or not. We Started and the horse went Much better than we expected. Charles went along to prove the Negro. We got to Hancock after night. Paid the ferry men double price to take us over being 5 cents. And when we got over there was some danger crossing the Railroad the Night being dark only sat[?] light[?] and 6 long Miles to Bath over a graded Mud Road.

10 O'clock at Night our horse and selves all tired. At length we arrived at Bath about 12 O'clock at Night. We tryed to get in at O'ferrels. They told us to go some where else Naming 2 or 3 plaices. We tryed but could get in now where and almost thought we Should have to sleep in the street. At length we got in at Mrs. Oferrel's. Our horse put up and we went to bed.

Got up next morning bright and early. Tryed to see our horse but couldn't find him. Went Round to the jail and wanted to know what was to be done. The jailor said he was committed as a Runaway and he had given his bond to keep him there till legally let out. Some 3 or 4 went with us to Duckwatts a lawyer. Stated the case to him. He asked us where we stayed. Said he would be down in a few Minutes. Came down after Some time and said we must give Notice to the Man Bersell who put him in so we put a boy on a horse and agreed to give him a ___ to ride 6 Miles to a deep cut on the Railroad where he was watching to keep the stone of the tract.

The Majestrits court was in session. I talked to the chief Judge as he came in and others on the bench. Court was called at length about 10 or 9 O'clock. The Matter was talked over. I was sworn I gave him priviledge to go and see his Mother. Charles was sworn to prove he was my slave. Another Man who crossed the River with him was sworn who testified he had questioned him and had no Idea he was a Runaway. This took him from under the law of Runaways and consequently the 10 per cent. He then came under the ___ [Jaliare?] regulations - any Negro found 3 Miles from home without a pass has a right to be

of Washington County, Maryland

taken up and put in Jail and his Master can't get him out unless he pays the jail fees.

The court waited some time till he came. I was introduced to him. We went into the court house and he paid a lawyer for the 10 per cent. Our lawyer made 2 little speeches before the court and the other one. The court gave us an order for the Negro by paying the Jail fees about 3 dol. I asked the lawyer what I owed him. He said 5 dol. So I laid him down 10 and he gave me 2 dol. back. So we went Round to the Jail and got Morris out and the horse and started for home about one.

The question was now, "Could we get home in time for the wedding?" Iona said he would put it off till Eight on our account. We walked up nearly all the big hills. We didn't stop to feed or water. The horse was nearly give out. We made the landing about 6 O'clock. One hour and a half to wash, shave, dress, blacken boots and go up. We were there, but it was like Judge Snyder getting into heaven - it was a d--m tight squeeze.

- The letter and diary of Otho Nesbitt was owned by Mrs. Florence Frantz in October 1975. The excerpts here were taken from a photocopy which was in the possession of Marguerite Doleman in December 1997.

Appendix G

Original Manumission Document

I, Simon Long, of Washington County, in the State of Maryland, do hereby manumit and set free, my negro slave, Airy Brooks, her freedom to commence from the thirteenth day of May, Eighteen hundred and sixty two - my negro slave Ellen Smothers, her freedom to commence from the fifteenth day of October, Eighteen hundred and sixty - my negro slave Martha Smothers, her freedom to commence from the fifteenth day of March, in the year, Eighteen hundred and Eighty two - my negro slave July Smothers, her freedom to commence from the first day of March, Eighteen hundred and Eighty - my negro slave Elijah Hammet, his freedom to commence from the first day of May, Eighteen hundred and sixty-five - my negro slave Abraham Brown, his freedom to commence from the first day of May, Eighteen hundred and sixty nine. - my negro slave, Sarah Jane Brooks, her freedom to commence from the first day of May

African American Manumissions

Eighteen Hundred and seventy two - my negro slave Lloyd Brooks his freedom to commence from the sixteenth day of August Eighteen hundred and seventy Three - my negro slave Van Brooks, his freedom to commence from the fifth day of February, Eighteen hundred and seventy six - my negro slave Serena Brooks, her freedom to commence from the fifteenth day of April, Eighteen hundred and seventy Eight - my negro slave Eliza Brooks, her freedom, to commence from the nineteenth day of June Eighteen hundred and Eighty two - my negro slave George Brooks, his freedom to commence from the first day of March, Eighteen hundred and Eighty five.

Witness my hand and seal this seventh day of July _____, Eighteen hundred and fifty seven.

Test. H.B., George Schley   Simon Long   *Seal*
State of Maryland   Washington County towit.

- The original of this manumission document was owned by Douglas G. Bast, Boonsboro, Maryland in December 1997. I made this transcription from a photocopy of the original.

Slave Bill of Sale from 1835

Know all men by these presents that I James J. Beatty of Washington County and State of Maryland for and in consideration of the sum of three Hundred and twenty five dollars to me in hand paid by Sarah Middlekauff and Susan Middlekauff of the said State and county at or before the sealing and delivery of these presents, the receipt whereof I the said James J. Beatty do hereby acknowledge have granted, bargained and sold and by these presents do grant bargain and sell unto the said Sarah Middlekauff and Susan Middlekauff their executors administrators and asigns a certain Negro woman slave named Cloe, supposed to be about nineteen years of age & a certain Negro child, female slave named Jill about three years of age. To have and to hold the said Negroe slaves named above bargained and sold or intend so to be, to the said Sarah Middlekauff and Susan Middlekauff their executors, administrators and assigns forever. and I the said James J. Beatty for myself, my heirs executors and administrators, the said Negro Woman & child female, as slaves, unto the said Sarah Middlekauff & Susan Middlekauff their executors, administrators and asigns, against me the said James J. Beatty

Deed of Manumission, Collection of Doug Bast, Boonsboro, Maryland

I, Simon Long, of Washington county, in the state of Maryland, do hereby manumit and set free, my negro slave Mary, that I'd her freedom to commence from this instant – my negro slave Tilly, Eighteen hundred and sixty – my negro slave Ellen Smothers, her freedom to commence from the thirteen day of March, Eighteen hundred and sixty – my negro slave Charlotte, Eighteen hundred and sixty – my negro slave Matthias, her freedom to commence from the fifteenth day of March, in the year Eighteen hundred and eighty five – my negro slave Stilly Mothery, her freedom to commence from the first day of October, Eighteen hundred and eighty eight – my negro slave Manuel, his freedom to commence from the first day of April, Eighteen hundred and eighty five – my negro slave Abraham Flower, his freedom to commence from the first day of May, Eighteen hundred and sixty five – my negro slave Jackson, his freedom to commence from the first day of May, Eighteen hundred and eighty – my negro slave Sarah, his freedom to commence from the first day of August Eighteen hundred and sixty nine – my negro slave Jackson to commence from the [illegible] day of August, Eighteen hundred and sixty three – my negro slave Ephraim, his freedom to commence from the first day of February, Eighteen hundred and sixty six – my negro slave Henry Harris, his freedom to commence from the thirteenth day of June, Eighteen hundred and eighty four, and my negro slave Henry Harris, his freedom to commence from the thirteenth day of June, Eighteen hundred and eighty four – my negro slave Eliza Harris, his freedom to commence from the first day of January, Eighteen hundred and eighty five, and my negro slave George Harris, his freedom to commence from the first day of [illegible], Eighteen hundred and eighty five – ____ Witness my hand and seal this seventh day of July ____ Eighteen hundred and fifty seven.

Simon Long {seal}

Test:
Geo. Phillip
Wm Ridenour

State of Maryland }
Washington County } I hereby certify

OLD STONE BLOCK DATES TO TIMES OF SLAVERY HERE

Historic Block Has Interesting History Connected With It.

ORIGINALLY STOOD ON JONATHAN STREET

Many Negroes Sold From It To City And County Bidders.

The "mysterious" old stone block, "covered by grass and underbrush" with a metal plate "almost illegible with age" has an interesting history connected with it.

But the metal plate is not illegible with age, having been placed on the stone within the past 6 or 7 years by Mrs. Julia Hamilton Briscoe, and there is no overgrowth of grass and weds covering the relic of the past, as it stands in the middle of the well-kept driveway at the home of Mr. John Stonebraker, "Oak Hill," formerly Governor Hamilton's home.

The crescent shaped block, standing 12 or 14 inches above the ground, could tell tragic stories of many slaves who have been sold from it, and if the stone could speak it might repeat oratorical flights of the great politicians and statesmen of the past.

Originally the stone stood on Johnathan street, at the spot in front of what is now the side entrance to the Hotel Hamilton, at that time either the Antietam House or the Old Eagle Hotel, said Mrs. Briscoe. It was used as a slave block and many negroes were sold from it to Hagerstown and county bidders. Important political debates took place from the stone, too, and Andrew Jackson and Henry Clay both visited Hagerstown in the year 1830, and both of them spoke standing on that stone, exhorting the citizens who frequented the hotel.

When the late Governor Hamilton tore down the Antietam House, he had the stone, which he prized very highly, realizing its historic value, moved to his estate at Oak Hill. Later Mrs. Briscoe had the bronze tablet made, stating that Jackson and Clay had spoken from it, and it has since remained planted in the driveway at Oak Hill.

Washington County Free Library, Hagerstown, Md.

of Washington County, Maryland

my executors and administrators and against all and every other person and persons whatsoever shall and will warrant and forever defend by these presents. In witness whereof I have hereunto set my hand and seal the 28 day of February 1835.
sealed and delivered in the presence of Nicholas Lowe

Slave Bill of Sale from 1841

Received May 14th 1841 of Miss Susan Middlekauff through the hands of Mr. Joseph Schnebly three hundred dollars for a Negro Girl named Ann who is a Slave for life

William Smith

Rent of Slave, Undated

Sir - The girls time that I hired to you was out on the first day of this month - you ought to have returned her home on that day - you must pay one Dollar for every week you keep her after the time she was hired to you for - please to pay ___? here to the bearer Mr. Talbott - and oblige yr ___? C.? Bagly, agent for J.T. Mason

- The originals of the preceding three documents are in the Western Maryland Room, Washington County Free Library, Hagerstown, Maryland. John T. Mason as well as Susan and Sarah Middlekauff later manumitted their slaves. See entries in Index.

Appendix H

FREEDOM TO SLAVES!

Whereas, the President of the United States did, on the first day of the present month, issue his *Proclamation* declaring *"that all persons held as Slaves in certain designated States, and parts of States, are, and henceforward shall be free,"* and that the Executive Government of the United States, including the Military and Naval authorities thereof, would recognize and maintain the freedom of said persons. *And Whereas*, the county of *Frederick* is included in the territory designated by the Proclamation of the President, in which the *Slaves should become free*, I therefore hereby notify the citizens of the city of Winchester, and of said

African American Manumissions

County, of said Proclamation, and of my intention to maintain and enforce the same.

I expect all citizens to yield a ready compliance with the Proclamation of the Chief Executive, and I admonish all persons disposed to resist its peaceful enforcement, that upon manifesting such disposition by acts, they will be regarded as rebels in arms against the lawful authority of the Federal Government and dealt with accordingly.

All persons liberated by said Proclamation are admonished to abstain from all violence, and immediately betake themselves to useful occupations.

The officers of this command are admonished and ordered to act in accordance with said proclamation and to yield their ready co-operation in its enforcement.

R.H. Milroy, Brig. Gen'l Commanding.
Jan. 5th, 1863.

The following proclamation was issued in Winchester, Virginia:
Proclamation!

IN pursuance of instructions from the Governor of Virginia, notice is hereby given to all whom it may concern,

That, as heretofore, particularly from now until after Friday next the 2nd of December, STRANGERS found within the County of Jefferson, and Counties adjacent, having no known and proper business here, and who cannot give a satisfactory account of themselves, will be at once arrested.

That on, and for a proper period before that day, stangers [sic] and especially parties, approaching under the pretext of being present at the execution of John Brown, whether by Railroad or otherwise, will be met by the Military and turned back or arrested without regard to the amount of force, that may be required to affect this, and during the said period and especially on the 2nd of December, the citizens of Jefferson and the surrounding country are EMPHATICALLY warned to remain at their homes armed and guard their own property.

Information received from reliable sources, clearly indicates that by so doing they will best consult their own interests.

of Washington County, Maryland

No WOMEN or CHILDREN will be allowed to come near the place of execution.

WM. B. TALLIAFERRO, Maj. Gen. Com. troops.
S. BASSETT FRENCH, Military Sec'y.
THOMAS C. GREEN, Mayor.
ANDREW HUNTER, Asst. Pros. Att'y.
JAMES W. CAMPBELL, Sheriff.

November 28th, '59

- I made the above two transcriptions from photocopies which were in the possession of Marguerite Doleman in December 1997.

Appendix I

NATIONAL ANTI-SLAVERY STANDARD
Vol. XXIV. No. 21.
New York, Saturday, October 3, 1863. Whole No. 1,1217.
NEWS DIRECT FROM RICHMOND

I have just had a visit from Wesley, one of the five of Gen. Lee's slaves who attempted to make their escape about four years ago and were captured, brought back to Arlington, taken to the barn and whipped, each fifty lashes, the open wound washed with salt and vinegar, and then sent down South. Wesley is brother of the girl whom Gen. Lee himself whipped, when the overseer refused to do so. He was sent to Tuscaloosa, Alabama; Mary to Richmond. It seems they have neither of them had a very hard life since then; he says he has never had a "lick" except the one Gen. Lee gave him. Gen. Lee's son, Curtis, gave him his pass, and he left Richmond last Friday, and reached his poor old father and mother at Arlington Tuesday morning. He says the Union soldiers at first were suspicious that he was a spy, that he was blindfolded and taken on a horse from Culpepper through the Union lines. He says there are no troops in Richmond, and the people are in constant alarm, fearing the Union soldiers will come; that there is the greatest destitution among them, and that he has seen ladies, who last year owned hundreds of slaves, *out barefoot, picking blackberries to sell for bread!* So we see the retribution. The tables are turned. As Wesley

African American Manumissions

says, they are now worse off than the slaves themselves. His sister, he says, is now waiting upon a lady at $16 a month, but that $2 here would be better for her; that they have their clothes packed ready to come North as soon as they can do so under a flag of truce. He showed me the pair of shoes he had on, for which he paid $25 Confederate money. I begged some of the money from him, as a relic. I asked him if he brought anything else that would be a curiosity; he said no, it " 'peared like he didn't want to bring anything away with him."

Wesley is a very truthful, honest fellow, and I should suppose might give much valuable information to government, and for which he certainly should be liberally rewarded.

He says he was never so happy in his life as he has been for the last two days; that he now feels free and like a man; and that he is going to school, the first thing he does, at the Freedmen's Camp at Arlington; says he can read a little now; that his father and mother never wish to leave the old place, but he is going where he can make the money.

Washington, Sept. 10   *Independent*

- The original newspaper that this article was excerpted from was located at the Washington County Historical Society Library in December 1997.

The American Farmer's Almanac
1831   No. X   Hagerstown, Maryland
Printed and sold by John Gruber, South Potomac Street:
Where German Almanacs can also be had.

Respecting the American Colonization Society
and the Colony of Liberia
Extracted from a late publication of said Society,
printed at Washington City in 1830

This Society was formed at Washington City in December 1816, for the purpose of colonizing, with their own consent, on the coast of Africa, or such other place as Congress shall deem expedient, the People of Colour in our country already free, and others who may hereafter be liberated by the humanity of individuals, or the laws of the States.

In Maine, New Hampshire, Connecticut, Vermont, New York, New Jersey, Pennsylvania, Maryland, Virginia, North

of Washington County, Maryland

Carolina, Alabama, Tennessee, Kentucky, Ohio and Indiana, State Societies have been formed, auxiliary to the American Colonization Society, besides upwards of 150 County and Town Auxiliaries.

It has hitherto had no direct assistance from the General Government. The income of the Society, during the 13 years of its existence, has been about 106,000 dollars. The contributions from January 1829 to January 1830 amounted to 20,295 dollars and 60 cents.

To say nothing of the assistance already afforded to the emigrants, in enabling them to establish themselves on the coast of Africa with so fair a prospect of future comfort and prosperity, the Society has accomplished great good by the diffusion of information, by provoking discussion, and by calling forth powerful sympathies in favor of the Africans generally. It has shown how manumissions can be effected without injury to any class of society; and of the emigrants which it has removed to Africa, more than 200 have been slaves liberated by their masters, for the purpose of colonization.

The Colony was established in December 1821. Dr. Elie Ayres and Capt. Stockton of the United States navy purchased the whole of Montserado, on the coast of Africa, and a most valuable tract of land on the river of the same name. The first settlers arrived at the Colony in June 1822. Mr. Ashmun took charge of the Colony as agent. To his zealous and persevering efforts is the Colony greatly indebted for its prosperity and success. After his death in 1828, Dr. Richard Randall succeeded him, who died soon after his arrival. Dr. Mechlin is the present agent. The population of the Colony is about 1500.

- *The original of this almanac is in the Western Maryland Room, Washington County Free Library, Hagerstown, Maryland.*

The Torch Light and Public Advertiser   **February 3, 1831**
Hagerstown, Maryland

Legislature of Maryland   House of Delegates
From the Maryland Republican of Saturday
Manumission and Colonization

Mr. Brawner submitted the following resolutions and order, which were severally ___? and adopted:

African American Manumissions

Resolved, That the increased proportion of the free people of colour in this state, ___? the white population, attests the evil growing out of the connection and unrestrained association with the slaves, their habits and manner of obtaining a subsistence, and their withdrawing a large portion of employment from the labouring class of the white population, are subjects of momentous and grave consideration to the good people of this state.

Resolved, That as philanthropists and lovers of freedom, we deplore the existence of slavery amongst us, and would use our utmost exertions to ameliorate its condition, yet we consider the unrestricted power of manumission as fraught with ultimate evils of a more dangerous tendency than the circumstance of slavery alone, and that any act, having for its object the mitigation of these joint evils, not inconsistent with other paramount considerations, would be worthy the attention and deliberation of the representatives of a free, liberal minded, and enlightened people.

Resolved, That we consider the colonization of free people of colour in Africa as the commencement of a system, by which, if judicious encouragement be afforded, these evils may be measurably diminished, so that in process of time, the relative proportion of the black to the white population, will hardly be matter for serious or unpleasant consideration.

Ordered therefore, That a committee of five members be appointed by the chair, with instructions to report a bill, based as nearly as may be, upon the principles contained in the foregoing, resolutions, and report the same to the consideration of this house. In pursuance whereof the speaker appointed Messrs. Brawner, Hawkins, Merrick, Bell and McMahon, the committe.

Mr. Brawner reported a bill in accordance on Thursday.

The bill goes to restrict manumission in this state in future, except upon condition of the payment of a sufficient sum to transport the persons manumitted to Liberia.

- *These preceding newspaper articles were taken from microfilm at the Washington County Free Library; bound indexes also are there. I have reproduced these excerpts exactly as they were printed, with no attempt to correct spelling or grammar.*

- *The Periodicals Department of the Enoch Pratt Library in Baltimore, Maryland has a large amount of information on the Maryland Colonization Society, including newspapers, manifests and the Liberia census.*

Jerry Summers, A Freed Slave from Washington County

A Registry of Artificates granted to such Negroes in Washington County under the act of Assembly passed at November session 1805. Chapter 66. Entitled an additional supplement to an Act, entitled an Act relating to Negroes, and to repeal the acts of assembly therein mentioned.

of Washington County, Maryland

Appendix J

Washington County Court Documents

Washington County Court Minutes and Proceedings, October 1811

October 29, 1811: page 18 - Negro Lydia and her three children, Richard, 10 years old, Patty, 7 years old and Elizabeth, 3 years old, are certified as the property of Thomas B. Evans.

Listing of Slaves in Washington County Land Records

Name of Negro	Name	Document Type	Liber Folio	Date
	Margaret A. Mason	B	IN1 141	1845
	Maria Oliver	D	IN2 640	1847
	Maria Oliver	D	IN2 641	1847
	John C. Unseld		IN7 213	1852
	Mary A. Moore		TT 269	1838
Emaline	George Hughes		TT 488	1838
	Josiah D. Flagg		TT 386	1838
Rose & Child	Samuel Silvers		TT 705	1838
	George S. Kennedy		TT 388	1838
	Samuel B. Harris		TT 800	1839
	Thomas G. Harris		TT 404	1838
	Samuel S. Cunningham		UU 452	1839
	Thomas G. Harris		UU 501	1839
	Adam Weaver	D	UU 706	1839
	Samuel B. Harris		UU 771	1840

- *General Index to Land Records - Washington County, Maryland, To December 31, 1932, Volume L, p. 231, "List of Slaves"*

Key to Document Type

DM = Deed of Manumission   C = Certificate of Freedom
R = Relinquish   M = Mortgage   L = List of Slaves
B = Bill of Sale   F = Freedom   D = Deed

African American Manumissions

*Editors's Note: The names in these tables are **not** indexed in the back of the book. Also, except as otherwise noted, all the following entries are Deeds of Manumission.*

Listing of Transactions Regarding African Americans in Washington County Land Records

Name of Negro	Name	Document Type	Liber Folio	Date
Ceaser	[blank]	C	K 674	1798
Bob	Thomas Prather	F	K 705	1798
Joe	Thomas Prather	F	M 115	1799
Margaret	Christian Eversole	F	N 107	1800
Poll	Christian Vansant	F	P 524	1804
Philis	Barnet Houser	F	P 574	1804
Nelly	John Henry	M	P 769	1804
Paul	Samuel DeButts	F	N 44	1800
Phebe	Frederick Hersh	F	N 314	1801
Grace	John Clagett	F	R 317	1805
Priscilla	Margaret Cook	C	R 224	1805
Betty	Frederick Shehann	F	R 354	1805
List of	Thomas Ringgold	R	R 505	1805
Caleb	Michael Fenceler	F	S 90	1806
William	Robert Smith	F	S 746	1807
Nelly	Thomas Allender	F	S 1058	1808
Samuel	John Stonebraker	F	S 1059	1808
Kate	Lydia Prather	F	T 231	1809
Susan	Mary Middlekauff	F	T 102	1808
George	John Lynch	F	T 249	1809
Frank	Arch McCoy	F	T 508	1808
Robert C.	Michael Kapp	F	W 426	1811
Sam	Charles F. Goll	F	W 494	1811
Mary	Abraham Moyer	DM	W 897	1811
Lucy	Christian T. Goll	F	W 912	1811
Thomas	Daniel Sprigg	F	W 915	1812
Nelly	Frederick Dorsey	F	Y 2	1812
Stephen	John Hershey	F	Y 116	1812
Henry	John Hershey	F	Y 117	1812
Nero	Nathan Sutten	F	Y 238	1812
Nelly	Richard Geary	F	Y 318	1812
Margaret	Robert McGinty	F	Y 429	1812

of Washington County, Maryland

Name of Negro	Name	Document Type	Liber Folio	Date
Vincient	Jacob Brosius	F	Y 919	1813
Farmer	Baltzer G. Goll	F	Z 479	1814
Prissey	Jacob Kern	F	Z 547	1814
Rachel	P. Humrichouse	F	AA 85	1814
Priscilla	C.L.D. Grinderman	F	AA 113	1814
Ann	Arch Irwin	DM	AA 191	1815
List of	Nathaniel Willis	F	AA 208	1815
Henly & Washington	Pendleton Heronimus	F	AA 320	1815
Nace	George Cellar	F	BB 35	1816
Anthony	William Heyser	DM	BB 89	1816
Richard	Leonard Snyder	F	BB 132	1816
Sarah	Thomas Shuman	F	BB 214	1816
List of	John R. Hyland	F	BB 246	1816
Peter	Thomas Shuman	F	BB 500	1816
Hezekiah & Sharper	Josiah Reilly	C	BB 501	1816
Beck	Nathaniel Posey	F	BB 570	1816
Sall	Col. Wm. Fitzhugh	F	BB 577	1816
James	Jacob Zeller	F	BB 636	1816
Jacob	Benjamin Edwards	F	BB 641	1816
Henry & Sarah	James Ringgold	F	BB 690	1816
Rachel & Sarah	Thomas Edwards	F	BB 784	1817
Fanny	Thomas Belt	F	BB 779	1817
Richard	William Fitzhugh	D	BB 993	1817
Rachel	William Fitzhugh	F	BB 993	1817
Nace	William Fitzhugh	F	BB 994	1817
Mary	Otho H. Williams	D	BB 995	1817
Maria	William Dillahunt	D	CC 148	1817
Thomas	E.G. Williams	F	CC 421	1818
Rachel	E.E.G. Williams	F	CC 422	1817
Sarah	[blank]	C	CC 467	1818
Nan	Christian Hilliard	F	CC 853	1818
Lucy	David Boyd	F	CC 977	1818
Hannah	Matthew VanLear	F	DD 19	1818
Jacob	Thomas Boteler	F	DD 378	1819
Washington	Matthew VanLear	F	DD 384	1819
Susan	Peter Zollinger	F	DD 400	1819

African American Manumissions

Name of Negro	Name	Document Type	Liber Folio	Date
Rachel	Elizabeth Easton	F	DD 627	1819
Nan	William Hammond	F	DD 633	1819
Priss	Peter Gilbert	F	EE 221	1819
Tom	Henry Lewis	M	EE 443	1820
Sarah	Hezekiah Cooper	F	EE 499	1820
Jack	Esther Eagleton	F	EE 507	1820
Lucy	Thomas Shuman	F	EE 833	1820
Charlotte	Daniel Schnebly	F	FF 284	1821
Fanny	Michael Avey	F	FF 605	1822
Ben	James Tenant	F	FF 606	1822
Nace	Benjamin Yoe	F	FF 662	1822
Patrick	Isaac Long	F	GG 49	1823
Lewis	Samuel M. Hitt	F	GG 322	1823
Susan	John Hogg, Jr.	F	GG 451	1823
Grace	Catharine Miller	--	GG 502	1823
Phoebe	Josiah Price	F	GG 676	1824
Butler	Benjamin Yoe	F	GG 682	1824
Theodotie	Josiah Price	F	GG 690	1824
Mahala	Elizabeth Miller	F	GG 728	1824
Nelly	Nancy Myers	F	GG 814	1824
Nelly	Nancy Myers	Indte	GG 815	1824
Rachel	E.G. Williams	F	GG 916	1824
Ann	Solomon Chase	DM	GG 1008	1824
Nace	Hezekiah Boteler	F	HH 117	1825
List of	Casper W. Weaver	F	HH 512	1825
Nathaniel	George Crouse	F	HH 529	1825
Nancy	Hanson Jones	F	HH 597	1825
List of	Jacob T. Towson	F	HH 942	1826
Fanny & Milly	Philip Reeder	F	HH 1056	1826
Abraham	Hannah Johnson	DM	HH 1157	1826
Jemima	William Gabby	F	II 272	1827
Mary	James Reeside	F	II 725	1827
Rebecca	George Thomas	F	II 726	1827
Charles & Hannah	Philip Reeder	F	II 834	1828
Yarga	Samuel Young	F	KK 54	1828
Polly	John Ridenour & wfF		KK 2116	1828
Charity	Daniel Sprigg	F	KK 324	1828
Sarah	Catherine Gierhart	F	KK 351	1828
Jacob	George Bean	F	KK 721	1829

of Washington County, Maryland

Name of Negro	Name	Document Type	Liber Folio	Date
Susannah	Nathaniel Summers	F	KK 739	1829
Letty	Michael Neikirk	F	LL 18	1829
Mary	Henry Martin	F	LL 531	1830
Fanny	Mary Dillahunt	F	LL 886	1830
Delia	William Clingan	F	LL 900	1830
Alfred	Maria A. Ringgold	F	MM 61	1830
Eloilet	Nathaniel Summers	F	MM 238	1831
Phebe	Mary Hershey	F	MM 303	1831
Delia	John Swartzwelder	F	MM 476	1831
William	William T. Compton	F	MM 783	1832
List of	John Kennedy	F	MM 864	1832
List of	Joseph Martin	F	MM 914	1832
Hetty	Daniel Schnebley	F	NN 283	1832
Joseph	George Bean	F	NN 639	1932
Ivis	Maria A. Ringgold	F	OO 245	1833
Mary	John Myers	F	OO 678	1833
List of	Gabriel Swan	F	PP 485	1834
Daniel Abel	Susanna Hughes	DM	SS 550	1837
Hannah Reeder	Henry Rice & wife	D	SS 580	1837
Daniel Brooks	Jacob Dunn		SS 703	1837
Notley Hopewell	Tobias Johnson		SS 838	1837
Emily & Charles	Joseph E. Snodgrass (List of Slaves)		TT 234	1838
Charlotte & Jane	Eve Moudy		TT 266	1838
Nan & Samuel	Jane Hillerd		TT 566	1837
Massa & Children	Lewis Howard		TT 568	1838
Herod Vowls	William F. Hebb		TT 578	1838
Dorcas	Samuel Buhrman		UU 518	1839
Dent Brown	Adam Weaver		UU 714	1839
Jacob Ross	John A. Adams		UU 715	1839
Letty	Charles Rice		YY 192	1841
Nancy	John Eakle		YY 595	1841
Benjamin	Isaac Breathed		OHW2 892	1845
Polly	Samuel Newcomer		IN1 305	1846
Arthur	Nathaniel Summers		IN1 363	1846
Samuel Bean	Daniel P. Miller		IN1 682	1846
Erasmus Taylor	Anthony Varner		IN2 123	1846
Thomas Clements	John VanLear, Jr. Exr		IN2 168	1846
Thomas Kane	Maria E. Reynolds		IN2 226	1846
Arnold J.	John T. Mason		IN2 245	1847

African American Manumissions

Name of Negro	Name	Document Type	Liber Folio	Date
Benjamin W. & Louisa & Isaac & Silva	Nathaniel Summers	IN2	446	1847
Thomas Williams & Richard Waters	Nathaniel Summers	IN2	447	1847
Sophia	Jacob K. Harry, Exr.	(B of S)	IN2 617	1847
Sarah Pearce	Benjamin Long		IN2 618	1847
Johon Barnes	Jacob Firey		IN2 634	1847
Ann B & Children	Thomas Bell		IN2 645	1847
Lucy	Ann Tarvia	Cert	IN2 665	1847
Agnes R.	John Witmer		IN2 667	1847
John Brown	Henry Fiery		IN2 698	1847
Cloe Dorsey & Maria Matthews & Thomas Jones	Elizabeth Laurence		IN2 735	1847
Loyd	Michael Swingley		IN2 746	1847
Maria Summers	Jacob Firey		IN3 123	1848
Ellen Binder	Virginia W. Mason		IN3 178	1848
Rachel Lindsay	John Nicodemus		IN3 283	1848
Moses Tabbs	J.H. Bowles		IN3 658	1848
Henry Hill	Joseph Long		IN3 695	1848
Ann B.	Isabella Finley		IN3 713	1848
William Harrison	Solomon James		IN3 734	1848
Rachael	Ruth S. Prather		IN3 766	1848
John Rozier	E. Stake		IN4 151	1849
Jim Shorter & wife	Virginia W. Mason		IN4 187	1849
John Brown	Warford Mann		IN4 317	1849
Maria VanLear	John Reel		IN4 353	1849
Joshua	Susan Harry		IN4 405	1849
Richard Hill	David Nikirk		IN4 444	1849
Thomas Sanders	Daniel Winters		IN4 444	1849
Louisa Abel	Daniel Winters		IN4 489	1847
Nancy Anderson	Daniel Winters		IN4 490	1849
Alexander P.	David Long		IN4 524	1849
Malinda James	Margaret Booth		IN13 550	1858
Benjamin S.	Michael Smith		IN4 657	1849
Mary E. Mahomett	Sarah A. Price	D	IN13 712	1859
Richard Pindle	Isaac Cane		IN4 788	1850
Levi Kane	J. Dixon Roman		IN5 70	1850
Harriet Smith	James A. Magrude		IN5 193	1850
Mary Phenix	Benjamin Witmer		IN5 214	1850

of Washington County, Maryland

Name of Negro	Name	Document Type	Liber Folio	Date
Chloe Chase		Susan Middlekauff	IN5 271	1850
William Brown		Sally Troup	IN5 278	1850
Limus Linch		Ann E. Cushwa	IN5 291	1850
Henry Walker		Joseph Krotzer	IN5 293	1850
Francis Kane & Ann M. Smith		Sarah A. Price D	IN5 310	1850
Mary M. Dorsey		Rutha & Thomas Dorsey Deed	IN5 336	1850
Sarah Wagoner		William H. Fitzhugh	IN5 394	1850
Tom		Jacob K. Harry	IN5 445	1850
Jane Cosey		Samuel W. Jones	IN5 449	1850
Arthur S.		John Mullendore	IN5 596	1851
Margaret Pierce		John VanLear, Jr.	IN5 699	1851
Alex C. & Nathan Mingo		John VanLear, Jr.	IN5 700	1851
Lewis Mills		Mary Schnebley	IN6 34	1851
Ann		George Keahhofer	IN6 557	1852
Mary Dunward		David H. Keedy	IN6 708	1852
Peter Stephens		E. Woltz	IN6 771	1852
George Porter		Samuel Mason	IN7 137	1852
Delia Johnson		Frederick Brian	IN7 453	1853
Catharine Campbell		Samuel Williams	IN7 703	1853
Mary C. Harper		Samuel Craig	IN8 179	1853
Geeorge Harrison		Richard Harrison	IN8 199	1853
Peter Sophers		Catharine Ridenour	IN8 605	1854
Clarisa Goeres		Susan E. Rench	IN9 58	1854
Jane Goens		Susan E. Rench	IN9 96	1854
Mark Marshall		James Tennant	IN9 118	1854
Emily Marshall		James Tennant	IN9 119	1854
James Dover		Nathaniel Summers	IN9 145	1854
George W. Bently		Michael Jones	IN9 411	1855
Jacob Brown		Catharine Schindel	IN9 521	1855
Ann M. H.		Henrietta Gaither	IN9 625	1855
Jacob Jeffrey		Jacob Ames	IN9 651	1855
Mathias Hanson		Esther Briscoe	IN9 675	1855
Mary Coon		Henrietta T. Tilghman	IN9 687	1855
John White		Jacob Dellinger	IN9 752	1855
Catharine Howard		Henrietta Gaither	IN10 150	1855
Andrew		Daniel Reichard	IN11 37	1856
Joseph Blake		John Campbell White	IN11 34	1856
Theophilus Green		Jacob Funk (of Jno)	IN11 51	1856

African American Manumissions

Name of Negro	Name	Document Type	Liber Folio	Date
Madison Goings		Susan E. Rench D	IN11 70	1856
Laurence Taylor		Elizabeth Kershner	IN11 167	1856
John Fletcher		Martha Huyett	IN11 291	1856
Mary Dickerson		Sarah & Julianna Gaither	IN11 292	1856
Mary Dickerson		Daniel Huyett & wife	IN11 292	1856
Abner Howard		James A. Magruder	IN11 605	1857
Dennis Lewis		Eliza Davis	IN11 695	1857
Eliza		Susan E. Rench	IN11 709	1857
Rebecca Johnson		Joseph Rench	IN11 796	1857
Charlotte		Isaac Butterbaugh	IN12 161	1856
Melvin Young & Charles		Isaac Butterbaugh	IN12 511	1857
Cath. Thompson		Mary M. Gelwicks	IN12 562	1857
Maria Green		Joseph Newcomer	IN12 723	1857
Lucy Lynch		J. Campbell White	IN12 780	1858
Peter Taylor		Henry Fiery	IN13 134	1858
Elizabeth Howard		E. Virginia Donnelly	IN13 192	1858
Elizabeth Howard		Sarah & Mary Donnelly	IN13 192	1858
Thomas Mills		Mary Schnebley	IN13 197	1858
William Gasper		Joseph S. Moore	IN13 197	1858
Cornelius Goings		Henry Goings	IN13 277	1858
Kitty Brooks & Caroline V. Brooks		John B. Kerfoot	IN13 298	1858
Hester A. Boteler		Susanna Magruder	IN13 538	1858
Eliza Brooks		Joseph Rench	IN13 554	1858
Comfort Cooper		George Feidt	IN13 597	1858
Elizabeth Brooks		John E. Shup	IN13 599	1858
Harriet McKey		Juliana Gaither	IN13 618	1858
Eliza Moxley & Joseph Moxley & Thomas Moxley & Allen Moxley		Louisa Dorsey	IN13 634	1859
Otho L. Taylor		David Zeller	IN13 649	1860
Otho Dockens		Elizabeth Kershner	IN13 649	1860
William Parks		William Colklesser	IN13 683	1859
Emma J. Mahomett & Emma Mahonnett & Jeremiah H. Mahomett		Sarah A. Price	IN13 712	1859
Fanny Gant & Heirs		David Gant	IN13 714	1859
Sstephen Stansbury		Joseph M. MIddlekauff	IN14 51	1859
Samuel Curtis		Mary A. McKinley	IN14 102	1859

of Washington County, Maryland

Name of Negro	Name	Document Type	Liber Folio	Date
Nancy Campbell		Andrew Miller	IN14 129	1859
Jacob Brown		Mary A. Shafer	IN14 158	1859
Frances Palmer & Ann Taylor		Julia A. Reichard	IN14 313	1859
Hanson Evans		William S. Stonebraker &wife	IN14 510	1860
Andrew Howard		Jonathan Thomas	IN14 520	1860
Rebecca		Stephen Puterbaugh	IN14 545	1860
Isaac Clemens		Matthew VanLear	IN14 564	1860
Isaac Clemens		Casper Shunk & wife	IN14 564	1860
Isaac Clemens		Sophia V.L. Findlay	IN14 564	1860
Isaac Clemens		Joseph T. VanLear	IN14 564	1860
Lewis Moody		Susan Middlekauff	IN14 641	1860
Mary Anderson		Michael Grimes	IN14 643	1860
David Lyles		Thomas H. Crampton	IN14 643	1860
Henrietta Sands		Henrietta Sands Sr.	IN14 643	1860
Lewis Dickerson & Samuel Chesley		Sarah Gaither	IN14 644	1860
Mary E. Williams		John & Benjamin Ingram	IN14 644	1860
James Twine & Mary V. Twine		Samuel Zeller	IN14 645	1860
Alcinda Campbell		Emma Merrick	IN14 645	1860
Antoinett Cane		Sarah A. Price	IN14 645	1860
Isabella Small		Mary J. Watson	IN14 645	1860
Betsey Fowler & Alice Fowler & John Fowler & Susan Fowler		Richard Ragan	IN14 646	1860
Mary Kalip		Elizabeth McClain	IN14 646	1860
Charles Chase & Benjamin Grant & John Chase & William Chase		Samuel Eichelberger	IN14 647	1860
Fanny Chase & Amos Grant & Louisa Chase & Mary Chase		Samuel Eichelberger	IN14 647	1860
H. Chase & Alex Chase & M.E. Grant		Samuel Eichelberger	IN14 647	1860
Frances Fellman		Harriet A. Hall	IN14 647	1860
George Brown		Mary Shafer	IN14 648	1860
Ellen Dockens & Eli & Nel Saunders		Elizabeth Kershner	IN14 648	1860
Alfred Mack		Eliza E. Williams	IN14 648	1860

African American Manumissions

Name of Negro	Name	Document Type	Liber Folio	Date
Cornelius Green & James Curtis & Robert Munsebaugh	David Zeller		IN14 649	1860
Elizabeth Munsebaugh & L. Munsebaugh & Malinda Munsebaugh & Margaret Munsebaugh	David Zeller		IN14 6499	1860
Daniel Tyler	John B. Eakle		IN14 650	1860
Grace	Catharine Miller		-- --- --	

- *General Index to Land Records - Washington County, Maryland, To December 31, 1932, Volume N - O, p. 119, "Negroes"*

Other information on this subject can be found in the text of the Deeds of Manumission and of the Certificates of Freedom in Wills.

The Hagerstown Mail   September 13, 1839
A Kidnapper Caught

A young man, named John P. May, was committed to the jail of this county, on Wednesday last, charged with kidnapping and offering to sell a free black boy, 18 or 19 years of age, of Mifflin county, Pa. We understand that May, some weeks since made a proposition to Mr. William Freaner of this place, to furnish him with negroes from Pennsylvania. A time and place was fixed upon for the first delivery. May was there agreeably to arrangement - and so was Freaner, and his brother officer Sheckles, but with authority to arrest the offender to be dealt with as the law directs. May induced the black boy to accompany him to this place, by telling him that they would here connect themselves with a Circus company.

The Torch Light and Public Advertiser, Nov. 15, 1827
Excerpt from page 2, column F
FOR LIBERIA

"The following coloured persons are passengers: From Baltimore – Anthony Wood, wife and child,...John Q Adams, (a recaptured African,)... Joseph Dickinson, wife and child, from Hagers-town [See A61c for manumission of Joseph Dickinson]...the slaves of Daniel Murray, Esq. manumitted."

African American Manumissions of Washington County, Maryland

Book A

of Washington County, Maryland

A1a - Inside Front Cover
It has been proven to my satisfaction that Sarah Ann Beltzhower and Henry Joseph Belthower are the children of Henry & Amelia Beltzhower, the said Amelia Beltzhower being a free woman of color manumitted by Thomas Prather of this County before the birth of said children - the said Sarah Ann was born on the 12th of March 1818 and Henry Joseph on the 13th of July 1819 in this County.
        Jany 9, 1830   J.S. Smith Dpy Clk

A1b
A Registry of Certificates granted to free Neg[roes] in Washington County under the act of Assembly passed at November session 1805. Chapter 66, En___[page broken off - could be "Entitled"?]an additional supplement to an act, entit[led?] an act relating to Negroes, and to repeal the acts of assembly therein mentioned.

A1c   State of Maryland, Washington County, Towit:
I hereby Certify that Sarah Butler, hath satis[fied] me by her own oath, that Cecelia Butler the bearer hereof who applies for this Certificate, is free born and of free condition, that she was born in St. Mary's County in the State of Maryland, and hath resided in Washington County about fourteen years, said Cecelia Butler is about five feet two Inches high, about twenty four years of age of a dark complexion, no notable marks
Certificate given the 15th day of August 1806
        Test O.H. Williams Clk

A1d   State of Maryland, Washington County, Towit:
I hereby Certify that it appears to me by the deposition of John Bryan taken before Thomas Kennedy one of the Justices of the peace for Washington County that Sarah Foster alias Sara_____ [corner of page broken off - doesn't appear to be room for a surname, however] the bearer hereof who applies for this Certi[ficate] born and of free condition, that she was born on the Eastern shore of the State of Maryland and hath some time since resided in Washington County said Sarah is about five feet two Inches high, of a yellowish complexion, about twenty one or

African American Manumissions

twenty two years of age has a Slight scar on her right arm below the elbow, and also a small scar on her left arm a little above the elbow.   Certificate given the 15th day of August 1806
         Test O.H. Williams Clk

A2a   State of Maryland, Washington County, Towit:
I hereby Certify that it appears to me by the last will and Testament of Mrs. Mary Ringgold deceased which said will appears to have been proven before the Register of Wills for Washington County aforesaid on the twentieth day of August 1805, that Jim Demby the bearer hereof is liberated, manumated and discharged from bondage and it further appears to me by the information of Samuel Ringgold Esquire that Jim Demby was born and brought up in Kent County Maryland, the said Jim Demby is about five feet six inches high about twenty six years of age of a dark yellow complexion, an open countenance, a small scarr above his left eye no other notable mark perceivable
         Certificate given the 10th day of September 1806
         Test O.H. Williams Clk

A3a   State of Maryland, Washington County, Towit:
I hereby Certify that it appears to me by the Land records of Washington County, that negro Richard the bearer hereof who now calls himself Richard Summers was liberated, manumitted and discharged from Servitude from and after the fifteenth day of August 1806 by his then Master Edward Breathed, said Negro Richard was born in Prince George's County, but has principally resided in Washington County in the State of Maryland he is about five feet six inches high, about twenty five years of age of a black complexion has a scar on his right temple about the size of a cent it has the appearance to have been occasioned by a burn, and another between his eyes which appears to have been a cut
         Certificate given the 13th day of September 1806
         Test O.H. Williams Clk

A3b
I hereby Certify that Dolly Shorter the bearer hereof hath satisfied me by sufficient evidence that she was born free in Charles County in the State of Maryland. The said Dolly Shorter is about five feet two Inches high, about twenty two years of age of a black complexion, a tolerable wide mouth and shows her teeth much when she laughs, a small scar about the size of a cent

of Washington County, Maryland

on her left Jaw occasioned by a Bile no other notable marks perceivable. Certificate given the 17th November 1806
Test O.H. Williams Clk

A4a
I hereby Certify that Richard Philpot the bearer hereof hath satisfied me by sufficient evidence that he obtained his freedom by serving a certain John Miller for the term of two years and six months by a contract between said Miller and a certain George C. Smoot whose property he formerly was which said contract expired some time about June 1798. the said Richard Philpot is about six feet high aged from about sixty five to seventy years of a black complexion was raised in Charles County in the State of Maryland, has three of his fingers on the right hand contracted in the first Joints occasioned by a burn no other notable marks perceivable.
Certificate Given the 24th day of November 1807
Test O.H. Williams Clk

A4b State of Maryland Washington County towit -
I hereby Certify that Thomas Harris the bearer hereof hath satisfied me by sufficient evidence that he was set free by Genl. Daniel Hiester previous to his removal from Pennsylvania to Maryland, and in consideration of which the said Thomas Harris served the said Hiester for the Term of six years as appears by a certificate of Indenture in the possession of the said Thomas Harris. The said Thomas Harris is six feet high, about forty five years of age, not very black, was sest free on the 18th March 1803 was raised in the State of New Jersey; he is marked with the small pox, has a scar maily[?] below the left eye, and a large scar below the calf of the left leg occasioned by a burn - speaks the German language.
Certificate given the 19th August 1809
Test   O.H. Williams Clk

A5a State of Maryland Washington county Towit, I hereby Certify that George Gray the bearer hereof hath satisfied me by Sufficient Evidence that he [rest of page is blank]

A6a State of Maryland, Washington County, Towit:
I hereby Certify that Harry Collins a negro the beaarer hereof hath satisfied me by sufficient evidence that he was born free

African American Manumissions

that he was bound to Col. Nathaniel Rochester of Elizabeth Town Washington County and state of Maryland as an apprentice to be taught the art and business of a nailer until he arrived to the age of twenty one years - The said Harry Collins is about five feet seven Inches high abut twenty four years of age of a black complexion a tolerable wide mouth and a good set of teeth a scar on his left arm a little above the wrist occasioned (he says) by the cut of sickle no other notable mark perceivable
Certificate given the 28th day of February 1807
        Test   O.H. Williams Clk

A6b   State of Maryland, Washington County, Towit:
I hereby certify, that Harry Johnson, a negro the bearer hereof, was raised in Washington county aforesaid, and that he hath satisfied me by sufficient evidence, that he is entitled to his freedom; the said Harry Johnson is about five feet six Inches high, about thirty five years of age, very black a tolerable wide mouth, and shews his teeth much when he laughs, lame in his left leg occasioned, he says, by pain, no other notable mark perceivable.
        cert. given 5 July 1809   Tests   O.H. Williams Clk

A7a   State of Maryland, Washington County, Towit:
I hereby Certify that Negroe Peter the bearer hereof was manumitted and set free by Adam Ott Esquire of Hagers Town in the County aforesaid on the Eighth day of December one thousand seven hundred and ninety four as appears by the records of Washington County Court said Peter is about five feet Eleven inches high has a scar under his right eye, is about twenty six years of age, of a black complextion, was born in Hagers Town and has always resided there
Certificate given 5th Sept. 1809. Test O.H. Williams, Clk

A7b   State of Maryland, Washington County, Towit:
I hereby certify that the Bearer hereof Negro James Young hath satisfied me by sufficient evidence that he was born free that he was born in Kent County in the State of Maryland and resided there until he was about fifteen years old and then removed into this County with his Father Samuel Young a free negro and has resided here ever since - The said James Young is about twenty five years old about five feet Seven and a half Inches high has a small scar on the left eyebrow and is of a Dark complextion

of Washington County, Maryland

Certificate given 17th Oct 1809
Test O.H. Williams Clk

A8a State of Maryland, Washington County, Towit:
I hereby Certify that the bearer hereof David Wilson a Black man has satisfied me by sufficient evidence that he was born free - that he was born in Kent County in the State of Maryland that he resided in Kent and Queen Anns County until the last Seven years which time he resided in Washington County (excepting five years which time he served in the Revolutionary War. The said Black man is about forty Six years old about five feet ten or Eleven Inches high has a scar over the right eye which appears to have been burnt and has a Scar on the upper part of his left arm near the shoulder which he says he received from a Sword in the Revolutionary War - has no other perceivable marks.
Test O.H. Williams Clk
Certificate given the 8th February 1810.

A8b State of Maryland, Washington County, Towit:
I hereby Certify that the Bearer hereof Simon Harris a Black man has satisfied me by sufficient evidence that he was set free by General Daniel Hiester, as also appears by an Instrument of writing dated 21st March 1797 recorded in my office - The said Simon is about 29 years of age, five feet nine inches and an half high stout built not very black, marked with the small pox, has a scar behind his right ear occasioned (as he says) by the bit of a Dog, has also a scar upon his upper lip & right cheek & speaks the German language.
Test O.H. Williams Clk   Certificate given 30' Oct. 1810.

A9a State of Maryland, Washington County, Towit:
I hereby certify that negro Prince the bearer hereof, is a free Man, that he has satisfied me by sufficient evidence , he was born in Kent County State of Maryland, that he was sold by his former Master for a term of years to McPherson and Brien at Antietam Works in Washington County and State of Maryland, with whom he finished his servitude.
The said Negro Prince is about twenty eight years of age, of a Black complexion, about five feet six Inches high, has the first joint of his left thumb off; no other notable mark perceivable.   Test O.H. Williams Clk
certificate given 8' Jany. 1812

African American Manumissions

A9b   State of Maryland, Washington County, Towit:
I hereby certify that the bearer hereof a molatto man named George Kreek was manumitted and set free by John Harry of Elizabeth Town Washington County and State of Maryland, as appears by a deed of manumission of this date, recorded in my office among the Land records. The said George Kreek formerly belonged to Samuel L. Che___ [page broken off] of Kent County in the State of Maryland, where he formerly lived, and was brought into this County by his Mistress about fifteen years ago, where he has since principaly resided, and was sold in November 1809 by Thomas M. Foaman administrator of Saml. L. Chew to Mr. George Ross of Elizabeth Town who transferred his right to John Harry - he is about five feet nine and a half Inches high about thirty four years old, he is sraight and well made, has a Scar about the size of a Dollar below his right knee, and another scar about an inch above his right eye, and a Scar on the left foot on his Instep occasioned by a Cut
Certificate given 22d Jany 1812   Test   O.H. Williams   Clk

A10a   State of Maryland, Washington County, Towit:
I hereby Certify that the bearer hereof James Butler a Mulatto Man has satisfied me by sufficient evidence, that he was Born free in Washington County and State of Maryland, that he was Bound to Richard Henderson & Compy [Company] of the County aforesaid until he arrived at age that he served said Richard Henderson and Co. some part of his time and was afterwards transferred to John McPherson & John Brien, with whom he finished his servitude -
The said James Butler is about Twenty one years of age of a yellowish complexion, about five feet nine Inches high, has a hole on the inside of his left knee accasioned, he says, by the white sweeling -
Cert. given 23rd Oct. 1811
Test   O.H. Williams   Clk

A10b   State of Maryland, Washington County, Towit:
I hereby certify that the bearer hereof Nancy Marke a Molatta Woman has satisfied me by Sufficient evidence that she was born free in Washington County and State of Maryland, that her mother was a white woman by the name of Molly Clarke, that she was bound by her mother to George Keishner of this County when about Six years old, and lived till she was free said Nancy

of Washington County, Maryland

Clarke is about twenty two years old a bright molatta about five feet three _nches [paper broken off] high, rather stout made, speaks the German and English Languages, and has always resided in this County
Cert. Given 16th Nov. 1811
Test   O.H. Williams   Clk

A11a   State of Maryland, Washington County, Towit:
I hereby certify that the bearer hereof Negro Milly, was Manumitted and set free by Rebecca Prather of Washington County and State of Maryland, as appears by a deed of Manumission dated Mar 28th day of November 1797. and Recorded in my office - The said Negro Milly is about thirty one years of age, of a black complexion, the little fingers of her right and left hand, some what stiff, no other notable mark perceivable.
Cert. given 23rd January 1812.

A11b   State of Maryland, Washington County, Towit:
I hereby Certify that the bearer hereof Jacob Jackson a blackman has satisfied me by Sufficient Evidence that he is entitled to his freedom that he has long resided and now resides in Washington County That he was born in Baltimore County in the family of John Bosley who removed to Somerset County in the State of Pennsylvania where the said Jacob Jackson was declared a free man by the decision of Somerset County Court the said Jacob is about twenty eight years of age five feet six inches high, dark complextion, a film on his right eye which covers near the half and injures the sight - one of the fingers of his right hand crooked with a Scar on the Joint - and a forgeman by Trade -
(Cert. Given 4th Aug. 1812.)

A12a   State of Maryland, Washington County, Towit:
I hereby Certify that the bearer hereof Negro Caleb who now calls himself Caleb Caff, was manumitted and set free by Michael Fansler of Washington County and State of Maryland, as appears by a Deed of Manumission dated the Eleventh day of April Eighteen hundred and Six and recorded in my office - the said negro Caleb Cuff is about twenty seven years old of a black complection, he appears to have had a cut on the knuckle of the little finger of his left hand, about Six feet high, and stout made, speaks German & English said Negro Caleb was born in

African American Manumissions

Pennsylvania and was brought to this County by Michael Fansler about twenty years ago, and has lived in this County ever since. (Cert. given the 30th day of Sept. 1812.)

A12b   State of Maryland, Washington County, Towit:
I hereby Certify that it appears by the records of Proceedings of Washington County Court in a Suit depending between Negro Jerry petitioner for freedom and Jean Carlisle Charlotte Carlisle and William Carlisle defendants at April Term one thousand seven hundred and ninty Six that the said Negro Jerry obtained his freedom by Judgment of the said Court against the said defendents   Said Negro Jerry who now calls himself Jerry Smith is about forty one years of age, five feet seven Inches high dark complection has a Scar on the top of his left wrist and a Scar on the top of his left hand - and has resided in this county since he obtained his freedom.   (Cert given 12th Oct. 1812)

A13a   State of Maryland, Washington County, Towit:
I hereby Certify that the bearer hereof Richard Hatton a negro man has satisfied me by sufficient evidence that he was born free in this County near Jacques furnace [several words written here but deliberately smeared out while still wet] where his mother Catharine a free woman now lives, that he was bound unto George Dragoonier on the thirteenth day of April Eighteen hundred and ten to serve said Dragoonier ten years. which term he served - said Richard is about 21 years of age five feet five Inches high rather stout made of a yellowish complection large feet and hands.(Cert. given 25th Nov. 1812)

A13b   State of Maryland, Washington County, Towit:
I hereby Certify that Maria James a Mulatto woman has satisfied me by Sufficient evidence that she was born free in this County at Hughes forge and has always lived in this County where her mother Tabitha James then lived. Said Maria is about twenty four years of age, about five feet four inches high; has a scar on the right side of her neck and a large Scar on the inside of her left arm near the elbow, and has lost the big toe of her right foot, cut off at the second Joint -
         (Cert. Given 10th Nov. 1813)

of Washington County, Maryland

A14a State of Maryland, Washington County, Towit:
I hereby Certify that the bearer hereof Hezekiah Clements has satisfied me by sufficient evidence that he was born free in Montgomery County State of Maryland where he was bound at three years of age by the orphans Court of said County to Charles McDade until he should arrive at the age of twenty one years, that the said McDade removed to this County some years ago and brought with him the said Hezekiah, and that the said Hezekiah lived with him until he was free and has ever since lived in this County - said negro man is about twenty two years of age about five feet ten Inches high, of a yellowish complection, and has a large Scar under the right Eye.
(Cert. given 29th Nov. 1813) -

A14b State of Maryland, Washington County, Towit:
I hereby certify that the bearer hereof Letty Butler has Satisfied me by Sufficient evidence that she was born free, and has lived in this County since her birth, that she resided with Mr. Daniel Gehr of this County from her infancy, said Letty Butler is about twenty three years of age about five feet five or six inches high, of a Dark complection, has a scar on the left arm above the elbow.
(Cert. given 17th June 1814)

A15a State of Maryland, Washington County, Towit:
I hereby Certify that the bearer hereof negro Rachel Young hath satisfied me by Sufficient testimony that she was born free in Kent County State of Maryland, and resided there until she was about thirteen years old, and then removed into this County and resided with her father Samuel Young a free man and has resided here ever since - The said negro Rachel is about twenty six years old, very black complection about five feet three Inches high.
Cert. Given 8th Augt 1815   O.H. Williams Clk.
[This next entry has been crossed out with several X's.]

A15b State of Maryland, Washington County, Towit:
I hereby Certify that it appears by the record of Washington County that the bearer hereof Robert Creek was manumitted by Michael Kieff of this County on the 16th day of May 1811 to be freed on the 1st January 1817 and it also appears that the said Robert Creek was transferred to Jacob Shahlot[?] of this County

African American Manumissions

deceased by Theobald Eichelberger of Washington County Administrator of Jacob Sholl deceased said Robert Creek is about [blank space here] years old

A16a   State of Maryland, Washington County, Towit:
I hereby Certify that the bearer hereof Jenny Cromwell a black woman has satisfied me by sufficient proof that she was born free, in Somerset County in this State, that when she was about two years old she was removed to this County by her mother Susanna Ridout a free black woman and has resided in this County ever since, said Jenny is about five feet five & a half Inches high about nineteen years of age, has a Scar on the upper part of her right breast about two Inches in length, and another scar on the left arm - said Jenny Cromwell has a male child about three years old called Henry Elie - Given under my hand this 11 Dec. 1815.

A17a   State of Maryland, Washington County, Towit:
I Otho Holland Williams, Clerk of the County Court of the County aforesaid, do hereby certify that negro Harry Curtis has satisfied me by good and sufficient testimony that he was born free in Saint Marys County in the State aforesaid and resided there until he was about ["fifty" has been crossed out and "21" written over top] 21 years old that he then removed to this county where he has ever since resided and still resides the said Harry is about fifty years of age about 5 feet 8 inches high, nearly black. his left ear is much smaller than the right, he having lost nearly all the external cartilage thereof in an obstinate battle fought by the said Harry some years since. He has also several other trophies or scars which may assist in identifying him to wit: a large gash on the inner side of his right arm just above the wrist and a cut across the left eyebrow -
and he is by trade a Stone quarrier
In Testimony whereof on the 27 day of January AD. 1815
          O.H. Williams Clk   C. C. Court

A18a   State of Maryland, Washington County, Towit:
I hereby Certify that the bearer hereof a Black man named Charles Brien was manumitted and set free by Christian Lantz of the County aforessaid as appears by a Deed of Manumission dated the Eleventh day of August 1815 and recorded in ____? office - The said Charles Brien is about thirty Eight or nine years

of Washington County, Maryland

of age, about five feet Eleven inches high, has a Scar about six inches long on his back under the shoulder blade of his left arm occasioned by the cut of a Scythe - was born in Prince Georges County in this State the property of the late Richard Pindell and on his decease became the property of Doctr. Richard Pindell who brought him to this County ___? thirty years ago, in whose possession he remained until a few years since when he was sold to the above named Chr. Lantz.
(Cert. given 28th Decr. 1815.)

A18b State of Maryland, Washington County, Towit:
I hereby certify that ___? appears by the Records of Washington County that the bearer hereof Negro Anna was manumitted by John T. Mason of the County aforesaid when she should arrive at the age of Eighteen - and Anna was sold by said J. T. Mason to Richard Ragan of Hagers Town w[?] Ato[?] whom she served until the 1 Jany. 1816 at which time she was to be free. the said Anna was born in St. Marys County the property of the late Richd Barns, and was brought to this County when she was a child where she has remained ever since is about five feet two inches high nearly black, is slender made, has a Scar on the right Eye brow.
    Cert. given 1 Feby 1816.

A19a State of Maryland, Washington County, Towit:
I hereby Certify that it appears by the records of Washington County that the bearer hereof Negro Henry Holland was manumitted and set free from slavery by Nathaniel Rochester of the County aforesaid on the 6th day of May 1808. the said Negro Henry Holland is about thirty four years of age not very black, the little finger on his left hand is crooked and also has the mark of a cut between the fore and middle finger. is a Nailer by trade about five feet seven Inches high, Stout made, was born in Annapolis and was brought to this County when a child and has remained therein ever since.
    (Cert. Given 22d August 1816.)

A19b State of Maryland, Washington County, Towit:
I hereby Certify that the bearer hereof David Booth hath satisfied me by sufficient evidence that he was born free in George-Town District of Columbia and resided there until he was about fifteen years old and then removed into this County with his mother

African American Manumissions

Rachel a free woman and has resided here ever since - the said David Booth is about twenty seven years old about five feet nine or ten Inches high a bright Mulatto, a Speck on the right eye which has destroyed the sight, has a scar on the upper part of his forehead above the right eye.
  (Cert. Given 31st Augt. 1816.)

A20a State of Maryland, Washington County, Towit:
I hereby Certify that it appears by the records of Washington County that the bearer hereof Susanna Imes was manumitted and set free by Mrs. Mary Middlecauff of the County aforesaid on the twenty ninth day of August 1808. to take effect on the 29th August 1816. the said Susanna is about twenty one years of age about five feet seven inches high, very stout, a bright Mulatto, one Joint on each of the small fingers of her right hand cut off, and the middle finger of the same hand crooked, has two large scars on the back of the left hand, was born in Washington County and has always resided therein.
  (cert. Given 3d. Septr. 1816.)

A20b State of Maryland, Washington County, Towit:
I hereby certify that it appears by the records of Washington County that the bearer hereof Negro Chloe was manumitted and set free by John T. Mason Esquire of this County after she should arrive at the age of Eighteen years, which would be on the first day of January 1817. That she was sold by Mr. Mason to Archibald M. Waugh Esquire of Hagers-Town on the twentieth day of November 1807. to serve until the said period and that Mr. Waugh has this day relinquished to the said Chloe all title to the remainder of her time. Said Chloe will be Eighteen Years old on the first day of January next about five feet two or three Inches high, not very black is a Stout chunky person. was born in Washington County and has always resided therein.
  (Certe. Given 18th Septr. 1816)

A21a State of Maryland, Washington County, Towit:
I hereby certify that the bearer hereof Sophia Creek and her two children Peggy and William were manumitted and set free by Col. Nathaniel Rochester of Washington County aforesaid as appears by a Deed of Manumission dated 17th May 1810. and recorded in my office - the said Sophia Creek is about 24 years of age about 5 feet 2 Inches high is not very black has long and

of Washington County, Maryland

straight hair formerly belonged to Samuel L. Chew of Kent County in this State, and was brought to this County about 19 years ago and has resided in this County ever since.
    (Certe. Given 2d Octr. 1816.)

A21b   State of Maryland, Washington County, Towit:
I hereby Certify that it appears from the records of Washington County that the bearer hereof Negro Vincent Montgomery was manumitted and set free by Jacob Broscius of the County aforesaid on the 18th day of October 1813 to be free in three years. The said Negro Vincent Montgomery, is about 33 years of age - about five feet seven Inches high rather a bright Mulatto complexion and very much pited with the small pox. was born in Saint Mary's County - formerly belonged to John Biles of Virginia and was brought to this County about four years ago and has resided in this County ever since.
In Testimony whereof __? the 21st day of October 1816
(Cert. given 21 Oct 1816) O.H. Williams Clk W_. Cty

A22a   State of Maryland, Washington County, Towit:
I hereby Certify that the bearer hereof James Booth a Mulatto Man hath satisfied me by sufficient Evidence, that he was born free in the District of columbia and resided there until he was about seven years old, and then removed to this County with his Mother Rachel a free Woman and resided in this County until about June last when he went to the District of Columbia and remained there about six months - the said James is about twenty years of age full six feet high, has a small scar on the left thumb across the Joint.
    (Certe. Given 10th Jany. 1817.)

A22b   State of Maryland, Washington County, Towit:
I hereby certify that it appears by the records of Washington County that the bearer hereof Negro Seala was manumitted and set free by John T. Mason Esq. of this County when she should arrive at the age of Eighteen years, that she was sold for that period to Mr. George Smith of Hagers Town with whom she served until the 1 January 1817. at which time she was Eighteen years of age - the said Selula is about five feet five inches high, the knuckel on her two small fingers of her right hand and the small finger on her left hand are very much sunk, which can be observed when she shuts her hand. she was born in St. Marys

African American Manumissions

County the property of Colo. [Colonel] Richard Barris and was brought to this County very young, and has remained here ever since.

   Certe given 22d Jany 1817.

A23a State of Maryland, Washington County, Towit:
I hereby certify that it appears by the records of Washington County that the bearer hereof Negro Jenny was manumitted and set free by John T. Mason Esqr. of this County when she should arrive at the age of Eighteen years of age, said Jenny hath also satisfied me by sufficient evidence that she was sold to Mr. Melcher Beltzhower near Pitsburgh in the State of Pennsylvania with whom she served until the 1 Jany. 1816 at which time she was Eighteen years of age - She is about five feet six Inches high, the small finger on each of her hands crooked was born in St. Marys county the property of Colo. Richard Barns and was brought to this County when young, and now resides in this County.

   Certe given 22d Jany. 1817.

A24a State of Maryland, Washington County, Towit:
I hereby certify that the bearer hereof Charles Millings a black man hath satisfied me by Sufficient testimony that he was born free in the town of Windsor in the State of Vermont were his relations now live, that he resided there until about three years ago. that he waited on Several officers during the late War in the North Western army of the United States, that he went on from the army with Doctor Bull to the State of Virginia, and came to this County about four or five months ago. said Charles Millings is about five feet five and a half Inches high rather slender made has what is called a Roman nose,["nose much more prominent than that of negroes generally" crossed out] the middle finger on the left hand has a scar on near the end, has also a scar on the left Eye brow.

   order given 19 Feby 1819

A24b State of Maryland, Washington County, Towit:
I hereby certify that it appears that the bearer hereof Negro Adam Tim was manumitted and set free by Henry Witmer on the 25th Jany. 1817. The said Adam Tim is about 5 feet 4 Inches high about forty three years of age has a small scar across the left eye brow has lost two front teeth in the upper jaw was born in

of Washington County, Maryland

Prince Georges County, and was brought to this County by Doctr. Pindell when young, and has resided in this County ever since.

(Certe. given)

A25a   State of Maryland, Washington County, Towit:
I hereby Certify that the bearer hereof Robert Creek was manumitted and set free by Michael Kapp of Hagers'-town in said County on the 14th day of March 1811. to serve until the 1' January 1817. a appears by a Deed of Manumission recorded in my office, said Robert Creek formerly belonged to Samuel L. Chew Esquire of Kent County in this State and was brought to this County by his Mistress about twenty three years ago and has since generally resided here - said Robert Creek is about thirty one years of age, about 5 feet 4 Inches high has a small mark of a cut at the upper part of his forehead - is rather slender made his knees bend back very much when he stands up his hair straighter and longer than the generality of a Black Man.

(Certe Given 8th March 1817)

A25b   State of Maryland, Washington County, Towit:
I hereby certify that the bearer hereof Betsey Booth a Mulatto woman hath satisfied me by sufficient Evidence that she was born in the District of Columbia and resided there until she was about nine years of age and then removed to this county with her mother Rachel a free woman and resided in this County ever since - the said Betsey Booth is about twenty two years of age about five feet seven inches high slender make a bright Mulatto has a small scar across the upper part of her forehead over the left Eye -   Certe. Given 11th March 1817)

A26a   State of Maryland, Washington County, Towit:
I hereby certify that it appears by the Records of Washington County that the Bearer hereof Richard Dutler a black man was manumitted by Peter Newcomer of Washington County on the 1st day of March Eighteen hundred - The said Negro Richard Dutler is about 65 years of age, six feet high, wears a long grey beard, his head is grey and a little bald, has lost nearly all his teeth, which causes his upper lip to sink and his under lip, which is thick, to project, has a scar upon his right wrist.

In Testimony, __? this 3d day of April 1817
O.H. Williams Clk W_____?

African American Manumissions

A26b   State of Maryland, Washington County, Towit:
I hereby certify that the Bearer hereof George Backstone a Yellow man has satisfied me by sufficient evidence that he was born free in the County at Hughes Forge where his mother Tabathey then lived that was was [sic] Colo. Hughes by his mother until he was of age and served his time with him and Mr. Jacob Rohrer - said George is about thirty four years old Stout made has a Scar on the left Cheek bone is about five feet [blank space] inches high
   In Testimony __? this 18th day of September 1817.
   O.H. Williams Clk W_____?

A26c   State of Maryland, Washington County, Towit:
I hereby certify that the bearer hereof Peter Blanchard has satisfied me by sufficient evidence that he was born free in the State of St. Lucia in the West Indies and that he arrived in Baltimore about eight years ago and lived there about a year, when he came to this County and has resided here ever since has a wife and family residing in Hagerstown in the County the said Peter Blanchard is a yellow man about twenty three years of age about five feet six and an half inches high has a scar on the upper lip on the right side his left hand is injured having lost a joint in the third finger the small finger crooked and the nail of the middle finger off, has his ears bored speaks french and broken english and blows very well on the trumpet and Buglehorn.
   In Witness this 26th Sept. 1817.
   O.H. Williams Clk W__? Md

A27a   State of Maryland, Washington County, Towit:
I hereby certify that it appears from the Records of Washington County that the bearer hereof Rachel Miller a Mulatto Woman was manumitted and set free by Robert Wilson on the 20th day of November last - The said Rachel Miller is about twenty two years of age about five feet four inches high, has a scar on the inside of her right arm above the elbow which appears to have been occasioned by a burn she was raised by Mr. Peter Light in Virginia near Williams Port and was transferred by him to his Son in Law Mr. Wilson -
   In Testimony __? this 9 Decr. 1817 -
   Certificate given   O.H. Williams Clk

of Washington County, Maryland

0A28a Washington County towit

I hereby certify that it appears by the records of Washington County Court that the bearer hereof a mulato woman named Rachel Blanchard was manumitted and set free by Edward G. Williams Esq. on the 7th day of Feby 1818 the said Rachel is about 27 years of age about 5 feet 6 Inches high rather corbulant has a small scar on the right elbow which appears to have been burnt is a very bright Mulato - was ___ed? by John T. Mason Esq. and was brought from the district of Columbia about 12 years ago and has resided in this County ever since.

   Certificate given 1 April 1818.

A28b Washington County towit

I hereby certify that it appears from the records of Washington County that the bearer hereof a Negro man named Thomas Russell was manumitted by Majr. Edward E. Williams of Washington County on the 7 day of February 1818 the said Thomas Russell is about 40 years of age five feet seven Inches high has a scar over the right Eye about one and a half Inches long, is not very black was born on the Eastern Shore of Maryland, and was brought to the County by Colonel Rawlings when he was about five years of age and has resided here ever since.

   Certificate given 7th April 1818.

A29a I hereby certify that it appears from the testimony of Samuel Hughes Jr. Esq. of this County that the bearer hereof Fanny Jackson formerly Fanny Creek is a free woman, she is about thirty years of age, five feet three or four Inches high, of a yellowish cast, her hair straighter and longer than the generallity of black persons, formerly belonged to Samuel L. Chew of Kent county in this State, was brought to this County by her mistress about twenty four years ago and was sold by Mr. Chew Administrator in the year 1809 to Samuel Hughes Jr. who sold her to Elie Williams Elliot for a limited period which is expired and has resided in this County ever since.

   Certe given 5 June 1818

[piece of paper glued directly below this:]

  I hereby certify that I sold Fanny Creek, who I purchased as a slave, to E.W. Elliott for a limited period only which has expired and after that time she was to be a free woman
Nov. 30th 1817 Saml Hughes Junr.

African American Manumissions

A30a   State of Maryland, Washington County, Towit:
I hereby certify that it appears by records of Washington County that the bearer hereof Negro John Moody was manumitted from Slavery by Robert Wilson and Enoch Jones on the 12 October 1817. Reference to Liber I.N. folio 595 one of the Land records of Washington County & it appears said John Moody is about thirty five years of age five feet ___? & 1/2 Inches high has a scar on the outside of his left leg which appears to have been occasioned by a burn was born in Prince Georges County in this State and was brought to this County about Eleven years ago and owned by ["several persons in this County" crossed out] John Irwin of Williams Port and was sold by his Executor to the aforesaid Wilson and Jones.

A30b   Washington County to wit
I hereby certify that it appears by the records of Washington County that the bearer hereof Negro Darky Jones was manumitted by John A. Hyland on the 11 May 1811, to be free on the 1st May 1817. the said woman is about 26 years of age five feet eight inches high and very large, was raised by said Hyland and his father about 6 miles from Hagers Town and always resided in this County - said woman ___? has a female child about five months old.
       Certe given 28th July 1818

A31a   Washington County to wit
I hereby certify that the bearer hereof Jenny Butler has satisfied me by sufficient evidence that she was born free in this County and has resided in this County ever since her birth and that she resided with Danial Schnebly Esq. since the year 1807. She is about seventeen years of age about five feet four inches high, slender and not to black as the generality of negroes.
       Cert. given 5 Aug 1818

A31b   Washington County to wit
I hereby certify that it appears by the records of Washington County that the bearer hereof a mulatto woman named Catharine Stewart was manumitted and discharged from Slavery on this day by Edward Stewart the said woman appears to be about 44 years of age a likely mulato woman about five feet four Inches high has a scar on the back of her right hand occasioned by a burn, was born in this County in Pleasant Valley, the

property of Posthumous Clagarte, by whom she was transferred to Docr. Zachariah Clagett who sold her to her husband the aforesaid Edward Stewart.
  Cert given 21 Aug 1818

A32a Washington County towit
I hereby certify that the bearer hereof who calls himself Jacob Miller has proved to my satisfaction that he was born free in this County. the said Jacob is about twenty three years of age five feet six Inches high, is a bright mulatoo, hazle Eyes, his mother is a white woman now living in this County and was at the time he was born the wife of a certain William Siren, the said Jacob is a rough Carpenter by trade. the said Jacob was raised and has always resided in this County - Cert not___[?] for -

A32b Washington County towit
I hereby certify that it appears from the records of Washington County that the bearer hereof Negro Aaren Cain was manumitted by Christian Lantz on the 25 January 1817. said Aarn is about 45 years of age five feet ten inches high Stout made is lame in the right hand occasioned by a cut on the inside of his wrist which has left a Scar thus W was brought to this County when a boy and lived with Genl. Thomas Shrigg until his death,
  Cert given 24 Octr 1818

A33a Washington County towit
I hereby certify that it appears by the records of Washington County that the bearer hereof a Negro man named James Young was manumitted by Samuel Mulien[?] on the 27th day of Jannay 1819. Said James Young is about thirty four years of age 5 feet 10 Inches high the middle Joint of the left hand appears to be stiff, has a rupture in the navel about the size of a hens egg. was born in and has always resided in this County
  Cert given 9th April 1819

A33b Washington County towit
I hereby certify that it appears by the records of Washington County that the bearer hereof a negro man named Levi Lee was manumitted by Mr. Posthumous Claggett and Doctr. Zachariah Clagett of Pleasant Valey in this County on the 25 day of March 1819. said Levi Lee is about twenty five years of age six feet high

African American Manumissions

____? made was born in this County in the family of Mr. Posthumous Clagett, and has always resided in this County -
   (Cert given 20th April 1819
   Cert given 2nd Dc. 1832

A34a   State of Maryland, Washington County, Towit:
I hereby certify that it appears from the records of Washington County that the bearer hereof a Negro man named Elijah Hopewell was manumitted by Mr. Posthumous Clagett of Pleasant Valey in this County on the 25th day of March 1819. said Elijah Hopewell is about 38 years of age five feet Eight Inches high has a remarkable scar on the upper lip appears to have been occasioned by a cut, very stout ___? and yellow complection was born in this County in the family of Mr. Clagett and has always resided therein.
   Certe given 20th March 1819

A34b   State of Maryland, Washington County, Towit:
I hereby certify that it appears from the Testimony of E___? Saml Saml Ringgold that the following married Negroes were born free in this County in the family of Saml Ringgold viz Isaac born on the 18th December 1799. said Isaac is about 5 feet Inches high - Mary a bright mulatto born 15 Oct 1801. Very slender and small - Catharine born 8th July 1804 black and chunky, Frances born 20th Sept 1806 - Edward born 10 Octr 1810. Elizabeth born 2d May 1815. the foregoing are the children of Diana Crawford who was manumitted in Philadelphia by Genl. Ringgold in the year 1793. the said negroes have always resided in this County.
   Witness 31 Augt 1819
   no certificate given - cert. given Mary Apr. 28. 1826

[Piece of paper glued below the preceding entry reads:]
A list of the ages of James and Diana Crawfords Children
Isaac was born on the 18th of December 1799
Mary was born on the 15th of October 1801
Catharine was born on the 8th of July 1804
Francis was born on the 10th of September 1806
Edward was born on the 10 of October 1810
Elizabeth was born on the 3rd of May 1815
Washington County   Decr. 2. 1818
I do hereby certify that in the year 1793 in the City of Philadelphia I manumitted the Mother of the above named

persons, they have all been born in my family and I request the Clerk of this County to give them certificates according to Law - The name of the mother is Dinah she is married to a black by the name of James Crawford - the second child Mary is a molatto The others are all black -

    Saml. Ringgold

A35a   State of Maryland, Washington County, Towit:
I hereby certify that the bearer hereof John Butler a mulatto man has satisfied me by sufficient evidence that he was born free in Washington County St of Md of a white woman by the name of Betsy Grub[?] that he was bound to Richard Henderson___? [& Co.] until he arrived of age that he served then some part of the time, and was afterwards transferred to McPherson & Brien with whom he served until he was of age - and afterwards bound himself to Isaac Keefers for two years to learn the business of Hammerman a drawer of Cast[?] Iron and served out that time with him - the said John Butler is about twenty four years of age & a yellowish complection about five feet six Inches high
    Certificate given 20 Sep 1819

A35b   State of Maryland, Washington County, Towit:
I hereby certify that it appears from the records of this County that the bearer hereof Betsy Plummer was manumitted by Henry McKinley of Washington County on the sixth day of November 1819 - said Betsy Plummer is about 35 years of age five feet 3 1/2 Inches high has a Scar on the left arm below her elbow about two Inches long came from the State of Virginia about Eleven years ago, and resided in Allegany County until about two years since
    Certificate given 8th Nov 1819

A36a   State of Maryland, Washington County, Towit:
I hereby certify that it appears from the Records of this County that the bearer hereof Jacob Homas a black man was manumitted by Thomas Boteler of Pleasant Valley in Washington County on the 9th day of January 1819. said Jacob Thomas is about 38 years of age - 6 feet 6 Inches high, and of slender statue - the first joint of the fore finger of the left hand cut off - the left aancle much enlarged, resides at present in Pleasant Valley in Washington County MD
    Given 29 Decr. 1819

African American Manumissions

A36b State of Maryland, Washington County, Towit:
I hereby certify that it appears from the Certificate of three Respectable Citizens of Washington County Maryland that the bearer hereof Thomas Duckett a black man is a free Man, born of a free Woman - said Thomas Duckett is about 28 years of age - five feet ten Inches high, rather chunky made, has a scar between the thumb and forefinger of the left hand - he was born in Pleasant Valley in Washington County, Md and resides there at present

A37a Maryland, Washington County Towit
I hereby certify that is appears from the Records of this County that the bearer hereof Tone Neilson a black man was manumitted by Major Henry Lewis of Hagers Town Washington County aforesaid on the eighth day of March Instant said Tone is about thirty five years of age five feet two & a half Inches high has a Scar on the upper part of his tro ss[?], and also a Scar on the left side of his head about the size of a cent - was brought to the County when about Seven years of age ["by the late Jacob Orndorff who transferred him to the late Jonathan Hager soon after and has resided" crossed out] and has resided therein ever since   Certe given 12 March 1820

A37b Maryland, Washington County Towit
I hereby certify that it appears from the records of this County that the bearer hereof a mulatto woman named Nelly was manumitted by Richard Geary on the 7 Augt 1812 and recorded in Liber   Y one of the Land record books of this County folios 318 & 319. the said Nelly is about thirty four years of age five feet Eleven inches high, very slender and is a very bright mulatto has a Scar on the inside of her ancle and was born in this County - Certe given 20 March 1820

A38a Washington County Towit
I hereby certify that it appears from the records of this County that the bearer hereof Vachel otherwise called Vachel Bostick was manumitted by Miss Susan Hughes of Hagers Town on this day. Said Vachel is of a yellow complection about forty years of age five feet Six inches high has a Scar about the size of a cent occasioned by a burn on the upper part of his left arm near the Shoulder blade - was born in Annapolis brought to this County by the late Colo. Hughes about twenty five years ago has resided

of Washington County, Maryland

in this County ever since and has been brought up as a Hammerman & drawer of ban Iron.
    Cert given 16 June 1820

A38b   State of Maryland, Washington County, Towit:
I hereby certify that the bearer hereof Bartley[?] Holmes a yellow man has satisfied me by sufficient evidence that he was born free of a free woman - said Bartley[?] is about twenty two years of age about five feet eight & one half Inches high, has a Cangr[?] Scar across the fore part of his left leg above the ancle, a scar on the right foot below the instep and several Scars on his hand occasioned by cuts - has always resided in the lower end of this County at McPherson & Brien Iron works and other bercy[?] in that neighborhood.   Cert. given 7 Augt 1820

A39a   State of Maryland, Washington County, Towit:
I hereby certify that it appears from a deed of manumission dated 4th Sebte 1818 and recorded in my office that the bearer hereof Negro Lucy was manumitted by David Boyd and Job Hunt, to be free on the 4th day of Sebtember, Instant, the said woman is about twenty four years of age is very black and chunky and about five feet high, was born in Frederick Town and resided there until about five years ago when she was brought to this County by Job Hunt and has resided with him ever since. She has a scar under the left Jaw near her neck.
    Certe given 9t Sebt 1820

A39b   State of Maryland, Washington County, Towit:
I hereby certify that the bearer hereof a black man named Joseph Brister has satisfied me by sufficient evidence that he was born free of a free woman named Rachel in this County, that he was bound to John[?] McNamee[?] by his mother when he was about nine years of age to serve until he was twenty one years of age, that his term of service expired on the 15th day of January last - said Joseph is about five feet ___? Inches high, has a scar on the inside of his third finger on the left hand, has very large full eyes, and is of a dark complection. says he understands and can speak German   Certe given 28 Sebt 1820

A40a   State of Maryland, Washington County, Towit:
I hereby certify that it appears by a Deed of Mannumission dated 1 January 1812 and recorded in my office that the bearer hereof a

African American Manumissions

yellow or Mulatto woman named Nelly was mannumitted by Doctr Frederick Dorey - The said woman is about thirty years of age about five feet five and a half inches high her right knee or leg appears to have been injured which causes her to limp when walking - was born in Prince Georges County and brought to this County when about eight or nine years of age - and has resided in this County ever since, has five children 4 males, and one female all born since she was set free.
        Certe given 9 Octr 1820

A40b   State of Maryland, Washington County, Towit:
I hereby certify that it appears by the Records of Washington County that the bearer hereof Cesar Russell was manumitted on the 16th day of February 1795. by Thomas May of the State of Deleware Iron Master, as by his Will filed amongst the papers of the Pennsylvania Incorporated Society for promoting the abolition of Slavery, will appear - The said Cesar Russell is about forty six years of age - five feet three & a quarter inches high - chunkey built - a large Scar on the right leg occasioned by a fracture - Resided in Washington County Md twenty five years, about 15 years of that time with Col. Daniel Hughes

A41a
I hereby certify that James Carroll the bearer hereof hath satisfied me by sufficient evidence that he is entitled to his freedom and that he was born free in the State of Pennsylvania and had to serve under the law of the said State of Pennsylvania until he arrived to the age of twenty Eight years. That the time of servitude of the said James was purchased by Alexander Moore and by said Moore about five years ago he was brought into the State of Maryland when said Moore removed his family from Pennsylvania to Washington County MD - said James is a dark skined Neegro about five feet nine Inches high - straight and well made Strong Beard & Whiskers has a scar on his left cheek bone

A41b   State of Maryland, Washington County, Towit:
I hereby certify that it appears by the records of Washington County that the bearer hereof a yellow woman named Mazy Lee was mannumitted by Mr. Posthumous Clagett and Docr Zachariah Clagett of Pleasant Valey in this County on the 5th day of December 1820 the said woman is about thirty five years

of age about five feet Seven inches high, has a scar on the back of her right hand has very long hair which is grey on the fore part of her head, She was born in this County in the family of Mr. Posthumous Clagett and has always resided therein.
Certificate given 15 Feby 1821

A42a State of Maryland, Washington County, Towit:
I hereby certify that it appears by a Deed of Manumission dated 13th February 1798 and recorded in my office that the bearer hereof a black man named Robert was manumitted by Thomas Prather of Washington County, MD. The said Negro Man is about 32 years of age, 5 feet 7 1/2 Inches high, a scar on the forefinger and thumb of his right hand - he is lame in the left leg and goes on tiptoe when walking, has a smile on his countenance when in conversation.
   Cert. given 25t July 1821

A42b State of Maryland, Washington County, Towit:
I hereby Certify that the bearer hereof a negro man named Alexander Swan has satisfied me by sufficient evidence that he was born free in the City of Washington, that his mother Nancy Swan is also a free woman, that he was brought to this County in the year 1804 by the late Genl. Daniel Heister, to whom he was bound by his mother until he should arrive at the age of twenty one years, that he lived with Mrs. Heister until her death in 1810, and with Mr. Philip Wingert one of the Executors in this County and Allegany County until his time of service expired which was on the 21st day of May last at which time he was twenty one years of age - the said Alexander is of a yellowish complection, is about five feet one and a half Inches high, has a large scar on the back of his neck on the left side occasioned by a burn, speaks English and German.   Cert. given 9 Augt 1821

A43a State of Maryland, Washington County, Towit:
I hereby certify that it appears by a Deed of manumission dated the 11th August 1821 and recorded in my office that the bearer hereof a negro woman named Nancy Moody was manumitted by Mrs. Margaret Smith of this County. the said woman is about twenty eight years of age Five feet high is very black the one of her right wrist enlarged in Consequence of a sprain, was brought to this County when a child from Prince Georges County by Mr.

African American Manumissions

Samuel Dayly and has resided here ever since. has a male child born since she was manumitted.
  Certificate given Novr. 17th 1821

A43b State of Maryland, Washington County, Towit:
I hereby certify that it appears from the records of this County that the bearer hereof Negro Ben was manumitted by John T. Mason Esqr. of this County on the 11 day of November 1808 when the said Ben should arrive at the age of Twenty two years - the said Ben was sold to Mr. John Oliver of this County for that time, who transferred him to Mr. Jacob Branchman with whom he lived until the 1st January Instant at which time he was twenty two years of age - The said Ben is about five feet high, stout and chunky make, has the mark of a Cut across his left cheek, he was born in this County the property of Col. Richd[?] Baines[?] and has always resided in this County.
  Certificate given 3d Jany 1822

A44a State of Maryland, Washington County, Towit:
I hereby certify that it appears from the records of Washington County Court and from evidence produced to me from Bedford County Court Pennsylvania, that the bearer hereof Nelly Digges was manumitted by Charles Carroll of Washington County on the 6th April 1815 on condition of her signing an Indenture to serve Hugh Dennison of Pennsylvania for the term of seven years - which term has since elapsed & she has accordingly been set at liberty by the Court of Pennsylvania - The said Woman is about fifty years of age, five feet two inches high, a dark Mulatto
  In Testimony whereof I have hereto subscribed my name and affixed the seal of my Office this 20th June 1822

A44b State of Maryland, Washington County, Towit:
I hereby certify that it appears from the records of this County that the bearer hereof Nancy Wilson a black woman and her daughter May aged about Sevin years were manumitted and set free by James H. Moore on the twentieth day of June Instant. the said Nancy is about thirty two years of age five feet one Inch high dark complection and very chunky, has a scar across the upper part of her nose, the said Nancy was born in this County the property of the late Col John Strite and at this death became the property of his son Daniel Strite who devised her to his daughter Emely who transferred her & her daughter May to the

of Washington County, Maryland

aforesaid James H. Moore, said Nancy has always resided in this County,
  Certificate given 21 June 1822

A45a State of Maryland, Washington County, Towit:
I hereby certify that the bearer hereof Solomon Chase a black man has satisfied me by sufficient testimony that he was born free of a free woman in this County, that he was bound to a certain David Bets until the age of 21 years to learn the trade of blacksmith, with whom he remained until the said term expired Said Soloman is about 26 years of age about five feet five Inches high slender and black, has a small scar over the left eye, he has always resided in this County.
  Certificate given 31 July 1822

A45b State of Maryland, Washington County, Towit:
I hereby certify that it appears from the records of Washington County that the bearer hereof a negro woman named Sarah Night was manumitted by Mr. Posthumous Clagett when an infant with her mother Marian on the 16th October 1799. Said Sarah is about twenty four years of age five feet four Inches high dark complection Stout make, has a scar across the middle finger of her right hand, she has always lived in this County and Frederick County near Middletown
  Augt 1 1822

A46a Washington County Towit
I hereby certify that by a deed of manumission dated on the 20th day of February 1817 and recorded in my office that the bearer hereof a coloured woman named Fanny Brien was manumitted by Thomas Belt[?] Esq. of this County the said Fanny is about thirty five years of age about five feet Six Inches high, has a very large scar occasioned by a burn above her right breast extending to her shoulder has also a small scar or mark between her Eye brows, she was raised in the family of Mr. Belt[?] and resided with him until the death of Mrs. Bett as a house servant, since which time she has resided in Hagers Town with her husband Charles Brien a free man of Colour.
  Certificate given 13 Augt 1822

African American Manumissions

A46b State of Maryland, Washington County, Towit:
I hereby certify that it appears from the records of Washington County Court that the bearer hereof a Mulatto Woman named Maria Thomas was manumitted by Mrs. Sophia Ducket on the 17 day of December 1822 the said Maria is about twenty five years of age 5 feet one Inch high a bright complexion is rather hard of hearing said Maria was born in Prince George's County is this State and was removed to this county by Mrs. Ducket about nine or ten years ago and has resided here ever since.
    Certificate given 20 Dec 1822

A47a State of Maryland, Washington County, Towit:
I hereby certify that it appears from the records of Washington County that the bearer hereof a negro man named Jacob Diggs was manumitted and set free by Christian Middlecauff of Leonard, [place which no longer exists - near St. James, a few miles south of Hagerstown] on the twenty Eighth day of August Eighteen hundred and twenty Two, the said Jacob is about thirty eight years of age, five feet Nine inches high, not very black, has a scar or cut on the little finger of his left hand, and a small Scar on his nose, was born in St. Marys County in this State, was brought to this County when a boy and has resided therein ever since.   Certe given 22d December 1822

A48a State of Maryland, Washington County, Towit:
I hereby certify that it appears by a deed of manumission dated on the 21 day of March 1816 and recorded in my office that the bearer hereof a Negro woman named Patience Summers was manumitted by John Stonebraker of this County, the said woman is about thirty four years of age five feet three Inches high, the ancle of her left foot has been injured by being frozen and is Stiff, has lost her upper front teeth, she was raised in this County the Property of Mr. Peter Huflich[?] in Hagers Town - has a feemale (sic) child about a year old also named Patience -
    Cert given 6 Feby 1823

A48b State of Maryland, Washington County, Towit:
I hereby certify that it appears from the records of Washington County aforesaid that the bearer hereof a negro woman named Esther Tarber was manumitted by Mrs. Sophia Duckett of Hagers Town in the County aforesaid on the Seventeenth day of December Eighteen hundred and twenty two, the said Esther is

about thirty one years of age, five feet three & an half Inches high dark comblection, she was born in Prince Georges County in this state the slave of Mrs. Duckett, and was removed to this County about four years ago.   Cert 6 March 1823

A49a   State of Maryland, Washington County, Towit:
I hereby certify that it appears from Records of Washington County Court that the bearer hereof a negro man named David Hopewell was manumitted by Mr. Jacob Russell of this County on the fifteenth day of April Instant the said David is about thirty five years of age five feet Eleven Inches high has a scar across the forefinger of his left hand and also a small scar on the upper part of his nose is very Stout, said David was born and raised in this County in Pleasant Valey, the slave of Mr. Posthumous Clagett.
       Certificate given 16 April 1823

A49b   State of Maryland, Washington County, Towit:
I hereby certify that it appears by the records of Washington County Court that the bearer hereof a negro man named Patrick Sile was manumitted by Aquila Neall on the 14th day of May 1803 to be free at the expiration of five years and two months from the said time, the said Patrick is now about forty nine years of age five feet Seven inches high, of a ____? complection has a small scar on his fore head and one on the side of his head above his left ear; said Patrick was born in Charles County in this State and was brought to this County when young, and has resided here ever since.
       (Certificate given 12th May 1823)

A50a   State of Maryland, Washington County, Towit:
I hereby certify that it appears from the records of my office that the bearer hereof a mulatto man named Lewis was manumitted by Mr. Samuel I.[?] Hete[?] of this County on the fourteenth day of June Eighteen hundred and twenty three, the said Lewis is stated in the Deed of manumission to be about thirty five years f age, five feet nine Inches high, has a Scar on the left knee below the knee ___? occasioned by the cut of a Sickle, has lost one of his front teeth in his upper Jaw, the said Lewis formerly belonged to Robert Smith[?] Esq. _____?, who devised him the said Samuel tob[?] Hite[?]
       Certificate given 1 Augt 1823

African American Manumissions

A50b   State of Maryland, Washington County, Towit:
I hereby certify that the bearer hereof David Hatton a negro man has satisfied me by sufficient evidence that he was born free in this County near Jacques furnace where his mother Catharine a free woman now resides that he was bound to George[?] Braggonien[?] until he was Twenty one years of age, which term expired about the first day of October Eighteen hundred and thirteen, said David is now about thirty one years of age five feet Six and a half Inches high dark complection, has a scar across the upper part of his right fore finger occasioned by the cut of a Sickle, the said David has always resided in this County -
Cert. given 29 Augt 1823

A51a   State of Maryland, Washington County, Towit:
I hereby certify that the bearer hereof Jacob Hatton a Negro man, has satisfied me by sufficient evidence that he was born free in this County near Jacques Furnace where his mother Catharine a free woman now resides said Jacob is about twenty six years of age five feet Seven Inches high dark complexion has a scar on his breast bone about the size of a dollar occasioned by a burn the said Jacob has always resided in this County
Cert given 29 Augt 1823

A51b   State of Maryland, Washington County, Towit:
I hereby certify that it appears by the records of Washington County that the bearer hereof named Charles Adams was manumitted by Doct. Zachariah Clagett of Pleasant Valey in this County on the twenty ninth day of November Eighteen hundred and twenty three the said Charles is of a Yellowish complexion about five feet nine Inches high Slender make has a Scar on the Little finger on his left hand has little hair on the forepart of his head was born in St. Mary's County in this State and was brought to this county about twenty four years ago and has resided in this County ever since and is at this time about forty four years of age -   Cert. given the 5th Decr. 1823

A51c   State of Maryland, Washington County, Towit:
I hereby certify that it appears from the records of Washington County that the bearer hereof a yellow man named Peter Hopewell was manumitted on the twenty ninth day of November Eighteen hundred and twenty three by Doct. Zachariah Clagett the said Peter is about five feet nine Inches

high about thirty two years of age very stout has a small scar on the side of his right eye brow one on the side of his left and one over his left eye brow is a blacksmith by Trade said Peter was raised in this County in Pleasant Valey the Slave of Mr. Posthumous Clagett and has always resided there -
   Cert. given 5th Decer. 1823

A52a State of Maryland, Washington County, Towit:
I hereby certify that it appears from the records of my office, that the bearer hereof, a mulatto man named John See, was manumitted by Doct. Horatis Claggett of this County, on the 18th day of July 1823. The said John See is stated in the deed of manumission to be about 32 years of age - He is five feet ten inches high, somewhat freckled, has a Scar on the left side of his upper lip, one between his eye brows and one in his forehead - Was raised and formerly belonged to Posthumous Clagett of this County, and by him sold to Doct. Horatio Clagett for a term of years, ["which has lately expired" crossed out] -
   Cert. given 9th Decemr. 1823

A52b State of Maryland, Washington County, Towit:
I hereby certify that it appears from the records of my Office that the bearer hereof a Mulatto man named Jesse Green was manumitted by Peter Newcomer on the 23d December 1820[? - or 1825?] The said Jesse Green by the Deed of Manumission is about twenty eight years of age five feet eight Inches high slender make has a Scar on his forehead above the left Eye was born in Montgomery County Maryland and was brought to this County about fourteen years ago sold to the aforesaid Peter Newcomer and has resided in this County ever since
   Certificate Given 14th Feby. 18224
   Ditto May 1828

A53a State of Maryland, Washington County, Towit:
I hereby certify that it appears from the records of this County that the bearer hereof Negro George was manumitted by Mr. John Lynch of this County on the 6t day of August 1808. the said George to be free in fifteen years from the 21 day of October 1807 at which time the said George was twenty one years of age, is about five feet one inch high, has two scars on his breast and a large Scar under the knee han[?] of his left leg was born in the County the property of said Lynch, who transferred him to Mr.

African American Manumissions

John Ashberry for the above term of fifteen years, with whom he lived till the death of Mr. Ashberry, when he was sold for the remainder of the said term to Mr. Roger[?] Snyder, and has resided in this County ever since
    Certe given 19 Fey 1824

A53b   State of Maryland, Washington County, Towit:
I hereby certify that it appears from the record of this County that the bearer hereof Negro Jack JJams was manumitted by David Angle of this County on the 19t day of January 1818 to be free on the first day of March Instant, the said Jack is about forty four years of age five feet Six Inches high of a yellow complection has a large scar on the shin of his right leg and a Scar on the Joint of his left wrist - has a large bald spot on the top of his head, was born in Ann Arundel County, brought to this County when young, and has resided thereof ever since
    Cert. given 2d March 24

A54a   State of Maryland, Washington County, Towit:
I hereby certify that it appears by the records of this County that the bearer hereof a negro woman named Theodocia was manumitted by Col. Josiah Price of this County on the first day of January Eighteen Hundred and twenty four the said Theodocia is about thirty seven years of age five feet Six Inches high dark complection and very Stout was born in the family of Col Price and has always resided with him in this County
    Cert 6 March 1824

A54b   State of Maryland, Washington County, Towit:
I hereby certify that it appears from the records of this County that the bearer hereof Letty Chase was manumitted by John Ridout of this County on the twentieth day of December Eighteen hundred and twenty thr[ee?] said Letty Chase is now about forty ["two" crossed out] one years of age about five feet high. a bright mulatto the first Joint of the middle finger of her ["right" crossed out] left hand is stiff, said Letty was born in Annapolis and was taken to Baltimore when about sixteen years of age and came to this County about fifteen years ago and has generally resided here ever since
    Cert 30t April 1824

of Washington County, Maryland

A55a   Washington County etc
I hereby certify that it appears from a deed of manumission dated on the first day of February ["January" crossed out] 1824 and recorded in Liber G.G. folio 676 that the bearer hereof a mulatto woman named Phebe was set free by Col. Josiah Price of this County, the said woman is slated[?] to be about forty ["thirty seven" crossed out] years of age five feet one inches high, slender has a scar or mark of a cut over the right eye brow and a mole on the inner part of her right cheek she is a yellow complection was born in this County the property of Col Price and has always resided therein.
    Cert 12 May 1824

A55b
I hereby certify that it appears from a Deed of manumission dated 29 Nov 1823 and recorded in Liber GG that the bearer hereof a negro woman named Hannah Verner was set free by Doct Zachariah Clagett the said woman is taken to be about thirty years of age five feet four inches high the said Hannah is of a yellow complection has a small scar near her right Eye, was raised by Posthumous Clagett of this County and sold to Doct Zachariah Clagett for a term of years -
    Cert Given 26 May 1824

A56a   State of Maryland, Washington County, Towit:
I hereby certify that it appears from the records of this County that the bearer hereof a negro man named John Snowden was manumitted by John Thompson Mason of this County on the 11th day of November 1808 when he the said John Snowden arrived at the age of twenty two years at which time the said John was aoubt Eight years old, he was sold to Col Josiah Price for the said term with whom he served until he was 22 yrs old as appears by the Certificate of Col Price, the said John is about 24 years of age five feet Seven & one half inches high of a Dark complection has a scar on the lower part of his chin on the right side of his face, was born and raised in this County -
    Cert given 13/10[? - 13 or 10] July 1824

A57a   Washington County etc.
I hereby certify that it appears by a deed of manumission recorded in my office 30th day of August 1822 that the bearer hereof a mulatto woman named Sheckey Dunmore was

African American Manumissions

manumitted Jacob Miller and other heirs at law of Tobias Miller (to be free on the twenty fourth day of May 1824) the said woman is about thirty years of age 4 feet 11 Inches high yellow complection a number of freckels on her face was born in this county in the family of Col William Fitzhugh and has alwaays resided in this County   Cert given 5 Oct 1824

A57b   Washington County etc.
I hereby certify that it appears by a Deed of Manumission recorded in my office dated on the 17th day of January 1824 that the bearer hereof a Negro man named Job Motts was manumitted by Nilly Motts the said Job is stated in the Deed of manumission to be forty four years of age, he is five feet 7 inches high, Stout make; the little finger of his left hand is crooked, he was raised in the family of Joseph Chaplain near Sharpsburgh and has always resided in this County.
    Cert given 27 Oct 1824

A58a   Washington County Towit:
I hereby certify that it appears by a deed of Manumission recorded in my Office the 3d day of September 1798 that the bearer hereof a negro man named James was manumitted by Isaac Long (to be free on the 3d day of September 1814) the said James is about forty three years of age, five feet nine Inches high, of a dark complexion, has a scar over his left eye - the upper part of his forehead is bald, he says he was born in Saint Marys County and was brought to this County by William S. Compton when very young and has resided here ever since
    Cert. given 6th Nov. 1824

A58b   Washington County etc.
I hereby certify that it appears by Deed of manumission recorded in my Office this 26th January 1825 that the bearer hereof a Negro Man named Nace was manumitted by Hezekiah Boteler on the said 26 Jany 1825 - The said Nace is about five feet three inches high, of a dark complexion. has a scar on his breast, is lame, the right leg being shorter than the left - is twenty eight years of age - was born at Pleasant Vally in Washington County -
    Cert given 26 Jany 1825
    Indentured himself to A.M Reed for life

of Washington County, Maryland

A59a   Washington County etc.
I hereby certify that it appears by a deed of manumission recorded in my office on the 22d day of February 1825, that the bearer hereof a negro woman Named Nancy Parker and her female child named ["Nancy P" crossed out] Caroline were manumitted by Jacob Myers on the 18th day of February 1825 - The said Nancy is about five feet two Inches high of a dark complextion ["said Nancy" crossed out] is about twenty nine years of age, was born in Price Georges County the property of Benjamin Oden Esq,. and brought to this County in the year Eighteen hundred and fourteen and sold to the above named Myers with whom she has lived ever since
        Cert given 22d Fby 1825

A59b   Washington County etc.
I hereby certify that it appears from a Deed of Manumission dated the 12t November 1812 and recorded in my office that the bearer hereof Margaret was manumitted on that day by Robert McGirty[?] of this County, the said Margaret is now about fifty five years of age about five feet four inches high of a light complection - robust in Stature, has a pleasant countenance - has a mark on the inside of her right arm, and black moles between her eyes - was born in Calvert County Md in the family of Andrew Duke -

A60a   Washington County etc.
I hereby certify that it appears by Deed of manumission records in my office on the 9t day of Nov 1818 in liber DD folio 169. that the bearer hereof a negro man, named Hanson Jones was manumitted the said Hanson is about thirty one eyars of age five feet ten Inches high, a Dark complection, the Joint of His fore finger of his right hand cut off. has a small scar under the left eye, was born in this County and has always resided here except the last five years that he has resided with Mr. John Eelwise[?] in Barkly [Berkeley] County Virginia

A60b   Washington County etc.
I hereby certify that it appears by a Deed of Manumission recorded in my office that on the 2d day of February 1819 the bearer hereof a Negro woman named Susan was manumitted by Peter Tollinger to be free in Six years from said date, the said Sarah[sic] appears to be about forty four years of age is about 5

African American Manumissions

feet 3 1/2 Inches high aid Susan is very ["dark" crossed out] black, Slender make the little finger on her right hand crooked - has resided in Frederick County near Emmitsburg except the last Six years that She lived with Mr. Nathan Muary[?] in Hagers Town Maryland.
    Cert given 3d Sept 1825.

A61a   Washington County etc.
I hereby certify that it appears by a Deed of Manumissiondated on the 26th day of March 1825 and recorded in my office that the bearer hereof a Negro woman named Esther Lear was set free with her husband Charles Lear [or Lean?] and their two children Juliet and Darnella[?] by Mr. Caspar W. Wever of this County said Esther is about thirty nine years of age five feet ___? Inches high of a yellowish complection and Stout make, was born in Berkly County Virginia near Lee Town and brought to this State about ten years ago by Mr. Wever and resided here ever Since. Said Esther has an female child born since she has been set free which is named Catharine -
    Augt 4t 1825

A61b   Washington County etc.
I hereby certify that it appears by a Deed of Manumission dated the 26th March 1825 and recorded in my office that the bearer hereof of negro man named Charles Lear was set free with his wife named Esther and their two children named Juliet[?] and Darnella by Mr. Casper W. Wever of this County said Charles is about forty three years of age dark complection five 5 feet 5 Inches high the little on his left hand is crooked occasioned by the cut of a sickle. was born in Jefferson County virignia, and was bought of Mr. Wager at Harpers ferry about ten years ago and brought to this County by Mr. Wever and has resided here ever since.

A61c   Washington County Towit:
I hereby certify that it appears by a Deed of Manumission recorded in my office dated the 13t day of October 1825 that the bearer hereof a negro man named Joseph Dickinson was manumitted on that day by Susan Hughes, Esther Hughes, Joseph Martin and Joseph J. Merrich of said County, the said Joseph is about thirty one years of age, five feet eight inches high of rather light complexion, has two scars under his left jaw, was

born on the Eastern Shore in Maryland and was brought to this County about twenty years ago by Col. Wm. Fitzhugh and Col. Daniel Hughes and has resided here ever since.
   Cert. given 26 Oct 1825

A62a Washington County Sct.
I hereby certify that it appears from a Deed of Manumission recorded in my office dated the 30t day of November 1825 that the bearer hereof a negro man named Joseph Shorter was manumitted on that day by James Neale, Richard McMahan, Charles Rice and Jesse Long of said County, the said Joseph Shorter is about twenty eight years of age five feet five inches high of ["rather" crossed out] dark complection has a very large swelling or enlargement of the bone on the left cheek extending from the lips to the left eye, was born in St. Marys County and brought to this County when he was a child, by Charles Herletin[?] of Williams port, and resided there ever since
   Cert. given 19 Decr. 1825

A62b Washington County etc.
I hereby certify that it appears by a deed of Manumission recorded in my Office dated the 20t day of January 1826, that the bearer hereof a negro man named George Washington was manumitted on that day by John E. Crampton and Elie Crampton of the County aforesaid, the said George is about forty four years of age, five feet, six and a quarter inches high dark complexion, has a mark on his left wrist occasioned by a burn, a blacksmith by trade, was born in this County and resided here every since
   Cert. given 7t May 1826

A63a Washington County fs
I hereby certify that it appears by a Deed of Manumission Dated the twenty second day of July eighteen hundred and twenty six and recorded in my Office, that the bearer hereof a negro man named Moses Collins was manumitted on that day by John Ash of Washington County - the said Moses Collins is stated in the Deed of Manumission to be about thirty seven years of age, five feet eight inches high - dark complexion - has a scar above his right eye and ohn on the back of his head occasioned by a burn, plays well on the violin, was born in Prince Georges County and

African American Manumissions

brought to this County while very young and has remained here ever since
        Cert. given 29 July 1826

A63b   State of Maryland, Washington County, Towit:
I hereby certify that it appears from the records of Washington County Court that the bearer hereof a negro woman named Judah Taylor was manumitted by Christian Fechtig Senr. of Washington County Maryland on the twelfth day of September eighteen hundred and twenty five The said Judah is about forty one years of age, five feet three inches high, has a small scar on the left arm at the elbow, very corprulent complexion rather more dark than the generality of Negroes.
        Cert. given 16 Augt 1826

A64a   Washington County etc.
I hereby certify that the bearer hereof Hannah Creek a black woman has satisfied me by Evidence that she was born free in this county and has lived in Hagers Town ["since the birth" crossed out] ever since, that she is the daughter of Rachel Young who also resided in Hagers Town aat this time and is a free woman, the said Hannah is now about twenty years of age very black. Slender person, four/five[? - four or five] feet four inches high   Cert given 29 Sept 18226

A64b   Washington County to wit:
I hereby certify that it appears by a Deed of Manumission recorded among the record of Washington County Court, that the bearer hereof a negro woman named Grace Frances was manumitted and set free on the fifteenth day of November in the year eighteen hundred and twenty three by Catharine Miller of this County - The said Grace is at this time about forty seven years of age about five feet two and a half inches high, yellow complexion, was born in the City of Annapolis and brought to this County about thirty years since and has remained here ever since   Cert. give 3 Octr. 1826

A65a   Washington County etc.
I hereby certify that it appears from a Deed of manumission dated the 26th July 1826 and recorded in my office, that the bearer hereof a negro man named Samuel Harrison was manummitted on that day by David Hess of Washington County

of Washington County, Maryland

- the said Samuel is stated in the deed of manumission to be about twenty four years of age - and is about five feet Six Inches high of a yellow complection, has two[?] small Scaar running across his nose, two small scars on the back of his neck, was born in this County and has always resided therein -
    Cert 23 Feby 1827

A65b   Washington County etc.
I hereby Certify that it appears from a Deed of Manumission dated on the 10t day of March 1827 and recorded in my office that the bearer hereof a negro man named Lewis Gross was manumitted on that day by Queenbery Johnston, Charlotte Johnston and Tobias Johnson of this County the said Levin is about thirty years of age five feet Eight Inches high of a very black complection has a Small scar on the back of the left hand above the middle finger, has very large and full eyes, and Slender person, was born in this county the property of Robert Johnson ["Deceased" crossed out] and descneded to the above persons on the decease of the said Robert Johnson.
    Cert given 17 March 1827

A66a   State of Maryland, Washington County, Towit:
I hereby certify that the bearer hereof Nancy Cole a Colored Girl was born free and of free condition in Williams port in this County, that her mother also now calls herself Sarah Young a free woman also now being in this County, the said Nancy is about five feet three inches high, has a scar aere[?] of the left eye lash & Eye brow - is about Seventeen years of age, of a yellowish complection - and has always resided in this County.
    Certificate given 23d Mar. 1827

A66b   Washington County to wit:
I hereby certify that the bearer hereof a negro woman named Rachel Brumley was manumitted by Thomas Edwards of this County on the fourth day of March in the year of our Lord one thousand eight hundred and seventeen - The said Rachel Brumley is about 35 years of age five feet, five inches high, light complexion, - was brought to this County by said Thomas Edwards from the Eastern Shore of Maryland about twenty years ago and has resided in this County ever since.
    Cert. given 30 Apr. 1827

African American Manumissions

A67a   State of Maryland, Washington County, Towit:
I hereby certify that the bearer hereof a mulatto Boy named William Campbell was born a ["free" crossed out] of a free mulatto woman named Nancy Coon in Haagers Town in the County aforesaid the said William is about 18 - years of age five feet - Seven inches high a yellow complection has a Scarr through the ["eye brow" crosssed out] left Eye brow. he was born in this County and has always resided therein -
   Cert. given 31 May 1827

A67b   Washington County to wit:
I hereby certify that the bearer hereof a negro woman named Charity Chase has satisfied me by sufficient evidence that she was born free of a free woman in this County - The said Charity is about 26 years of age 5 feet 3 inches high, very black, no perceivable marks
   Cert. given 11 June 1827

A67c   Washington County to wit:
I hereby certify that it appears by a Deed of manumission recorded in my office dated the 26t day of April 1820 that the bearer hereof negro Jack who calls himself Jack Gates was manumitted by Mrs. Sarah Prather to be free on the first day of July 1826 to which time he was sold to Mr. Joseph Tookman[?] of this County the said Jack Eaty is now about thirty eight[?] years of age four feet ten Inches high of a Dark complection has a scar on the right hand above the middle finger and s small mark of a Cut at the end of the forefinger on the left hand, was born in Allegany County, but resided in this County about twenty years, has been in Ligoyed[?] in Steering or managing boats on the Potomac River from Williams port to George Town for the last ten years or upwards.
   Cert given 16t July 1827

A68a
I hereby certificy that that the bearer hereof a mulatto woman named Jane Clemens wife of Hezekiah Clemens was born free of a negro woman named Sarah Butler that she was born free in St. Marys County in this State, and came to this County with her mother when she was a child, and resided here ever since as a free person; the said Jane is about five feet ten[?] Inches high

about thirty five years of age, a dark complection no notable marks.   Cert given 18t July 1826

A68b
I hereby certify that the bearer hereof a negro man named Robert Butler was born free of a negro woman named Sarah Butler. the said Robert is about twenty five years of age five feet nine inches high of a dark complection, has a scar on his forehead a little above the left eye. has followed boating from Williams Port to George Town on the Potomack for many years.
      Cert. given 18. July 1827

A69a   State of Maryland, Washington County, Towit:
I hereby certify that it appears from a Deed of manumission recorded in my office that the bearer hereof Negro George Hanson was manumitted by Mr. John Lynch on the 6t day of August in the year 1808 to be free on the 21 day of October 1822 to which time he was sold by Mr. Lynch to John Ashberry of this County, the said George is now aboaut forty years of age Six feet three Inches high of a Dark complextion has a Scar across his left leg under the knee - a scar over the left eye, and also a Scarr on the upper part of his left arm; was raised in this County and has always resided therein -
      Cert given 1 Augt 1827

A69b   State of Maryland, Washington County, Towit:
I hereby certify that it appears from a Deed of manumissionin my office that the bearer hereof Negro Jeremiah was manumitted by Mr. William Gabby of this County on the 27t day of March 1827. the said Jeremiah is about thirty five years of age five feet [unknown word crossed out] high of a dark complection, pitted with the small pox thick lips. was brought to this County when a ["young" crossed out] child and has resided therein ever since the said Jeremiah has also three black children with her that are also free, the oldest a girl named Fredericke aged about 8 years - another a girl named Ann Maria aged about 5 years and the youngest boy named Simon aged about Eighteen Months.
      29 Augt 1827

A70a   State of Maryland, Washington County, Towit:
I hereby certify that it appears from the records of Washington County that the bearer hereof a negro woman named Clare was

African American Manumissions

manumitted by John Thompson Mason Esquire of this County on the Eleventh day of November Eighteen hundred eight when she the said Clare should arrive at the age of Eighteen years (being at that time about Seven years of age) said Clare was transferred untill she should be free unto Mr Thomas S. Dunn who at that time lived in this County and who afterwards removed her to Franklin County State of Pennsylvania, where she served out her time the said Clare is now about twenty five years of age five feet two Inches high not very black, freckeled on the face, Slender person - has a male child about two years of age named William Henry of a yellow complection, aid Clara has always resided in this County except when she lived with Mr. Dunn in Pennsylvania
  Cert 5 Sept 1827

A71a State of Maryland, Washington County, Towit:
I hereby certify that it appears from the Records of Washington County Court that the bearer hereof William Callihan was manumitted by Mr. Otho W. C. Strite on the 6t of April 1815 which said man was then Seventeen years of age to be free when he should arrive at the age of twenty Eight years, and it also appearing by a certificate from Wm. Reynolds of Bedford County Pennsylvania thaby a Deed of Manumission recorded in my officethe said man served out his said term - The said man is now about twenty nine years of age five feet 3 1/2 inches high. ["The said man" crossed out] a bright mulatto waas born in this County and ["was bought from Mr. Stube" crossed out] resided there until he was Seventeen years of age, when he was sold for the balance of his time to the said Mr. Reynolds and resided in this ____? in Bedford County ever since.
  Cert given 29 Sept 1827

A72a State of Maryland, Washington County, Towit:
I hereby certify that it appears by a Deed of manumission recorded in my officer that the bearer hereof a negro woman named Susan Johnston was manumitted and set free by Eleanor Beall of Washington County on the 19 day of July 1825. The said Susan Johnston is now about twenty six years of age five feet, six inches high, with thick lips, the forefinger on her left hand crooked at the first joint, flat nose, was born in the City of

of Washington County, Maryland

Washington and brought to this County when very young and has remained in this County ever since.

   No Cert. given ["1 Decr. 1827" crossed out]

A72b Washington County etc.
I hereby certify that it appears by a Deed of Manumission recorded in my office that the bearer hereof a negro woman named Rebecca was manumitted and set free by Emory[?] Thomas of this County on the 17t day of August 1827 the said Rebecca is now about Eighteen years of age five feet four Inches high of a yellowish complextion was born ["in this County" crossed out] near Boonsborough in this County and has always resided therein, her female Child now about Seventeen months also named Maria was also manumitted at the same time

   Cert given 11 Dec 1827

A73a State of Maryland, Washington County, Towit:
I hereby certify that the bearer hereof a negro man named Elie Washington has satisfied me by the testimony of Elie Crampton Esq. of this County that the said Elie was born free on the farm of his father the late Thomas Crampton Esq. of a free woman now residing ["in the neighborhood" crossed out] near the said Crampton - the said Elie is about twenty five years of age of a yellow complection of sturdy make, had a cut across the first Joint on the second finger of the left hand, is about five feet Seven Inches high, he has always resided in this County

   Cert given 11 Dec 1827

A73b State of Maryland, Washington County, Towit:
I hereby certify that it appears from the records of my office, that the bearer hereof a negro man named Chargo Gross was manumitted and set free by Docr. Samuel Young of this County on the seventeenth day of May eighteen hundred and twenty eight, - The said Chargo is now in his twenty eighth year of age, five feet and six inches in heighth. of dark complexion, has a scar on his left arm below the elbow, occasioned by the cut of a sickle, also one other scar on the forefinger of the right hand immediately upon the 2d joint was born in this County in the family of Docr. Young and has always resided in said County

   Cert. given 17 May 1828 Cert. given 24 June

African American Manumissions

A74a   State of Maryland, Washington County, Towit:
I hereby certify that the bearer hereof a negro man named Lives Clark was sold by John Thompson Mason Esqr of this County to Daniel Miller of Franklin County Pennsylvania on the first day of January 1808, at which time the said Lives was of the age of seven years, to serve until he should arrive at the age of twenty two years, at which time he was to be free, I further certify that it appears by the certificate of said Daniel Miller that the said Lives has served his term of servitude, and has been released by said Miller, the said Lives was twenty seven years of age on the 1 day of January last, five feet, seven inches in heighth, very black, has a small scar about half an inch in length, in his forehead, immediately above the nose -
    Cert. given 31 May 1828

A75a   State of Maryland, Washington County, Towit:
I hereby certify that it appears from the records of my office that the bearer hereof, a negro man named Oliver Chesley was manumitted and set free by Joseph Stonebraker of said County, on the twenty fourth day of June eighteen hundred and twenty eight; The said Oliver is now about thirty four years of age, five feet and ten inches in height, dark complexion, has a small lump under the right ear, and a scar on the calf of the left leg occasioned by a burn whilst a child, was born in Charles County Maryland and brought to this County about fifteen years ago and has resided here ever since
    Cert. given 15 July 1828

A75b   State of Maryland, Washington County, Towit:
I hereby certify that it appears from the records of my office that the bearer hereof, a negro woman named Polly Hinton was manumitted and set free by John Ridenour and Dorothy his wife of said County on the 29th day of July 1828. The said Polly is now about twenty five years of age, five feet and six inches in heighth of dark complexion, was born in this County in the family of said Mr. Ridenour and has always lived in said County.
    Cert. given 30 Jany 1829

A76a   State of Maryland, Washington County, Towit:
I hereby certify that it appears from the records of Washington County Court, that the bearer hereof a negro man, named

of Washington County, Maryland

Benjamin Gross, was manumitted and set free by Charles Shaffner of the County aforesaid on the eighth day of February eighteen hundred and twenty eight, - The said Benjamin is at this time about thirty years of age, five feet seven inches and one half in height, light complexion - has a scar on the thumb of his left hand, occasioned by a cut, was raised in Saint Mary's County in the State aforesaid in the family of Dr. Tabbs, he was brought to this County some years since by Moses Tabbs Esqr and has resided here ever since -
    Cert. given 13 Octr. 1828

A76b   State of Maryland, Washington County, Towit:
I hereby certify that it appears from the records of my office, that the bearer hereof, a negro woman, named Sarah Robinson, was manumittted and set free by Catharine Gearhart of the County aforesaid on the twenty second day of October eighteen hundred and twenty eight - The said Sarah is at this time about forty four years of age, five feet and one half inch in height, of light complexion, was born in this County and has always resided therein.
    Cert given 1 Nov 1828

A77a   State of Maryland, Washington County, Towit:
I hereby certify that it appears from a deed of Manumission recorded in my office, that the bearer hereof a negro man named William Duncan, was manumitted and set free by Greenbury Johnston of Washington County, on the tenth day of March eighteen hundred and twenty seven. The said William is now about thirty two years of age, five feet, four and one half inches high, of dark complexion, has a small scar on his left hand near the wrist of triangular form, was brought to this County from Prince Georges County, whilst very young by Robert Johnston and has lived here ever since.
    Cert given Decr 24, 1828

A77b   State of Maryland, Washington County, Towit:
I hereby certify that it appears from a Deed of Manumission recorded in my office, that the bearer hereof, a negro man named John Marshall was manumitted and set free by John Wolf of Washington County, onthe seventh day of March eighteen hundred and twenty nine. The said John Marshall is now about twenty two years of age, five feet, seven inches high of copper

African American Manumissions

complexion, flat nose, has a small scar on his forehead about an inch in length, and several scars about his knee on the right leg, occasioned by a burn, was born in Loudon County, Virginia, and was brought to this County about thirteen years ago by his master John Wolf, has remained here ever since.
Cert 7 Mar. 1829

A78a Washington County to wit:
I hereby certify that it appears from a deed of manumission recorded in my office that the bearer hereof, a negro man named Jeremiah Smothers, was manumitted and set free by Mrs. Louisa Prather of Washington County on the twenty eighth day of May eighteen hundred and twenty nine - The said Jeremiah is now about forty three years of age 5 feet 11 1/2 inches high of very dark complexion, slender make, has a scar on his right leg below the knee occasioned by the cut of a cradle and one small scar near the corner of his left eye, was born in Frederick County Maryland, and brought to this County about ten years ago -
Cert given 28 May 1829

A78b Washington County to wit
I hereby certify that it has been proven to my satisfaction that the bearer hereof Zachariah Moles is the son of Eleanor Moles who was manumitted by Doct. Frederick Dorsey on the 1st January 1812 - that he was born on the 10th of August 1814 in Hagers Town and has been residing therein ever since - He is a bright mulatto five feet 4 1/2 inches high, has a thick bushy head of hair, is slender stature has hazle eyes, a small mole on his face near the right side of his nose, and a large black mole on his left arm -
Cert. given 7 July 1829

A79a State of Maryland, Washington County, Towit:
I hereby certify that it appears from a deed of Manumission recorded in my office that the bearer hereof a negro woman named Mahala Edwards was manumitted and set free by Mrs. Elizabeth Edwards of this County on the 18t day of March 1827. The said Mahala is now about thirty years of age 5. feet 5 1/2 inches in height, she is a light mulatto, has a scar on the right side of her neck immediately below the ear, has but two teeth in front on the upper jaw, was born in Montgomery County

of Washington County, Maryland

Maryland, and brought to this County when about seven years of age and has resided here ever since -
Cert given 9 July 1829

A79b   State of Maryland, Washington County, Towit:
I hereby certify that it has been provento my satisfaction that the bearer hereof a negro man named John Ross is the son of Joseph and Phoeba Ross who were manumitted by Thomas Prather of this County on the fourth day of July 1799 - the said John was born on the 17 day of October 1806 in said County and has been residing therein ever since he is five feet, ten inches high, has several marks on his right hand occasioned by cuts, one on his middle finger across the knuckle about an inch in length another on his wrist and one other on his little finger occasioned by the cut of a sickle -   Cert. given 15 July 1829

A80a   State of Maryland, Washington County, Towit:
I hereby certify that it appears from a deed of Manumission recorded in my office that the bearer hereof a negro man named Jacob, otherwise called Jacob Welcome was manumitted, liberated and set free by Benjamin Edwards of Washington County on the 20 day of September 1816, to serve twelve[?] years, from the 25 December following, from which time it would be the 25 Decr. 1828. The said Jacaob is now about forty two years of age, 5 feet, seven inches in height, has a mark on his left leg above the ankle occasioned by the cut of a cradle whilst in the harvest field, bald on the top of the head
Cert. given 17 July 1829

A80b   State of Maryland, Washington County, Towit:
I hereby certify that it appears from a deed of manumission recorded in my office that the bearer hereof a mulatto woman named Ellen Jenkins was manumitted and set free by Col. Frisby Tilghman of Washington County aforesaid on the twenty seventh day of July 1829 - The said Ellen is about thirty two years of age five feet, one inch in height - she is a bright mulatto - her middle finger on the left hand somewhat crooked - she was born in the County aforesaid and always resided therein.
Cert given 3 Augt 1829

A81a   State of Maryland, Washington County, Towit:
I hereby certify that it appears from a Deed of Manumission recorded in my office, that the bearer hereof a negro man, named

African American Manumissions

Isaac Cole, was manumitted, liberated and set free by Abraham Newson of Marion County in the State of Ohio (late of Washington County Maryland,) on the fourth day of January 1830. The said Isaac Cole is now about twenty two years of age, five feet and six inches in height of very dark complexion, has a cut about one inch in length on the left side of the head immediately above the eye, occasioned by the cut of a knife, he was born in this County in the family of Mr. John Newson and has always lived in this County.
  Cert. given 4 Jany 1830

A81b State of Maryland, Washington County, Towit:
I hereby certify that it has been proven to my satisfaction that the bearer hereof a negro man named Joseph Grimes, was born free in this County the said Joseph was forty five years of age onthe fourth day of July last, he is five feet and five and one half inches in height, has an impediment in his speech, his right leg is considerably shorter than the left occasioned by the while swelling whilst very young, his left ear was frost bitten several years since which has changed its natural colour - the said Joseph was born in Sharpsburgh in the County aforesaid -
  Cert given 30 Jany 1830 Test O. Williams

A82a State of Maryland, Washington County, Towit:
I hereby certify that it appears from a deed of Manumission recorded in my office, that the bearer hereof a negro man named Jesse Key, was manumitted and set free by Daniel Thomas of the County aforesaid on the twenty third day of October eighteen hundred and twenty nine. The said Jesse is now about thirty four years of age, five feet and four inches in height of copper complexion, he has a scar on his left arm occasioned by a burn, and one on the left side of his face about the sise of a large pea on the lower jaw - he was born in Prince Georges County in this State and brought to this County about nineteen years ago and has lived here ever since.
  Tesst O H Williams Clk   May 13. 1830 cert given

A82b State of Maryland, Washington County, Towit:
I hereby certify that it has been proven to my satisfaction that the bearer hereof a negro man named David Norman, was born free in this County, the said David is about twenty years of age, he is about five feet and one and one half inches in height, he has a

of Washington County, Maryland

small scar on his left cheek and another on the right side of his face near the lower end of the ear about the sise of a large pea, - The said David was born in this County and has always resided therein -   Cert given 24 May 1830

A83a   State of Maryland, Washington County, Towit:
I hereby certify that it has been proven to my satisfaction by good and sufficient testimony that the bearer hereof a mulatto woman named Jane Lane was born free in this County (of a a free woman named Charity,) in the family of Mr. John Wagoner, the said Jane was sixteen years of age on the first day of December last, she is five feet three inches high, she is a bright mulatto of slender make, no perceivable marks, she has lived in this County from her birth to the present time
Test O H Williams Clk   July 26 1830 cert given

A83b   State of Maryland, Washington County, Towit:
I hereby certify that it appears from a deed of Manumission recorded in my office that the bearer hereof a negro man named Jacob Hicks was manumitted and set free by Mr. John Beall Clagett of This County on the 23d day of August 1830. The said Jacob Hicks is now about forty one years of age, five feet four inches in height, thickly built - flat nose - has two small warts on the right side of his neck of copper complexion - he was born in Calvert County and brought to this County when he was seven years of age and has resided here ever since -
       Augt 28. 1830

A84a   State of Maryland, Washington County, Towit:
I hereby certify that it has been proven to my satisfaction by good and sufficient testimony, that the bearer hereof a negro man named John Chase, was born free in this County of a free woman named Esther Chase, The said John was twenty three years of age on the nineteenth day of July 1830, he is five feet, five and three fourth inches in height, dark complexion, slendar make, he has a small scar on his left wrist and another about one half inch in length on his left cheek, he has lived in this County from the time of his birth to the present time -
       Cert given 28 Decr. 1830 Test O H Williams Clk

African American Manumissions

A84b   State of Maryland, Washington County, Towit:
I hereby certify that it appears by a deed of Manumission recorded in my office that the bearer hereof a negro man named John Groce was manumitted and set free by Mrs. Mary Johnston of this County on the 17th day of March 1828. The said John Groce is about five feet, six inches high, he has a small scar on his left arm near the hand and another on the right side of his head near the eye, he has a pleasant countenance and is well made - he is now about thirty one years of age, was born in this County and lived in the family of Mrs. Johnston from his birth to the present time
   Test O H Williams Clk

A85a   State of Maryland, Washington County, Towit:
I hereby certify that it appears by a Deed of Manumissionr in my Office that the Bearer hereof Richard Harrison a Negro Man was manumitted and set free by James B. Ditto of this County on the sixth day of January 1831 - The said Richard Harrison is about five feet, four inches high, stout built, the little finger of the right hand is crooked, has lost two or three of his upper front teeth, is a man of good countenance - He is now about forty three years of age, was born in Saint Marys County, and ever since his resssidence in this County he has lived in the family of Abrahm Ditto until his decease, since then he has lived with James B. Ditto - Cert. given 11. Jany. 1831
esst O H Williams Clk.

A85b   State of Maryland, Washington County, Towit:
I hereby certify that it appears by a Deed of Manumission recorded in my office, that the bearer hereof, a negro man named Elias Young, was manumitted and set free by John Ridenour of this County on the tenth day of November 1828. The said Elias is six feet in height, stout and well made, pleasing countenance - the middle finger of his right hand is stiff. occasioned by the breaking thereof - He is now between twenty four and five years of age, was born in this County in the family of Mr. Ridenour and lived therein until the death of him the said Ridenour
      Mar. 12 1831   Test O H Williams Clk

A86a   State of Maryland, Washington County, Towit:
I hereby certify that it appears by a deed of manumission recorded in my office that the bearer hereof a negro man named

of Washington County, Maryland

Samuel Harrison was manumitted and set free by David Hess of the County aforesaid on the twenty sixth day of July eighteen hundred and twenty six. The said Samuel is about five feet seven inches high, yellow complexion, he has two small scars on the back of his neck and two of his fingers of the left hand are crooked occasioned by the cut of a sickle, he ["is now about" crossed out] was 28 years of age in December last, was born in this County and has always resided therein -
  Test O H Williams Clk   May 16 1831

A86b State of Maryland, Washington County, Towit:
I hereby certify that it appears by a deed of manumission recorded in my office that the bearer hereof a mulatto woman named Delia was manumitted and set free by Isaac Swartzwalder[?] and William Weis of the County aforesssaid on the first day of June 1831. The said Delia is a bright mulatoo, five feet two inches in height about forty years of age, has two small moles or warts on her face, one at the lower end of the nose on the left side thereof and the other on the right cheek near the nose. she was born in Annapolis in this State and brought to this County when an infant and has resided here ever since - Test O H Williams Clk June 3. 1831

A87a State of Maryland, Washington County, Towit:
I hereby certify that it appears by a deed of Manumission, recorded in my office, that the bearer hereof a negro man named Alexander Robertson was manumitted and set free by John Langbridge of the County aforesaid on the twenty fifth day of April in the year eighteen hundred and thirtyone. The said Alexander Robertson is now about forty years of age, light complexion five feet and eight inches in height, - good countenance, prominent cheek bones, he has a mole on the lower end of his nose on the left side and another near the right corner of his mouth, he was born in this County and always has resided therein -
  Test O H Williams Clk   July 30. 1831

A87b State of Maryland, Washington County, Towit:
I hereby certify that it has been proven to my satisfaction that the bearer hereof a negro man named Josiah Brown, was born free in this County of a free woman named Jane. The said Josiah was twentyone years of age on the 26th day of January 1831. he is

African American Manumissions

five feet, eight and a quarter inches in height, very dark complexion, good countenance, he has a scar on his left leg, immediately below the knee, occasioned by a burn or scald he has resided in this County from his birth to the present time
    Test O H Williams Clk   15 Sepr. 1831.

A88a   State of Maryland, Washington County, Towit:
I hereby certify that it has been proven to my satisfaction by good and sufficient evidence that the bearer hereof a negro woman named Mary Green, is free born and of free condition - that she was born of a free woman named Sarah Cole in the town of Williams Port in this County in the fall of the year 1808 - The said Mary is now about 23 years of age, four feet 10 1/2 inches high - copper complexion chunky made, has a small mole oor indentation on the left cheek about the size of a squirel shot - she has always resided in this County -
Test O H. Williams Clk   17 Octr. 1831

A88b   State of Maryland, Washington County, Towit:
I hereby certify that it has been proven to my satisfaction by good and sufficient testimony that the bearer hereof a mulatto woman named Mary Creek is free born and of free condition that she was born of a free woman named Sophia Creek in the County aforesaid in the year 1813. The said Mary was eighteen years of age in September last, five feet two inches high, a bright mulatto, has several small moles on each cheek and one on the front of her neck
    Test O H Wms Clk   22 Oct4 1831

A89a   State of Maryland, Washington County, Towit:
I hereby certify that it has been proven to my satisfaction by good and sufficient testimony that Eleanor Nimmy, the bearer hereof, who applies for this certificate, is free born and of free condition, that she was born of a free woman in the County of Washington aforesaid on the 27 day of March eight hundred and eight and has resided in said County from her birth to the present time - The said Eleanor is five feet, five inches high, was twenty three years of age in March last, of yellowish complexion has a slight scar on the left cheek and another in the corner of the right eye, she is slendor made and a good person - lips rather thick -
    Test O H Wms clk. 12 Novr 1831

of Washington County, Maryland

A89b
I hereby certify that it has been proven to my satisfaction that the bearer hereof a negro woman named Jane Hatton who applies for this certificate, is free born and of free condition, that she was born of a free woman in this County in the month of November 1808. and has lived in this County from her birth to the present time. The said Jane is five feet and ["inches" crossed out] high, about twenty three years of age, of yellowish complexion, has two small moles on her nose and another on the right side of her neck.
   Test O H W. Clk   19 Nov 1831

A90a State of Maryland, Washington County, Towit:
I hereby certify that it has been proven to my satisfaction by good and sufficient testimony that the bearer hereof a mulatto woman named Eleanor Booth is free born, that she was born of a free woman named Rachael Booth in the County aforesaid on or about Christmas day in the year eighteen hundred and seven and has has resided in said County from her birth to the present time - The said Eleanor is about five feet six and one half inches in height was twenty three years of age on or about last Christmas of yellow complexion, slender made she has lost the first joint of her little toe, on the left foot, occasioned by a burn - no other prominent marks -
   Test O H Williams Clk
   12 Decr. 1831

A90b I Otho H. Williams Clerk of Washington County Court hereby certify to all whom it doth or may concern that it appears by the records of the County aforesaid that a certain Maria Antoinette Ringgold of the said County, by her certain deed of Manumission, bearing date on the eighth day of December in the year of our Lord eighteen hundred and thirty, did manumit, Liberate, set free and discharge form Slavery a Mulatto boy named Alfred, born in or about the month of December eighteen hundred and eleven -

   I further certify that a bright mulatto boy now present the bearer hereof, aged about twenty years, five feet three and a half inches high, has lost part of the first joint of his thumb on the left hand occasioned by its being marked - who is stout made and whose hair is curley) has proved by testimony which is satisfactory to me that this the identical person mentioned and

African American Manumissions

described in the deed of manumission above referred to, and that he was born in the City of Richmond in the family of George Hay Esqr. and brought to this County by his daughter Maria A. Ringgold aforesaid when he was about two years of age -
   In Witness &c.   Mar. 2 1832 Cert given

A91a State of Maryland, Washington County, Towit:
I hereby certify that it has been proven to my satisfaction by good and sufficient testimony that the bearer hereof Thomas C. Motts who applies for this certificate, is free born, that he was born of a free woman named Ellen Motts in the County aforesaid on the eleventh July eighteen hundred and ten and has resided in this County from his birth to the present time - The said Thomas is about five feet, eleven and three quarter inches in height was twenty two years of age last July of dark complexion stout made, has a mole on his left cheek several scars on his left hand, no other prominent marks. -
   Test O.H. Williams Clk   Cert. given April 4, 1832

A91b State of Maryland, Washington County, Towit:
I Otho H. Williams, Clerk of Washington County Court, hereby certify to all whom it doth or may concern that it appears by the records of the County aforesaid that a certain Ludwick Thomas of the said County by his certain deed of Manumission, bearing date the twenty fourth day of March in the year of our Lord one thousand eight hundred and thirty two, did manumit, liberate, set free and discharge from slavery a negro woman named Lydia Hamilton.
   I further certify that a negro woman now present, the bearer hereof aged about nineteen years, about five feet high, has a scar on her left arm, between the elbow and wrist, who is stout made and rather light complected, has proved by testimony that is satisfactory to me, that she is the identical person mentioned and described in the deed of Manumission above referred to, and that she was born in the County of Washington aforesaid and resided within the same frm her birth to the present -
   Test O.H. Williams Clk 10 Apr 1832 Cert given

A92a State of Maryland, Washington County, Towit:
I Otho H. Williams Clerk of Washington County Court in the State of Maryland, hereby certify to all whom it doth or may concern, that it hath been proved by testimony which is

of Washington County, Maryland

satisfactory to me that the beaerer hereof a negro girl named Diana Dorothy Jane Motts, who was fourteen years of age on the fourteenth day of February last - five feet and one inch high of dark complexion, has a large scar on her forehead above the left eye, occasioned by a burn - and stout made, was born free and raised in Washington County Maryland -
  Test O H Williams Clk Cert given 21 Apr. 1832

A92b State of Maryland, Washington County, Towit:
I Otho H. Williams Clerk of Washington County Court in the State of Maryland, hereby certify to all whom it doth or may concern, that it hath been proved by testimony which is satisfactory to me that the bearer hereof a negro boy named Robert Motts who was sixteen years of age on the fourteenth day of October ["last State of Maryland, Washington County, Towit:" crossed out] 1831 five feet and eight inches high dark complexion - slender form, thick lips - has a scar on the third finger of the left hand about an inch in length, was born free and raised in Washington County Maryland -
  Test O.H. Williams Clk Cert. given 21 Apr 1832

A93a State of Maryland, Washington County, Towit:
I Otho H. Williams Clerk of Washington County Court hereby certify to all whom it doth or may concern that it appears by the records of the County aforesaid that a certain Jacob Guting of the said County by his certain deed of Manumission, bearing date the fourth day of January eighteen hundred and thirty two, did manumit, liberate, set free and discharge form slavery a negro man named Isaac Wilson -
  I further certify that a negro man now present, the bearer hereof, aged about twenty six years, five feet nine and an half inches in height, has a small scar in the corner of each eye, and a larger one on his right wrist, of dark complexion and pleasing countenance has proved by testimony which is satisfactory to me, that he is the identical person mentioned and described in the deed of Manumission above referred to, and that he was born and raised in Washington County aforesaid -

A94a State of Maryland, Washington County, Towit:
I Otho H. Williams Clerk of Washington County Court hereby certify to all whom it doth or may concern that it appears by the records of the County aforesaid that a certain James Adley of the

African American Manumissions

said County, by his certain deed of Manumission, bearing date the twenty ninth day of April eighteen hundred and twenty eight, did manumit, liberate, set free and discharge from slavery a negro man named Charles Adley -

    I further certify that a negro man now present the bearer hereof aged about twenty eight years, five feet five inches in height, has a small scar in the middle of the forehead, of dark complexion and pleasing countenance has proved by testimony which is satisfactory to me, that this is the identical person mentioned and described in the deed of manumission above referred to, and that he was born near Charles Town in Virginia and formerly belonged to Mr. Charles Yates.
Cert given 3 May 1832

A94b   State of Maryland, Washington County, Towit:
I Otho H. Williams Clerk of Washington County Court hereby certify to all whom it doth or may concern that it appears by the records of the County aforesaid that a certain Daniel Schnebly of Said County, by his certain deed of Manumission bearing date the [blank] day of May eighteen hundred and thirty two did manumit, liberate, set free and discharge from slavery a negro woman named Hetty Stewart -

    I further certify that a negro woman now present the bearer hereof, aged about forty three years five feet eight and an half inches in height, of light complexion and slender made, thin visage, nose very flat between the eyes, has proved by testimony which is satisfactory to me, that she is the identical person mentioned and described in the deed of Manumission above referred to, and that she was born in Saint Mary's County in this State and raised in Washington County aforesaid -
test O.H. Williams Clk   Certificate given May 16. 1832

A95a   State of Maryland, Washington County, Towit:
I Otho H. Williams Clerk of Washington County Court hereby certify to all whom it doth or may concern that it appears by the records of the County aforesaid, that a certain John Snider of said County, by his certain deed of Manumission bearing date the eighteenth day of May eighteen hundred and thirty two did manumit liberate, set free and discharge from slavery a negro woman named Maria Datcher.

    I further certify that a negro woman now present the bearer hereof, aged about thirty two years five feet four inches

and an half in height of dark complexion & has four moles on the left side of her face, has proved by testimony which is satisfactory to me, that she is the indentical person mentioned and described in the deed of Manumission above referred to, and that she was born and raised in Washington County aforesaid.
    Cert. given May 19t 1832 Test O.H. Williams Clk

A95b State of Maryland, Washington County, Towit:
I Otho W. Williams Clerk of Washington County Court hereby certify to all whom it doth or may concern that it has been proved by testimony which is satisfactory to me, that the bearer hereof a negro man named William Butley, who applies for this certificate was born free in this County of a free woman named Letty Butley.

  The said William Butley is five feet seven and a quarter inches in height of a dark complexion stout made, thick lips, and has a black mark on one of his finger nails on the right hand, he was twenty two years of age on the twenty seventh day of May instant and has lived in the County of Washington from his birth to the present time -
    Cert given 28 May 1832 Test O.H. Williams Clk

A96a State of Maryland, Washington County, Towit:
I Otho W. Williams Clerk of Washington County Court hereby certify to all whom it doth or may concern that it has been proved by testimony which is satisfactory to me that the bearer a negro woman named Elisabeth Wise, who applies for this certificate was born free in this County of a free woman named Nancy

  The said Elisabeth Wise was twenty two years of age in January last. five feet. two inches high. of a dark complexion, and good countenance has no notable marks, she was born and raised in the County of Washington aforesaid - cert. given 26 May 1832 O.W. Williams Clk

A96b
I Otho Holland Williams Clerk of Washington County Court hereby certify to all whom it doth or may concern that it has been proved by testimony which is satisfactory to me that the bearer hereof a mulatto woman named Charity Green who

African American Manumissions

applies for this certificate was born free in this County of a free woman named Jane Green

The said Jane Green is about twenty one years of age, five feet and one inch high, a bright mulatto, has a small scar on her forehead and a mole on her left cheek was born and raised in Washington County -
cert given 26 May 1832   Test O.W. Williams Clk.

A97a   State of Maryland, Washington County, Towit:
I Otho Holland Williams Clerk of Washington County Court hereby certify to all whom it doth or may concern that it has been proved by testimony which is satisfactory to me that the bearer hereof a negro woman named Mary Hatten who applies for this certificate was born free in the County aforesaid

The said Mary Hatten is now about twenty four years, five feet and one inch in height of a light complexion, has several scars on the left side of her neck occasioned by a burn - she has lived in the County aforesaid from her birth to the present time -
cert given 26 May 1832   Test O.W. Williams Clk

A98a   State of Maryland, Washington County, Towit:
I Otho H. Williams Clerk of Washington County Court hereby certify to all whom it doth or may concern, that it appears by the records of the County aforesaid that a certain Charles L.D. Gunderman of said County by his certain Deed of Manumission bearing date the sixteenth day of November eighteen hundred and fourteen, did manumit, liberate, set free and discharge from slavery a mulatto girl named Jane A. Gunderman.

I further certify that a mulatto woman now present, the bearer hereof, who was seventeen years of age on the first day of September last, five feet and three inches in height. of a very light complexion, of pleasing countenance has no notable marks, has proved by testimony which is satisfactory to me that she is the identical person mentioned and described in the deed of manumission above referred to. and that she was born and raised in Washington County. (no cert. given)

A98b   State of Maryland, Washington County, Towit:
I Otho Holland Williams Clerk of Washington County Court hereby certify to all whom it doth or may concern that it has been proved by testimony which is satisfactory to me that the

of Washington County, Maryland

bearer hereof a mulatto girl named Elisabeth Barnes who applies for this certificate was born free in the County aforesaid.

The said Elisabeth was eighteen years of age on the fifth day of the present month of May, five feet and two inches in height of light complexion has a small scar on her upper lip and a great many freckles in her face, she was born and raised in the County of Washington aforesaid -
cert. given 29 May 1832 O.H. Williams Clk

A99a State of Maryland, Washington County, Towit:
I Otho Holland Williams Clerk of Washington County Court hereby certify to all whom it doth or may concern that it has been proved by testimony which is satisfactory to me that the bearer hereof a mulatto girl named Eleanora Barnes who applies for this certificate, was born free in the County aforesaid

The said Eleanora was fourteen years of age about the last of January last, five feet high a very bright mulatto, has several scars on her left arm occasioned by the bite of a dog, red hair and a number of freckles in her face - she was born and raised in Washington County aforesaid -
cert given 29 May 1832 Test O.H. W Clk

A99b State of Maryland, Washington County, Towit:
I Otho Holland Williams Clerk of Washington County Court hereby certify to all whom it doth or may concern that it has been proved by testimony which is satisfactory to me that the bearer hereof a negro man named Lloyd Collins, who applies for this certificate was born free in this County -The said Lloyd is now about twenty one years of age, five feet ten and an half inches in height, of dark of complexion, has an impediment in his speech, has a small scar on his thumb on the right hand, and small eyes, he was born and raised in Washington County -
cert given 30 May 1832 O.H. Williams Clk

A100a State of Maryland, Washington County, Towit:
I Otho Holland Williams Clerk of Washington County Court hereby certify to all whom it doth or may concern that it has been proved by testimony which is satisfactory to me that the bearer hereof a mulatto man named Otho Snyder who applies for this certificate was born free in this County.

The said Otho was twenty one years of age in August last, five feet eleven inches in height, has several small scars on

African American Manumissions

his thumb and one on his little finger on the right hand of light complexion, red hair and a great many freckles in his face, he was born and raised in the County aforesaid
cert. given 30 May 1832 O.H. Williams Clk

A100b   State of Maryland, Washington County, Towit:
I Otho H. Williams Clerk of Washington County Court, hereby certify to all whom it doth or may concern, that it appears by the records of my office that a certain Jacob Zellar of said County by his certain deed of Manumission bearing date the twenty third day of June eighteen hundred and twenty six did liberate, manumit, set free and discharge from slavery a negro man named Brister Anderson. I further certify that a negro man now present (the bearer hereof) called Brister Anderson about forty two ["forty two" is underlined and "39" is inserted] years of age - five feet and five inches high, has a small scar near the corner of his left eye and several on his right wrist, of dark complexion has a small lock of grey hair on the fore part of his head - has proved by testimony which is satisfactory to me that he is the identical person mentioned and described in the deed of Manumission and described in the deed of Manumission above referred to and that he was born and raised in Washington County aforesaid
In testimony 23 Aug 1832

A101a   Washington County to wit:
I Otho Holland Williams Clerk of Washington County Court hereby certify to all whom it doth or may concern that it has been proved by testimony which is satisfactory to me that the bearer hereof a negro man named Thomas Hall, who applies for this certificate was born free in this County

The said Thomas was twenty one years of age on the 14th day of April last Six feet and one inch in height, has two Small Scars on his thumb on the right hand and a small mole on his neck under the left jaw - slender make, and of good form dark complexion and pleasing countenance he was born and raised in this County -   In Testimony 16 Octr. 1832

A102a   Washington County to wit:
I Otho Holland Williams Clerk of Washington County Court hereby certify to all whom it doth or may concern that it has been proved by testimony which is satisfactory to me that the

of Washington County, Maryland

bearer hereof a negro man named Isaiah Hall was born free in this County

The said Isaiah is now about twenty years of age, six feet three and one half inches in height, strait and well made and of good and open countenance, has several Small scars on both hands, he was born and raised in the County aforesaid -
In Testimony 16 Octr. 1832

A102b Washington County to wit:
I Otho Holland Williams Clerk of Washington County Court hereby certify to all whom it doth or may concern that it has been proved by testimony which is satisfactory to me that the bearer hereof a negro woman named Catharine Welch was born free in Anne Arundel County Maryland -

The said Catharine is now about eighteen years of age 5 feet and three inches in height dark complexion, thick lips and flat nose - her two little fingers are both crooked, no other perceivable marks -   In Testimony 16 Novr. 1832

A103a State of Maryland, Washington County, Towit:
I Otho Holland Williams Clerk of Washington County Court hereby certify to all whom it doth or may concern that it has been proved by testimony which is satisfactory to me that the bearer hereof a negro woman named Sophia Butter who applies for this certificate was born free in this County

The said Sophia will be twenty five years of age on the seventh day of March next, five feet and five inches in height, has a small scar on her left arm slender form - dark complexion and was born in the Town of Williams Port in the County of Washington aforesaid   19 Jany 1833   Test O.H. Williams Clk

A103b State of Maryland, Washington County, Towit:
I Otho Holland Williams Clerk of Washington County Court hereby certify to all whom it doth or may concern that it appears by the records of my office that a certain George Webb of said County by his certain deed of Manumission bearing date on the 10th day of December 1829 did liberate, manumit set free and discharge from slavery a mulatto man named Patrick Tiernan, born on the fourth day of April 1803.

I further certify that a bright mulatto man, now present, the (bearer hereof) called and known by the name of Patrick Tiernan aged about thirty years, five feet, seven and one half

African American Manumissions

inches in height, stout and well made, straight black hair, who has a defect in his left eye which has nearly deprived him of the sight thereof, has proved by testimony which is satisfactory to me, that he is the identical person mentioned and described by the name of Patrick Tiernan in the deed of Manumission above referred to, and that he was born and raised in the County aforesaid   Test O.H. Williams Clk   23 July 1833

A104a   State of Maryland, Washington County, Towit:
I Otho Holland Williams Clerk of Washington County Court hereby certify to all whom it doth or may concern that it appears by the records of my office that a certain William D. Bell Esq. of said County, by his certain deed of Manumission, did liberate, manumit, set free and discharge from slavery a mulatto man named Lewis Chase, born on or about the first day of December 1805.

    I further certify that a bright mulatto many now present, (the bearer hereof) called and known by the name of Lewis Chase being of the age of twenty seven years and upwards five feet and eight inches high, has a Small Scar above the left eye, well made, and a good countenance and by trade a printer, has proved by testimony which is satisfactory to me that he is the identical person mentioned and described by the name of Lewis Chase in the deed of Manumission above referred to, and that he was born in Baltimore City Md
    Test   O.H. Williams Clk Aug 1 1833

A105a   State of Maryland, Washington County, Towit:
I Otho Holland Williams Clerk of Washington County Court hereby certify to all whom it doth or may concern that it has been proved by testimony which is satisfactory to me that the bearer hereof a negro man named Samuel Kizen who applies for his certificate is free

    The said Samuel will be thirty one years of age on the second day of February next, five feet & five inches in height, has a mark on his right Shoulder from a bile & also a mark on his left thumb below the second joint, & a mark on his right leg, complexion not very dark, and was born in Washington County aforesaid   14t Octr. 1833   Test O.H. Williams Clk

A105b   State of Maryland, Washington County, Towit:

of Washington County, Maryland

I Otho Holland Williams Clerk of Washington County Court hereby certify to all whom it doth or may concern that it has been proved by testimony which is satisfactory to me that the bearer hereof a negro woman named Polly Winters who applies for her certificate is free.

The said Polly was thirty years of age last October, five feet & four inches in height, bright mulatto of a pleasing countenance, and was born in Boonsborough in Washington County aforesaid. She became free in the year 1831.
Test O.H. Williams Clk				November 28t. 1833

A106a State of Maryland, Washington County, Towit:
I Otho Holland Williams Clerk of Washington County Court hereby certify to all whom it doth or may concern that it appears by the records of my office that a certain Frisby Tilghman Jr. Esq. of said County, by his certain deed of Manumission, did liberate, manumit set free and discharge from slavery a black man named Richard Smith born in Anne Arundel County near Annapolis. -

I further certify that a black man called and known by the name of Richard Smith being of the age of thirty eight years and upwards, five feet eight and an half inches high, has a scar on right leg from a burn about the length of his hand, nose flat mouth large and thick lips, has proved by testimony which is satisfactory to me, that he is the identical person mentioned and described by the name of Richard Smith, in the Deed of Manumission above referred to, -
		Test	O.H. Williams Clk			Decr. 9t 1833

A106b State of Maryland, Washington County, Towit:
I Otho Holland Williams Clerk of Washington County Court hereby certify to all whom it doth or may concern that it appears by the records of my office that a certain John Myers of said County by his deed of Manumission did liberate manumit set free and discharge from slavery a molatto Woman named Mary born in Washington County Maryland -

I further certify that a Molatto Woman now present the bearer hereof called Mary being of the age of thirty two years, four feet eleven inches high, has a scar on her right ear, of a chunkey stature and of good countenance has proved by testimony that she is the identical person mentioned in the deed of Manumission above referred to
		Test O.H. Williams Clk Dec 13t 1833

African American Manumissions

A107a State of Maryland, Washington County, Towit:
I Otho Holland Williams Clerk of Washington County Court hereby certify to all whom it doth or may concern that it appears by the records of my office that a certain William Towson of said County by his deed of Manumission did liberate manumit, set free and discharge from Slavery a black man named Nace Brooks born in Washington County Maryland

    I further certify that a black man now present the bearer hereof called Nace Brooks of the age of Thirty Eight years five feet seven inches high with a scar on his wrist, nose & forehead and of a good countenance has proved satisfactorally that he is the identical person mentioned in the deed of Manumission above referred to.   Test O.H. Williams Clk Dec. 23 1833

A107b State of Maryland, Washington County, Towit:
I Otho Holland Williams Clerk of Washington County Court hereby certify to all whom it doth or may concern that it appears by the records of my office that Mary Jane Johnston a negro Girl has been manumited by Henry A. Leonard and set free and discharged from all Manner of Slavery.

    ["I further certify" crossed out] The said Mary Jane Johnston was twelve years of age on the fourth day of January 1834 and was born in Washington County Md. and became free in the year 1829 of a jet Black, and fine countenance -
    Test O.H. Williams Clk   Feb. 17 1834

A108a State of Maryland, Washington County, Towit:
I Otho H. Williams Clerk of Washington County Court hereby certify to all whom it may or doth concern that Susan Johnston a Black Girl now present was born free in the year 1826, and that the said Susan Johnston was 12 years of age the 26 January 1834, [please note that the age and date of birth do not match] of a surly countenance, thick lips and very Black.
    Test O.H. Williams Clk   Feb. 17 1834

A108b State of Maryland, Washington County, Towit:
I Otho H. Williams Clerk of Washington County Court hereby certify to all whom it may or doth concern that Cecelia Elizabeth Jordon a Molatto Girl now present was born free and that she will be 9 years of age on the 6 April next of a fine countenance, large and sprighley eye, and which has been proven satisfactorally to me.   Feb. 28 1834   Test O.H. Williams Clk

Book B  of Washington County, Maryland

B1a - Inside cover
Mary Dorsey - born Febr 10th 1800 - 5 feet 4 1/2 inch.
Mary Theodosin Dorsey was born July 23 1831.
Evelina Dorsey was born 14 Dec 1837 -
Margaret Eliza Jane Dorsey born Oct 12 1839 -
I have always known Mary Dorsey to be a free woman and her children to be free born.
    S A Price

B1b - Inside cover
Mr. Nesbitt -
Isaiah Hughes Cain born Jan 7 1840
Eliza Jane Wagoner Feb 25 1840
Thomas Calvin Wagoner 17 years - 15 Jan 1859

I certify that I know these three children to be free born - Isaiah was Eliza Williams adopted child
    S A Price

B1c   State of Maryland, Washington County, Towit:
I hereby certify that it appears from a deed of Manumission recorded in my office that the bearer hereof a Negro man named Jeremiah Domanak was manumitted and set free by Adam Hains of the county aforesaid on the thirtieth day of March 1831 he being at that time forty three years of age. The said Jeremiah is of a dark complexion five feet two and one fourth inches high, has a large scar on the right side of his forehead, a scar on his right knee and one on the instep of his right foot occasioned from the cut of an axe, and of a good countenance.
    Test O.H. Williams Clk
August 18 1834

B1d   State of Maryland, Washington County, Towit:
I hereby certify that it appears from a deed of Manumission recorded in my office that the bearer hereof a Negro Woman named Fanny now Fanny Hughes was manumitted and set free by Mary Dillehunt of the County aforesaid on the ninth day of October Eighteen hundred and thirty she being at that time aged about thirty five years of age. The said Fanny is of a dark

African American Manumissions

complexion five feet 1 Inch in height has a scar under the left eye and of a good countenance.
     Oct. 7 1834   Test O.H. Williams Clk

B2a   State of Maryland, Washington County, Towit:
I Otho Holland Williams Clerk of Washington County Court hereby certify to all whom it doth or may concern that it has been proved by testimony which is satisfactory to me that the bearer hereof a Negro man named Elias Jones who applies for his certificate is free and free Born -
     The said Elias Jones is about 26 years of age 5 feet 9 inches high, sparcly made, has his ears pierced, a scar on each thigh from the cut of a knife thick lips and of dark complexion.
     Test   O.H. Williams Clk   Oct. 21. 1834.

B2b   State of Maryland, Washington County, Towit:
I hereby certify that it appears from a Deed of Manumission recorded in my office that the bearer hereof a Negro man named Anthony Porter was Manumited and set free by Jeremiah Mason of the County and State aforesaid on the twenty second day of December Eighteen hundred and thirty four he being at that time about the age of thirty five years of age. The said Anthony is of a dark complexion five feet nine and one half inches high Slight scar on his left cheek and rather a down look when spoken to
     Test OH Williams Clk   Jan. 13 1835

B3a   State of Maryland, Washington County, Towit:
I Otho Holland Williams Clerk of Washington County Court hereby certify to all whom it doth or may concern that it has been proved by testimony which is satisfactory to me that the bearer hereof a Negro Man named Frank Worthy who applies for his Certificate is free.
The said Frank Worthy is about 44 years of age 5 feet 6 inches high, a Bright Molatto flat nose a good countenance and the first Joint of his third finger on left hand stiff from a cut
     Test O.H. Williams Clk Jan. 13 1835

B3b   State of Maryland, Washington County, Towit:
I Otho H. Williams Clerk of Washington County Court, hereby certify to all whom it doth or may concern, that it appears by the records of my office that a negro man John Kettle was Manumited and set free by Benjamin Oswald on the 11 day of

of Washington County, Maryland

March 1835. The said John Kettle is 32 years of age a dark Molatto flat nose good countenance and the thumb nail on his right hand is crooked from a felon. [See explanation of "felon" in Author's Notes.]
Test O.H. Williams Clk March 13 1835

B4a   State of Maryland, Washington County, Towit:
I Otho Holland Williams Clerk of Washington County Court hereby certify to all whom it doth or may concern that it has been proved by testimony which is satisfactory to me that the bearer hereof a Negro man named Moses Lake, who applies for his certificate was born free in this County of a free woman named Charity Lake.

The said Moses Lake was thirty three years of age in October last, five feet, eight inches high, a bright Molatto and good countenance, has no notable marks, he was born and raised in Washington County aforesaid.
   O.H. Williams Clk   May 29 1835

B4b   State of Maryland, Washington County, Towit:
I Otho Holland Williams Clerk of Washington County Court hereby certify to all whom it doth or may concern that it has been proved by testimony which is satisfactory to me that the bearer hereof a Negro man named Joseph Briscoe, who applies for this certificate was born free in this County

The said Joseph Briscoe was Born January 15 1796, is five feet Seven and a half inches high, has a scar on the left side of his forehead and one on the third finger of his left hand from it having been broken a good countenance and speaks German tolerably well. July 17 1835 O.H. Williams Clk

B5a   State of Maryland, Washington County, Towit:
I O.H. Williams, Clerk of Washington County hereby Certify to all whom it may or doth concern that it appears from a Deed of Manumission recorded in my Office that the bearer hereof a negro Woman named Mary Winkley, was manumitted and set free by Philip Reeder on the 6th day of June 1836 - The said Mary Winkley is 25 years of age - five feet two and a half inches high - a dark Mulatto, with a good countenance, a small scar under the right eye, a full suit of hair - she was born and raised in Washington County Maryland.
   Aug 11 1835 O.H. Williams Clk

African American Manumissions

B5b State of Maryland, Washington County, Towit:
I Otho Holland Williams Clerk of Washington County Court hereby certify to all whom it doth or may concern that it has been proved by testimony which is satisfactory to me that the bearer hereof a Molatto boy named Lewis P.F. Able ["is a free man" crossed out] who applies for a Certificate is a free man. The said Lewis Able is five feet nine inches high about twenty three years of age a dark Molatto, ["thick lips" crossed out] has a scar upon his forehead and one upon the first finger of his left hand and a crooked nail on the second finger of his right hand he was born and raised in Washington County Maryland.
   Sept. 5 1835 O.H. Williams Clk

B6a State of Maryland, Washington County, Towit:
I Otho Holland Williams Clerk of Washington County Court hereby certify to all whom it doth or may concern that it has been proved by testimony which is satisfactory to me that the bearer hereof a Negro man named Henry Barns who applies for his certificate is a free man.
   The said Henry Barnes is about 35 years of age 5 feet 4 1/2 inches heigh has a scar on his left cheek, he was born in Washington County Maryland ["and was set free by" crossed out]
Sept 116 1835 O.H. Williams Clk

B6b State of Maryland, Washington County, Towit:
I Otho Holland Williams Clerk of Washington County Court hereby certify to all whom it doth or may concern that it has been proved by testimony which is satisfactory to me that the bearer hereof a Molatto Girl named Sophia Wagoner was born free, Said Sophia is about 17 years of age 5 feet 1 inch high, a bright molatto no marks that are perceivable and a good countenance
Sept 21 1835 O.H. Williams Clk

B6c State of Maryland, Washington County, Towit:
I Otho Holland Williams Clerk of Washington County Court hereby certify to all whom it doth or may concern that it has been proved by testimony which is satisfactory to me that the bearer hereof a Negro Man named Samuel Lake is a free Negro Said Samuel Lake is 5 feet 7 inches heigh 43 years of age has a

of Washington County, Maryland

mark below left cheak from being lanced and of good countenance
     O.H. Williams Clk   Oct. 15 1835

B7a   State of Maryland, Washington County, Towit:
I hereby certify that it has been proven to my satisfaction that the bearer hereof a Negro Woman named Gertrude Ross is the daughter of Joseph & Phoeba Ross who were manumitted by Thomas Prather of this County on the fourth day of July 1799. The said Gertrude Ross is about 34 years of age, five feet four inches high, has a scar on her neck occasioned from a burn, and is now residing in said County in which she was born.
     Test   O.H. Williams Clk   Nov. 19 1835

B7b   State of Maryland, Washington County, Towit:
I Otho H. Williams Clerk of Washington County Court do hereby Certify to all whom it may or doth concern that it appears from the Records of Washington County Court as well as from the testimony of James Fleming also on Record, that the bearer hereof a Mulatto Girl named Harriett, was sold to the said Fleming by Margaret Hagan for the term of seven years, which term has expired and she is now free - said Harriett is 18 years of age - 5 feet high, a bright Mulatto, a mark on her left hand occasioned by a burn, also a scar on her right cheeck - She was born in Frederick County, Md in the family of Francis Hagan -
Jany 9 1830   Test O.H. Williams Clk fee not paid

B8a   State of Maryland, Washington County, Towit:
I, Otho H. Williams Clerk of Washington County Court do hereby certify to all whom it may or doth concern that it appears from the Records of Washington County Court, that the ["bearer hereof" crossed out] a Negro Woman named Sarah Saucer was sold to William Van Lear for the term of 4 years which term has expired and she is now free - said Sarah is about 47 years of age 4 feet 11 Inches high a scar on the right side of her neck occasioned from the Kings evil.
     Test O.H. Williams Clk   March 19 1836

B8b   State of Maryland, Washington County, Towit:
I Otho Holland Williams Clerk of Washington County Court hereby certify to all whom it doth or may concern that it has been proved by testimony which is satisfactory to me that the bearer hereof a Negro Man named Perry Scott was born free in

African American Manumissions

Washington County Maryland, Said Perry Scott was 23 years of age in December last, 5 feet 1 3/4 inches in height, flat nose, large thick lips has a slight scar above the left eye and has lost one of his front teeth.
        Test O.H. Williams Clk   April 2. 1836

B9a   State of Maryland, Washington County, Towit:
I Otho H. Williams Clerk of Washington County Court do hereby Certify to all whom it may or doth concern that it appears from the Records of Washington County Court that the bearer hereof a Dark Molatto boy named William Cook was set free and manumitted from Slavery by Joseph Martin of said County. Said William Cook will be 8 years of age on the 13 day of December next, 4 feet 6 inches high has several scars on the left side of his neck, under the left jaw and on the back of his neck from the Scorpula.
April 4 1836   Test O.H. Williams Clk

B9b   State of Maryland, Washington County, Towit:
I Otho H. Williams Clerk of Washington County Court do hereby Certify to all whom it may or doth concern that it appears from the Records of Washington County Court that a Molatto man named Noah Collins is free, said Noah was manumitted by William T. Brown who purchased him from Doct. Frederick Dorsey and Jane Randall Administrators of Vachell W. Randall deceased. Said Noah is 5 feet 8 inches high and will be 34 years of age on the 22 of June next, has a lump on the nuckle of his fore finger on the right hand resembling a vein, and a scar on the crown of his head from a cut.
May 18 1836   O.H. Williams Clk

B10a   State of Maryland, Washington County, Towit:
I Otho Holland Williams Clerk of Washington County Court hereby certify to all whom it doth or may concern that it has been proved by testimony which is satisfactory to me that the bearer hereof a Negro Man named Samuel Nimmy who applies for his certificate is a free man -
The said Samuel Nimmy is 5 feet 4 inches high, 36 years of age, having the two forefingers on the left hand stiff from being broken and s small venn [sic] on the left rist [sic].
June 4 1836   Test O.H. Williams Clk

B10b State of Maryland, Washington County, Towit:
I Otho Holland Williams Clerk of Washington County Court hereby certify to all whom it doth or may concern that it has been proved by testimony which is satisfactory to me that the bearer hereof a Molatto boy name Jarrett Galloway who applies for his certificate of freedom was born free. - Said Jarrett will be ninteen years of age on the 17 day of July next, five feet eight inches heigh and has a scar on his right eye brow from a cut, no other perceivable marks.
June 6 1836   Test   O.H. Williams Clk

B11a State of Maryland, Washington County, Towit:
I Otho H. Williams Clerk of Washington County Court do hereby Certify to all whom it may or doth concern that it appears from the Records of Washington County Court that a certain Benjamin Yoe of said County by his certain Deed of Manumission bearing date on the 3 day of April 1822 did liberate, manumit, set free and discharge form Slavery a Negro Man named Nace Diggs. -

    I further Certify that a Negro Man now present (the bearer hereof) called and known by the name of Nace Diggs being of the age of thirty two years, about five feet two inches high, a small scar on the upper lip; and also a large one on the back of his right hand from a burn, and the left leg shorter than the right, has proved to me by testimony which is satisfactory to me, that he is the identical person mentioned and described by the name of Nace Diggs in the Deed of Manumission above referred to.
    July 12 1836   Test O.H. Williams Clk

B11b State of Maryland, Washington County, Towit:
I Otho H. Williams Clerk of Washington County Court do hereby Certify to all whom it may or doth concern that it appears from the Records of Washington County Court that a certain Caspar W. Wever of said County by his deed of Manumission did liberate, manumit, set free and discharge from Slavery a Negro Woman named Dorcas Lear. And I further certify that a Negro woman present the bearer hereof called Dorcas Lear being 23 years of age on the 7 January last five feet, one and a half inches high, not having any ["particular" crossed out] perceivable marks has proved satisfactorally to me that she is the

African American Manumissions

person mentioned and described by the name of Dorcas Lear in the Deed of Manumission above referred to.
   August 4 1836 Test O.H. Williams Clk

B12a State of Maryland, Washington County, Towit:
I Otho H. Williams Clerk of Washington County Court do hereby Certify to all whom it may or doth concern that it appears from the Records of Washington County Court that a certain Juliet Anderson of said County by her deed of Manumission bearing date the second day of August 1836 did liberate manumit set free and discharge from slavery a Negro man named Hillery Bell. And I further certify that a negro man now present (the bearer hereof) called Hillery Bell being about twenty two years of age of a dark complexion about five feet nine and a quarter inches in hight the small fingers on each hand crooked two cuts on the right wrist, has proven satisfactorily to me that he is the person mentioned in the deed of manumission above referred to
   Test O.H. Williams Clk Sept 9 1836

B12b State of Maryland, Washington County, Towit:
I Otho Holland Williams Clerk of Washington County Court hereby certify to all whom it doth or may concern that it has been proved by testimony which is satisfactory to me that the bearer hereof that the bearer hereof a negro man named Charles Little who applies for his Certificate is free.
  The said Charles was eighteen years of age last August, about five feet ten inches in height, a bright mulatto of a pleasing countenance with a Scar above the right eye and a scar on his tongue, and was born in Washington County aforesaid
   Test O.H. Williams Clk Sept 16 1836

B13a State of Maryland, Washington County, Towit:
I Otho Holland Williams Clerk of Washington County Court hereby certify to all whom it doth or may concern that it has been proved by testimony which is satisfactory to me that the bearer hereof a negro girl named Letty Barnes who applies for her certificate is free
  The said Letty is about sixteen years of age five feet and an half inch in heighth. dark complection, a scar on the left arm and was born in Washington County aforesaid
   Test O.H. Williams Clk Sept 22 1836

of Washington County, Maryland

B13b State of Maryland, Washington County, Towit:
I Otho H. Williams Clerk of Washington County Court do hereby Certify to all whom it may or doth concern that it appears from the Records of Washington County Court that a certain Juliet Anderson of said County by her deed of Manumission bearing date the 2 day of August 1836 did liberate, manumit, set free and discharge from slavery a Negro Man named William Bell. And I further certify that a negro man now present (the bearer hereof) called William Bell about 20 years of age of a dark complexion, five feet eleven inches high has several scars on his forehead and a scar from a burn on his right wrist, has proven satisfactorally to me that he is the person mentioned in the deed of Manumission referred to.
    Test   O.H. Williams Clk   Sept 27 1836

B14a State of Maryland, Washington County, Towit:
I Otho Holland Williams Clerk of Washington County Court hereby certify to all whom it doth or may concern that it has been proved by testimony which is satisfactory to me that the bearer hereof a Negro Man named Ned Forrest who applies for his certificate is free.

The said Ned Forrest was 36 years of age on the 25 day of April last part, five feet nine inches heigh has a scar on the bald of his thumb on right hand, no other perceivable marks.
Oct. 31. 1836   Test O.H. Williams Clk

B14b State of Maryland, Washington County, Towit:
I Otho Holland Williams Clerk of Washington County Court hereby certify to all whom it doth or may concern that it has been proved by testimony which is satisfactory to me that the bearer hereof a Molatto Man named Mathias Snyder who applies for his certificate is free, he being the son of Betsy Snyder who was set free under the Will of Richard Barnes her time having expired in the year 1807. The said Mathias Snyder is 5 feet 6 inches high, was 22 years of age in March last a bright Mulatto, sandy[?] haired and face considerably freckeled.
Nov. 8 1836   Test O.H. Williams Clk

B15a State of Maryland, Washington County, Towit:
I Otho Holland Williams Clerk of Washington County Court hereby certify to all whom it doth or may concern that it has been proved by testimony which is satisfactory to me that the

African American Manumissions

bearer hereof a Negro Woman named Harriett Williams who applies for her certificate is free. The said Harriett Williams is about thirty five Years of age five feet one inch in hight has a slight scar from a cut across the back of her right hand no other marks perceptible
December 5 1836   Test O.H. Williams Clk

B15b State of Maryland, Washington County, Towit:
I Otho Holland Williams Clerk of Washington County Court hereby certify to all whom it doth or may concern that it has been proved by testimony which is satisfactory to me that the bearer hereof a Negro Man named Mount Joy William Jackson who applies for his certificate is free.
The said Mount Joy William Jackson was 18 years of age in June last 5 feet 5 1/2 inches in height has a scar on his forehead, one on his forefinger of his left hand and three scars below the left knee, no other marks perceptible
January 28 1837 O.H. Williams Clk

B16a State of Maryland, Washington County, Towit:
I Otho Holland Williams Clerk of Washington County Court hereby certify to all whom it doth or may concern that it has been proved by testimony which is satisfactory to me that the bearer hereof a Negro Girl named Pruelender Dixon is a free Girl.
The said Pruelender will be 25 years of age in March next 4 feet 10 inches high no perceptible marks.
Jan. 28 1837   O.H. Williams Clk

B16b State of Maryland, Washington County, Towit:
I Otho H. Williams Clerk of Washington County Court do hereby Certify to all whom it may or doth concern that it appears from the Records of Washington County Court that a bright Mulatto Man named Lewis Wright who applies for his certificate is free. The said Lewis Wright was ["aged" crossed out] twenty one years of age in July last past, five feet, Seven and a half inches high, has a scar on his right arm from the bite of a dog and a scar on the small finger of the left hand from a cut of a Syckle.   March 3 1837   O.H. Williams Clk

of Washington County, Maryland

B17a   State of Maryland, Washington County, Towit:
I Otho Holland Williams Clerk of Washington County Court hereby certify to all whom it doth or may concern that it has been proved by testimony which is satisfactory to me that the bearer hereof a Negro man named ["Henson Graham" crossed out] Michael Henson who applies for his certificate is free.
The said ["Henson Graham" crossed out] Michael Henson is five feet nine and a half inches high, thick lips, has a scar above the left eye and a scar on the back of the right hand and was twenty five years of age on the 12 of May last.
March 4 1837   O.H. Williams   Clk

B17b   State of Maryland, Washington County, Towit:
I Otho H. Williams Clerk of Washington County Court do hereby Certify to all whom it may or doth concern that it appears from the Records of Washington County Court that a Negro Woman named Rebecca Butler who applies for her certificate is free.
     The said Rebecca Butler is about thirty four years of age, five feet two inches high, has a scar on the right arm from a cut, and a large mould behind the left ear.
March 20 1837   O.H. Williams   Clk

B18a   State of Maryland, Washington County, Towit:
I Otho Holland Williams Clerk of Washington County Court hereby certify to all whom it doth or may concern that it has been proved by testimony which is satisfactory to me that the bearer hereof a negro woman, named Sarah Johnson who applies for her certificate is free.
     The said Sarah is thirty eight years of age, about five feet 5 1/2 inches in height, of a dark complexion, pleasing countenance, and has a mark of a burn on the right hand and a lancet mark on her chin, and was born in Washington County
March 25, 1837   Test   O.H. Williams   Clk

B18b   State of Maryland, Washington County, Towit:
I Otho H. Williams Clerk of Washington County Court do hereby Certify to all whom it may or doth concern that it appears from the Records of Washington County Court that a certain Susan Hughes, Isabella Hughes, Rebecca Hughes, Letitia Hughes & H. Courtenay Hughes, by their Deed of Manumission bearing date the tenth day of February, 1837, did liberate, manumit and

African American Manumissions

set free and discharge from slavery a Negro Man named Daniel Able. And I further certify that a Negro man now present (the bearer hereof) called Daniel Able, about 37 years of age, of a dark complexion, five feet six and a quarter inches high, has a slight scar over his left eye, produced by a blow, a scar on the left side of his head, upon which the hair does not grow; the fore finger of the right hand stiffened in the first joint by a cut, has proven satisfactorily to me that he is the person mentioned in the Deed of Manumission referred to.
Test   O.H. Williams Clk
April 4. 1837

B18c   State of Maryland, Washington County, Towit:
I Otho Holland Williams Clerk of Washington County Court hereby certify to all whom it doth or may concern that it has been proved by testimony which is satisfactory to me that the bearer hereof a Negro Man named Alexandrice Mitchell is a free man. The said Alexandrice Mitchell is six feet one inch high, about twenty six years of age, has a ["burn"crossed out] scar on his right arm from a burn and of a good countenance
March 24 1837   Test   O.H. Williams Clk

B19a   State of Maryland, Washington County, Towit:
I O.H.Williams Clerk of Washington County Court do hereby certify to all whom it may or doth concern that it appears by the Records of Washington County aforesaid, that a certain Christian Eversole by his deed of manumission, bearing date the 13th day of August 1800, did liberate manumit and set free and discharge from Slavery a Negro Man named Abraham Valentine Hess. The said Abraham Valentine is 37 years of age, a dark mulatto, 5 feet 11 inches in height, has a scar on his right leg, produced by the cut of a scythe, a mole on the right cheek near the nose, and has proven to me satisfactorily that he is the person mentioned in the deed of manumission referred to. Test O.H. Williams Clk
    June 29. 1837

B19b   State of Maryland, Washington County, Towit:
I Otho H. Williams Clerk of Washington County Court do hereby Certify to all whom it may or doth concern that it appears from the Records of Washington County Court that a certain John R. Hyland, by his deed of Manumission bearing date the 11th day of May 1816, did liberate, manumit, and set free and

of Washington County, Maryland

discharge from Slavery, on the third day of July 1837, a Negro Man named Jonathan J. Myers. The said Jonathan is 24 years of age, five feet seven inches high, stout built, of a dark complexion and pleasing countenance. a miller by trade, and his hands are marked by steel picks, produced by dressing Burrs. He has proven to me satisfactorily that he is the person mentioned in the Deed of Manumission referred to and of his having faithfully served out his time.
July 4. 1837   Test   O.H. Williams Clk

B19c State of Maryland, Washington County, Towit:
I Otho H. Williams Clerk of Washington County Court do hereby Certify to all whom it may or doth concern that it appears from the Records of Washington County Court that a Mulatto boy named Joseph Moles was born free, said Joseph is the son of a Molatto Woman named Nelly who was manumitted by Doct. Frederick Dorsey of this County. the said Joseph is five feet, five inches high has no marks perceptible. and will be 20 years of age 24 Dec. next   July 18 1837   Test   O.H. Williams Clk

B20a State of Maryland, Washington County, Towit:
I Otho Holland Williams Clerk of Washington County Court hereby certify to all whom it doth or may concern that it has been proved by testimony which is satisfactory to me that the bearer hereof a Negro Man named Samuel Barnes, is free.
    The said Samuel is about 28 years of age, 5 feet 11 1/2 inches high, has a scar on his right leg, produced by the cut of an axe; a mark, encompassing the Second toe of the right foot, produced by being caught by the cogs of a Wheel attached to bolting gears in a Mill. His left thigh was once broken, which has made One leg shorter than the Other, and causes him to limp.   Aug. 10. 1837   Test   O.H. Williams Clk

B20b State of Maryland, Washington County, Towit:
I Otho H. Williams Clerk of Washington County Court do hereby Certify to all whom it may or doth concern that it appears from the Records of Washington County Court that a Negro Woman named Eliza Bell is free, she having been Manumitted by Juliett Anderson on the Second day of August 1836. The said Eliza Bell is five feet 3 1/2 Inches high, about twenty five years of age, has a scar on her left cheek and two scars under the right ear.   Test O.H. Williams Clk   Augst 12 1837

African American Manumissions

B20c State of Maryland, Washington County, Towit:
I Otho Holland Williams Clerk of Washington County Court hereby certify to all whom it doth or may concern that it has been proved by testimony which is satisfactory to me that the bearer hereof a Molatto Woman named Charity McCubbins is a free Woman, being the daughter of Prissy Beall who was manumitted by Samuel B. Beall of Allegany County in the year 1801. The said Charity McCubbins is five feet, four and a half inches high about 25 years of age, has several Marks about her neck from the Kings Evil which she has at this time
Sept 26 1837   Test   O.H. Williams Clk

B21a State of Maryland, Washington County, Towit:
I Otho H. Williams Clerk of Washington County Court do hereby Certify to all whom it may or doth concern that it appears from the Records of Washington County Court that Mary Pindell is a free Woman. The said Woman was set free by a Deed of manumission bearing date the 29th day of April 1817. and recorded in Liber BB folio 995 - She is a bright mulatto, with straight black hair, five feet two and the quarter inches in height, aged thirty eight years, and has a scar on her left hand occasioned by a burn
   Test   O.H. Williams Clk   November 7 1837

B21b State of Maryland, Washington County, Towit:
I Otho H. Williams Clerk of Washington County Court do hereby Certify to all whom it may or doth concern that it appears from the Records of Washington County Court that a certain Tobias Johnson of said County by his deed of Manumission bearing date on the 22 day of May 1837 did liberate manumit, set free and discharge from slavery a Negro man named Notley Hopewell. I further certify that a Negro man now present (the bearer hereof) called Notley Hopewell of the age of about 23 years about 5 feet 4 inches in height has a scar on side of his right eye and a moule upon his nose has proved to me by testimony which is satisfactory to me that he is the person named in said deed of Manumission
Dec 27 1837   Test   O.H. Williams Clk

B22a State of Maryland, Washington County, Towit:
I Otho H. Williams Clerk of Washington County Court do hereby Certify to all whom it may concern that it appears from

the records of Washington County Court, that the bearer hereof William Murray is a free man, having obtained his freedom on petition to the Court aforesaid, by a Verdict of a Jury and the Judgement of said Court -

The said William Murray is about twenty five years of age, five feet nine inches and a half in height, is a bright mulatto, has black curly hair, has a scar on his left elbow occasioned by a fall, and a small scar on the little finger of the left hand, occasioned by a cut

Test Otho H. Williams Clerk   Feby. 27. 1837

B22b   State of Maryland, Washington County, Towit:

I, Otho H. Williams, Clerk of Washington County Court, do hereby certify to all to whom it may or doth concern, that it hath been proven by testimony that is satisfactory to me, that the bearer hereof a Mulatto Man named Benjamin Stuart, is free.

The said Benjamin is about 5 feet 3 inches in height, twenty one years of age the 31st day of August last, has a scar on the third finger of the left hand - and a bright Mulatto.

March 16, 1838. Test   Otho H. Williams Clerk

B23a   State of Maryland, Washington County, Towit:

I, Otho H. Williams, Clerk of Washington County Court, do hereby certify to all whom it may or doth concern, that it hath been proven by testimony that is satisfactory to me, that the bearer hereof a dark mulatto man named Henry Green, is free. The said Henry is about 5 feet 5 inches high; has a bare forehead, and an indentation on the right side of the bare spot, occasioned by a blow: is about 37 years of age.

Test = Otho H. Williams Clerk   March 24, 1838

B23b   State of Maryland, Washington County, Towit:

I Otho H. Williams, Clerk of Washington County Court do hereby Certify that it has been proven to my satisfaction by good and sufficient testimony that the bearer hereof a negro Woman named Kitty Chase was born free in this County of a free woman Esther Chase. The said Kitty is about twenty six years of age, she is five feet one inch in height, has a mark on the right wrist occasioned by a burn, and is slightly pitted with the small pox, has a sprightly countenance, and thick head of wool.

Test Otho H. Williams Clerk

March 28, 1838

African American Manumissions

B23c   State of Maryland, Washington County, Towit:
I, Otho H. Williams, Clerk of Washington County Court, hereby certify to all whom it may or doth concern that it hath been proven by testimony that is satisfactory to me, that the bearer hereof a Negro Man named Nathan Jonson, is free.

The said Nathan is about five feet nine inches high, twenty two years of age, has a scar two inches long immediately under the left eye, also a scar under the cheekbone on the right side of the face, produced by being cut with an axe, and is of a copper complexion.
   Test Otho H. Williams Clerk   March 29, 1838

B24a   State of Maryland, Washington County, Towit:
I Otho H. Williams Clerk of Washington County Court do hereby Certify to all whom it may concern that it appears from the Certificate of Daniel Schnebly Esquire, Register of Wills for Washington County, and from other testimony satisfactory to me, that the bearer hereof, Henry Rossier, a Negro man was set free by Van S. Brashier late of Washington County deceased and that he is a free man - Said Henry is about forty two years of age, five feet four inches and a half high, has a small scar on his forehead, and a scar over each eye & a small wart on the left side of his neck, wears whiskers, and has a pleasant countenance
.Test Otho H. Williams Clerk   April 5. 1838

B24b   State of Maryland, Washington County, Towit:
I, Otho H. Williams Clerk of Washington County Court do hereby certify to all whom it may concern that it appears from the certificate of Daniel Schnebly Esqr. Register of Wills for Washington County that the bearer hereof a Negro man named Stephen was manumitted and set free from slavery by Maria Brasher late of Washington County deceased. Said Stephen is about 30 years of age, five feet, seven inches in height, has a small scar upon his left cheek no other marks worth noticing.
   Test   Otho H. Williams Clerk April 9. 1838

B25a   State of Maryland, Washington County, Towit:
I, Otho H. Williams Clerk of Washington County Court, do hereby certify to all whom it may concern, that it appears from the certificate of Jas. H. Kennedy and from other testimony satisfactory to me, that the bearer hereof a negro Man named Henry Wagoner, is free. Said Henry is about 22 years of age, five

feet ten inches in heighth, has a scar on the top of the left foot, produced by being cut with an axe, and has a calm, collected and pleasant countenance.
Test   Otho H. Williams Clerk April 11, 1838

B25b   State of Maryland, Washington County, Towit:
I, Otho H. Williams Clerk of Washington County Court do hereby certify to all whom it may concern, that it appears from the certificate of Daniel Schnebly, Esquire, Register of Wills for Washington County, and from other testimony satisfactory to me, that the bearer hereof Richard Baker, was set free by Van S. Brashear, late of Washington County, deceased, and that he is a free man. Said Richard is about thirty eight years of age, five feet high, of dark complexion; and his left leg considerably shorter than the right, producing evident lameness.
Test   Otho H. Williams Clerk April 16, 1838

B25c   State of Maryland, Washington County, Towit:
I, Otho H. Williams Clerk of Washington County Court do hereby certify to all whom it may concern, that it appears from the certificate of Thomas Duckett, satisfactory to me, that the bearer hereof Williams Duckett is a free man. Said William is about 20 years of age, has a mark on his right wrist produced by being cut in a fall, a scar on the left leg below the knee; cut by a mowing scythe, and 5 feet 9 1/2 inches high.
Test   Otho H. Williams Clerk July 21, 1838.

B26a   State of Maryland, Washington County, Towit:
I Otho Holland Williams Clerk of Washington County Court hereby certify to all whom it doth or may concern that it has been proved by testimony which is satisfactory to me that the bearer hereof Nathaniel Cyrus[?] alias Daniel Fox is a free man. Said Daniel is about 20 years of age, has a mark on his head, covering the temple and part of his forehead, on the right side, produced by a burn, and five feet three and a half inches in heighth.   Test   Otho H. Williams Clerk Aug. 6. 1838.

B26b   State of Maryland, Washington County, Towit:
I Otho Holland Williams Clerk of Washington County Court hereby certify to all whom it doth or may concern that it has been proved by testimony which is satisfactory to me that the bearer hereof Otho Sewall, is a free man. Said Otho was 21 years

African American Manumissions

old on the 4th July last, has a mole on the left side of his breast, a scar on the big toe of the right foot, and five feet nine and a half inches high.
Test   Otho H. Williams Clerk August 7, 1838.

B26c   State of Maryland, Washington County, Towit:
I Otho Holland Williams Clerk of Washington County Court hereby certify to all whom it doth or may concern that it has been proved by testimony which is satisfactory to me that the bearer hereof a Negro Woman named Elizabeth Russell, is a free Woman, from birth. Said Elizabeth is about 31 years of age, 5 feet and one half inch in height, has a scar upon the elbow of her right arm. Said Elizabeth has two children named William Russell & Mary Russell. Said William Russell being a Mulatto 18 years of age, stout built, sandy hair, and has a scar on one of his eye brows.
Test   Otho H. Williams Clerk August 16, 1838.

B26d   State of Maryland, Washington County, Towit:
I, Otho H. Williams Clerk of Washington County Court do hereby certify to all whom it may concern, that it appears from the certificate of Daniel Schnebly Esqr. Register of Wills for Washington County and from the testimony satisfactory to me that the bearer hereof a Mulatto Woman named Mary Rosier was set free by Va S. Brashears late of Washington County deceased and that she is a free woman. Said Mary Rosier is about 37 years of age, 5 feet 4 1/2 inches in height has a scar on here left breast and has a good countenance.   Test   Otho H. Williams Clerk August 27 1838   said Mary has an infant child named Van Maria Rosier which is also free.

B27a   State of Maryland, Washington County, Towit:
I Otho H. Williams Clerk of Washington County Court, do hereby certify to all whom it may or doth concern, that it appears from a Deed of Manumission, by a certain Upton Laurence, recorded in Liber H.H. folio 32, one of the Land Record Books of Washington County, that the bearer hereof, a Negro Woman named Lucy Brown, is free. The said Lucy is about sixty one years of age, a bright mulatto, of good countenance, 5 feet in height.
Test   Otho H. Williams Clerk August 31, 1838.

of Washington County, Maryland

B27b   State of Maryland, Washington County, Towit:
I Otho Holland Williams Clerk of Washington County Court do hereby certify to all whom it doth or may concern that it has been proved by testimony which is satisfactory to me that the bearer hereof James Jenkins, is free. The said James was 21 years of age in August last, has two small scars on either side of his forehead, is 5 feet 5 inches high, and a bright mulatto, of handsome appearance.
Test   Otho H. Williams Clerk October 17, 1838.

B27c   State of Maryland, Washington County, Towit:
I Otho Holland Williams Clerk of Washington County Court do hereby certify to all whom it doth or may concern that it has been proved by testimony which is satisfactory to me that the bearer hereof a negro Woman named Charity, is a free woman. The said Charity was 22 years of age last May, five feet one inch in height, has a slight scar on the right cheek occasioned by a scratch from a child, as also a mark on her left wrist. Her color is somewhat light for persons who come under the denomination of Negroes, and her appearance indicates an amiable disposition.
Test   Otho H. Williams Clerk October 29, 1838.
said Charity has a child 3 years old in May, named Mary Ellen, who is also free.

B27d   State of Maryland, Washington County, Towit:
I Otho H. Williams Clerk of Washington County Court, hereby certify to all whom it doth or may concern that the bearer hereof George Duffin, has been satisfactorily proven to me to be a free man. The said George is about 25 years of age, dark complexion, has several scars on his forehead and opposite his right eye, produced he says by creeping through a Window pane, when a lad; he is five feet six and a half inches high, and has a good countenance.
Test   Otho H. Williams Clerk November 3, 1838.

B28a   State of Maryland, Washington County, Towit:
I Otho H. Williams Clerk of Washington County Court, hereby certify to all whom it doth or may concern, that the bearer hereof, a negro man named James Barnes, having been proven so, by testimony which is satisfactory to me. Said James is about twenty three years of age, five feet four inches high, has a scar on

African American Manumissions

the fore finger of the left hand from a cut, has his ears bored and wears rings in them; his complexion is black.
Test   Otho H. Williams Clerk December 17, 1838.

B28b   State of Maryland, Washington County, Towit:
I Otho H. Williams Clerk of Washington County Court, hereby certify to all whom it doth or may concern, that the bearer hereof, a negro man named Charles Barnes, is a free man, having been proven so by testimony which is satisfactory to me. Said Charles is about five feet four and a half inches high, twenty five years of age, no marks perceptible, colour black.
Test   Otho H. Williams Clerk December 17, 1838.

B28c   State of Maryland, Washington County, Towit:
I Otho Holland Williams Clerk of Washington County Court do hereby certify to all whom it doth or may concern that it has been proved by testimony which is satisfactory to me that the bearer hereof a Negro man named Henry Beltzhour is free and was free born. The said Henry Beltzhour will be 20 years of age on the 14 July next, is 5 feet 10 inches in height, has a scar along by his left ear, and a scar on the left arm from a burn and a good countenance.
Test   Otho H. Williams Clerk March 19 1839.

B28d   State of Maryland, Washington County, Towit:
I Otho H. Williams Clerk of Washington County Court, hereby certify to all whom it doth or may concern, that it appears by the records of Washington County Court that the bearer hereof a Molato Man named Samuel Robinson is a free man. Said Samuel was manumitted by William Price Esqr. of said County is 23 years of age 5 feet 6 1/2 inches high and has a bone felon on his left thumb.
Test   Otho H. Williams Clerk 12 April 1839

B28e   State of Maryland, Washington County, Towit:
I hereby certify that it appears by testimony which is satisfactory to me, that the bearer hereof a Negro man named Moses Reilly is a free man. The said Moses is about twenty two years of age, tolerably dark, five feet six inches high, and has a mark on the right cheek bone produced by a stone being thrown at him, and has a good countenance, and altogether likely.   Test
        Otho H. Williams Clerk Nov. 18, 1839.

of Washington County, Maryland

B29a State of Maryland, Washington County, Towit:
I Otho H. Williams Clerk of Washington County Court, hereby certify to all whom it doth or may concern, that it appears by the records of Washington County Court that the bearer hereof a Negro Man named Isaac Kane is a free man. Said Isaac Kane was manumitted on the 12 January 1837 by Sarah Barnett, is 32 years of age, 5 feet 10 inches in height, stout built and has a copper complexion, no marks that are perceptible
Test   Otho H. Williams Clerk April 22 1839.

B29b State of Maryland, Washington County, Towit:
I Otho H. Williams Clerk of Washington County Court do hereby certify that the bearer hereof a Negro Man named George Brown who applies for his certificate of freedom is a free man, said George Brown was manumitted in the year 1832 by Jacob B. Motter has two small scars on his right cheek, one small one on his forehead immediately above his nose and black spot on his tow on the left foot.
Test   Otho H. Williams Clerk April 29 1839

B29c State of Maryland, Washington County, Towit:
I Otho H. Williams Clerk of Washington County Court do hereby certify that the bearer hereof a Molatto Woman named Hannah Reeder who applies for his [sic] certificate of freedom is a free woman, said Hannah was manumitted in the year 1828 by Philip Reeder as appears from the Records of Washington County court said Hannah is a fair Molatto and has no marks perceptible.
Test   Otho H. Williams Clerk [no date]

B29d State of Maryland, Washington County, Towit:
I, Otho H. Williams Clerk of Washington County Court do hereby certify that the bearer hereof a Negro Man named Isaac Kane who has applied for his certificate of freedom is a free man. Said Isaac was manumitted in the year 1837 by Sarah Barnett as appears from the records of Washington County, said Isaac is five feet nine inches in height, has a swelling or Vene[? - Vein?] on the back of his neck, and is about thirty two years of age.
    Test   Otho H. Williams Clerk Augst 3d 1839

African American Manumissions

B30a   State of Maryland, Washington County, Towit:
I Otho H. Williams Clerk of Washington County Court, hereby certify to all whom it doth or may concern, that the bearer hereof a Negro Man named Charles Barnes is free as appears from the Record of said County. The said Charles Barnes was manumitted on the tenth day of April Eighteen hundred and thirty nine, is in his 29 year of age, five feet, Six inches in height and has a scar on his right thigh from a cut
Test   Otho H. Williams Clerk August 31. 1839

B30b   State of Maryland, Washington County, Towit:
I Otho H. Williams Clerk of Washington County Court, hereby certify to all whom it doth or may concern, that the bearer hereof a Molatto Man named John W. Brooks who who [sic] applies for his certificate has been proven by testimony that is satisfactory to me that he is a free man. Said John W. Brooks will be 21 years of age in May next Six feet one inch in height, has Several Scars on his left hand, has a scar on the left side of his chin and a scar on the left foot & leg.
Test   Otho H. Williams Clerk Sept 4 1839

B30c   State of Maryland, Washington County, Towit:
I hereby certify to all whom it may or doth concern that it appears from the records of Washington County that the bearer hereof a Molatto Woman who applies for her certificate of freedom is free having been manumitted by Charles Adamson the 19 March 1839. The said Harriett Lynch is five feet four inches in height and has a scar upon her forehead
   Test   Otho H. Williams Clerk Oct 18 ["17" crossed out] 1839 Certificate given 30 Apl 1845

B31a   State of Maryland, Washington County, Towit:
I Otho H. Williams Clerk of Washington County Court, hereby certify to all whom it doth or may concern, that the bearer hereof a Negro man named Moses Lair is free, as appears from the record of said County. The said Moses Lair was manumitted by Caspar W. Wever, Esq. in the year 1825 [or 1823?]; he is about 25 years of age, five feet seven inches high, tolerably dark, and has a scar on his right cheek bone, produced by a burn.
Test   Otho H. Williams Clerk Dec. 3, 1839

of Washington County, Maryland

B31b   State of Maryland, Washington County, Towit:
I Otho H. Williams Clerk of Washington County Court, hereby certify to all whom it doth or may concern, that the bearer hereof a Negro Woman named Ann Eliza Lear is free as appears from the records of said County - The said Ann was manumitted by Casper W. Wever Esqr in the year 1825 she is 21 years of age five feet high, tolerably dark and no perceivable marks.
Test   Otho H. Williams Clerk   April 13 1840

B31c   State of Maryland, Washington County, Towit:
I Otho H. Williams Clerk of Washington County Court, hereby certify to all whom it doth or may concern, that the bearer hereof, a Negro Woman named Henrietta Gross, is free, as appears from the Records of said County. The said Henrietta is about forty years of age, four feet ten and a half inches high, has a flesh mole on the right nostril and is of copper complexion.
Test   Otho H. Williams Clk   April 29, 1840.

B31d   State of Maryland, Washington County, Towit:
I Otho H. Williams Clerk of Washington County Court, hereby certify to all whom it doth or may concern, that the bearer hereof, a Woman named Louisa Brown, is free, as appears by a deed of Manumission on record in Washington County Court. The said Louisa is about twenty three years of age, five feet high, has a flesh mole on the right cheek bone, is of a yellow complexion and in appearance rather likely.
Test   Otho H. Williams Clerk   May 1, 1840

B32a   State of Maryland, Washington County, Towit:
I Otho H. Williams Clerk of Washington County Court, hereby certify to all whom it doth or may concern, that it appears from the Records of the Registers office of this County that the bearer hereof Maria Curtis a Negro Woman is free. The said Maria Curtis was 33 years of age in January last has a Scar on her right foot, a scar on her forehead and a Scar on the left ear.
Test   Otho H. Williams Clerk   June 1. 1840

B32b   State of Maryland, Washington County, Towit:
I Otho H. Williams Clerk of Washington County Court, hereby certify to all whom it doth or may concern, that it appears from evidence which is satisfactory to me that the bearer hereof a yellow woman named Catharine Dorsey, (formerly Catharine

African American Manumissions

Point) is a free woman, from her birth. The said Catharine is about 27 years of age, 5 feet 4 inches high, of a yellow complexion, has a felon mark on the forefinger of the left hand, no other marks perceivable; stout built and rather good looking.
Test   Otho H. Williams Clerk June 22, 1840.

B32c   State of Maryland, Washington County, Towit:
I Otho H. Williams Clerk of Washington County Court, hereby certify to all whom it doth or may concern, that it appears from the Records in my office that the bearer hereof a Mulatto man named Nathan Kelly is free, he being manumitted by Susan Hammer[?] on 20 February 1837. The said Nathan Kelly is about 34 years of age 5 feet 9 inches in height and no perceptible marks upon him   Test   Otho H. Williams Clerk June 30 1840

B32d   State of Maryland, Washington County, Towit:
I Otho H. Williams Clerk of Washington County Court, hereby certify to all whom it doth or may concern, that it appears from the evidence of Elie Crampton which is satisfactory to me that the bearer hereof a Mulatto man called John H. Washington is a free man and born free. Said John H. Washington is five feet ten 1/2 inches in height aged about 28 years and has a scar on his right wrist.   Test   Otho H. Williams Clerk July 28 1840

B33a   State of Maryland, Washington County, Towit:
I Otho H. Williams Clerk of Washington County Court, hereby certify to all whom it doth or may concern, that it appears from evidence which is satisfactory to me that the bearer hereof a Negro Woman named Rachael Jones was born free of a free woman. The said Rachael Jones is five feet and one half inches in height has a scar on the left side of her neck, a scar on the left side of forehead and very stout made.
Test   Otho H. Williams Clerk August 19 1840

B33b   State of Maryland, Washington County, Towit:
I Otho H. Williams Clerk of Washington County Court, hereby certify to all whom it doth or may concern, that it appears from the records of Washington County that the bearer hereof a Negro Woman named Elizabeth Robertson is a free Woman. Said Elizabeth Robertson is five feet two inches in height, aged about thirty four years and has no perceptible marks, and rather spare made Woman.
Test   Otho H. Williams Clerk August 19 1840

of Washington County, Maryland

B33c State of Maryland, Washington County, Towit:
I Otho H. Williams Clerk of Washington County Court, hereby certify to all whom it doth or may concern, that it appears from the records of Washington County that the bearer hereof who applies for his certificate of freedom is free named James Brown. The said James Brown was 19 years of age on the 14 February 1840 five feet Seven inches high, has a scar under his chin, a scar on his right eye brow and a mould in the palm of his left hand.
Test   Otho H. Williams Clerk August 31 1840

B34a State of Maryland, Washington County, Towit:
I Otho H. Williams Clerk of Washington County Court, hereby certify to all whom it doth or may concern, that the bearer hereof a Mulatto Woman named Mary Gurnin[?] is free as appears from the records of this County said Mary Gurnin[?] was manumitted by Henry Martin on the 23 April 1830 is five feet three inches in height Aged about 37 years of age and no perceptible marks.
Test   Otho H. Williams Clerk Sept 1. 1840

B34b State of Maryland, Washington County, Towit:
I Otho H. Williams Clerk of Washington County Court, hereby certify to all whom it doth or may concern, that it appears from the Records of Washington County aforesaid that a certain John R. Hyland by his deed of Manumission bearing date the 11 of May 1816 did set free his negro Girl Elizabeth Myers ["Mary Myers" crossed out]. The said Elizabeth was 24 years of age on the 2d of April 1840 is five feet One inch in height and has no perceptible marks.   Test   Otho H. Williams Clerk
       Oct 10 1840

B34c State of Maryland, Washington County, Towit:
I Otho H. Williams Clerk of Washington County Court, hereby certify to all whom it doth or may concern, that it appears from the Records of Washington County Court that the bearer hereof a Mulatto Woman named Hannah Farmer is free, having been manumitted this 27 October 1840 by William Gabby[?]. The said Hannah Farmer is ["23" crossed out] about 23 years of age, four feet eleven inches high has a small scar on her nose, no other perceptible marks.
Test   Otho H. Williams Clerk 27 Oct. 1840

African American Manumissions

B35a   State of Maryland, Washington County, Towit:
I Otho H. Williams Clerk of Washington County Court, hereby certify to all whom it doth or may concern, that the bearer hereof a Mulatto Woman named Sophia Moles is free as appears from the Records of Washington County. The said Sophia Moles is about 25 years of age 5 feet 2 3/4 inches in Height has a small scar above the right eye.
Test   Otho H. Williams Clerk Dec. 1. 1840   Not pd

B35b   State of Maryland, Washington County, Towit:
I Otho H. Williams Clerk of Washington County Court, hereby certify to all whom it doth or may concern, that it hath been proven satisfactory to me that the bearer hereof a Dark Mulatto Woman named Jane Spalden is a free Woman. The said Jane Spalden is about 14 years of age five feet one inch in height has a small scar on her forehead, no other perceptible marks and a dark Mulatto.
Test   Otho H. Williams Clerk Feb. 9 1941

B35c   State of Maryland, Washington County, Towit:
I Otho H. Williams Clerk of Washington County Court, hereby certify to all whom it doth or may concern, that it appears from the records of Washington County Court that the bearer hereof a Negro Woman named Sophia James is a free woman The said Sophia James was manumitted on the 29 April 1831 by John Oswald, is five feet one inch in height about 40 years of age and has no perceptible marks.   Test   Otho H. Williams Clerk
         Feb. 26 1841

B35d   State of Maryland, Washington County, Towit:
I Otho H. Williams Clerk of Washington County Court, hereby certify to all whom it doth or may concern, that it appears from testimony which is satisfactory to me that the bearer hereof a Bright Mulatto Woman named Elizabeth Miller is a free woman and born free. Said Elizabeth Miller will be 22 years of age on the 13 March inst. is five feet three inches in height, has a large wart and a scar on the back of her neck.
Test   Otho H. Williams Clerk March 8 1841

B36a   State of Maryland, Washington County, Towit:
I hereby certify to all whom it may or doth concern that it has been proven by testimony that is satisfactory to me that the

of Washington County, Maryland

bearer hereof a Bright Mulatto Woman named Susan Keller and her five children named Solomon, Elizabeth[,] Rebecca, Aaron & Ann Rosane are all free born. Said Susan Keller was 28 years old in November last is five feet Seven and three quarter inches in heighth has no perceptible marks.
Test   Otho H. Williams Clerk March 8 1841

B36b   Washington County to wit:
I hereby certify to all whom it may or doth concern that it has been proven by testimony that is satisfactory to me that the bearer hereof a Negro Man named Thomas Diggs who applies for his certificate of freedom is a free man and born free. Said Thomas Diggs is twenty five years of age, five feet, Nine inches in height and has no perceptible marks.
Test   Otho H. Williams Clerk March 18 1841

B36c   Washington County to wit:
I hereby certify to all whom it may or doth concern that it appears from the Records of Washington County Court that the within named Margaret Dorsey is a free woman, she having been manumitted by Otho H.W. Stull on the 12 day of April 1841.
The said Margaret Dorsey is four feet eleven and a half inches in height aged 25 years and has no perceptible marks.
Test   Otho H. Williams Clerk April 13 1841

B37a   Washington County to wit:
I Otho H. Williams Clerk of Washington County Court, do hereby certify to all whom it may or doth concern, that it appears from the Records of Washington County Court that the bearer hereof a Negro Man named Abraham Lindsay is a free man. Said Abraham Lindsay was manumitted by Thomas Keller on the 29 December 1840 is about forty three years of age five feet ten and one half inches in height and has no perceptible marks.
Test   Otho H. Williams Clerk April 14 1841

B37b Washington County to wit:
I Otho H. Williams Clerk of Washington County Court, hereby certify to all whom it may or doth concern, that it appears from the Records in my office that the bearer hereof a Molatto Woman named Mary G. Jenkens is a free woman. She is 17 years of age,

African American Manumissions

five feet and one half inches in height a bright Molatto and has no perceptible marks
Test   Otho H. Williams Clerk June 7 1841

B37c   State of Maryland, Washington County, Towit:
I Otho H. Williams Clerk of Washington County Court, hereby certify to all whom it may or doth concern, that the bearer hereof a Negro man named Philip Barnes, is a free man having been proven so by testimony which is satisfactory to me; said Philip is about five feet eight inches high, twenty one years of age, has a Scar on the left hand near the thumb and one above the left eye on the forehead, his complexion is black.
Test   Otho H. Williams Clerk July 21st 1841

B37d   State of Maryland, Washington County, Towit:
I Otho Holland Williams Clerk of Washington County Court do hereby certify to all whom it doth or may concern, that it has been proven by testimony that is satisfactory to me that the bearer hereof Jane Howard a Mulatto Woman, is a free Woman, being the daughter of ["Henry Galloway who was manumitted by James Prather of Allegany County. The said" crossed out] Pressy Beall who was manumitted by Samuel B. Beall of Allegany County in the year 1801. The said Jane Howard is five feet five and three quarter inches high, about 27 years of age, has several large scars on the right side of her neck. It further appears that the said Jane has two children, one named James Henry Howard, about 11 years, and the other, Alfred, about 3 years of age.
Test   Otho H. Williams Clerk [no date]

B38a   State of Maryland, Washington County, Towit:
I Otho Holland Williams Clerk of Washington County Court do hereby certify to all whom it doth or may concern, that it has been proven by testimony that is satisfactory to me that the bearer hereof a Mulatto Woman named Sivilla Galloway, is a free woman, being the daughter of Pressy Beall who was manumitted by Samuel B. Beall of Allegany County in the year 1801. The said Sivilla is ["about" crossed out] five feet five inches high, 22 years of age, has no perceptible marks about her, but is a little deaf and has a slight impediment of speech.
Test   Otho H. Williams Clerk [no date]

B38b State of Maryland, Washington County, Towit:
I hereby certify to all who it may or doth concern that it appears from the records of Washington County that the bearer hereof a Mulatto Woman named Ann Brown, who applies for her Certificate of freedom, is free, having been manumitted by her Mother Lucy Brown on the 23d day of September 1841. The said Ann Brown is five feet and one half inches high; aged about 25 years and has a slight scar on the forehead near the right eye.
   Test   Otho H. Williams Clerk [no date]

B38c State of Maryland, Washington County, Towit:
I Otho H. Williams Clerk of Washington County Court, do hereby certify that the bearer hereof a Mulatto woman named Maria Reeder, who applies for her certificate of freedom is a free Woman - having been manumitted in the year 1828 by Philip Reeder, as appears from the records of Washington County Court, Said Maria is five feet four and an half inches high, 25 years of age, and has no perceptible marks about her.
   Test   Otho H. Williams Clerk [no date]

B38d State of Maryland, Washington County, Towit:
I hereby certify to all whom it may or doth concern that it appears from Liber Y.Y. folios 455 & 456, one of the Land Records of Washington County, that the bearer hereof a Negro Woman, named Terry Wicks, who applies for her certificate of Freedom, is free, having been manumitted, by Isaac D. Eavey surviving Executor of Christian Eavey, on the seventh day of July 1841. The said Terry Wicks is five feet, one and three quarter inches high, about forty years of age, dark complected, and has no visible marks about her.
   Test   Otho H. Williams Clerk [no date]

B39a State of Maryland, Washington County, Towit:
I Otho H. Williams Clerk of Washington County Court, do hereby certify that the bearer hereof a Mulatto man named Charles Watts who makes application for his Certificate of freedom, is free, having been manumitted by Wm. H. Fitzhugh of Washington County, Maryland, on the fourth day of January in the year 1842, as will more fully appear by reference being had to the Land Records of said County. Said Charles is about twenty four years of age, five feet three and a half inches high, has two scars on the left hand between the thumb and wrist, and

African American Manumissions

a large scar on the right leg over the Calf occasioned by a fracture.   Test   Otho H. Williams Clerk Jany 4th 1845

B39b   State of Maryland, Washington County, Towit:
I Otho H. Williams Clerk of Washington County Court, hereby certify to all whom it may or doth concern, that the bearer hereof a Negro man named Frank Sansbury, who applies for his certificate of Freedom, is free - he having been manumitted by Archibald McCoy, now deceased, in the year 1809, as will more fully and at large appear by reference being had to said Deed of Manumission, recorded in Liber F. folio 508, one of the Land Records of Washington County. The said Frank is about sixty two years of age, five feet, six inches high, and has two scars on his forehead been the eyes.
Test   Otho H. Williams Clerk Jan. 31st 1842

B39c   State of Maryland, Washington County, Towit:
I hereby certify that it has been proven satisfactorily to me by good and sufficient testimony that the bearer hereof a Mulatto Girl named Maria Booth is free born, that she was born of a free woman named Eleanor Booth in the County & State aforesaid, and has resided in said County from her birth to the present time. the said Maria is 19 years of age, five feet, three inches high, a Dark Mulatto, and has no perceptible marks about her.
Test   Otho H. Williams Clerk [no date]

B39d   State of Maryland, Washington County, Towit:
I Otho H. Williams Clerk of Washington County Court, hereby certify to all whom it doth or may concern, that the bearer hereof a Mulatto man named William Dunmore, who applies for his Certificate of freedom, is free; he having been manumitted in the year 1822 by Jacob Miller & others as will more fully appear by reference to Liber F.F. folio 756 & 757, one of the Land Records of Washington County The said William is a bright Mulatto, five feet six 3/4 inches high, about thirty years of age, and has a scar on the forehead above the left temple, being the only visible mark about him.
Test   Otho H. Williams Clerk [no date]

B40a   State of Maryland, Washington County, Towit:
I Otho H. Williams Clerk of Washington County Court, hereby certify to all whom it doth or may concern, that   the bearer

of Washington County, Maryland

hereof a Negro Woman, named Harriet Blue formerly Harriet Miller who applies for her certificate of Freedom, is free - having been manumitted by Samuel Middlekauff and others, as will fully appear by reference to a Deed of Manumission recorded on the 21st day of March 1842, in one of the Land Records of Washington County. The said Harriet is a dark Mulatto, five feet, five inches high, will be 21 years of age, on the 27th day of June next, & has a large Scar on the left wrist, occasioned by a cut - said Harriet has a Son, named Owen Blue, about 3 years of age who is free born.
Test   Otho H. Williams Clerk [no date]

B40b   State of Maryland, Washington County, Towit:
I hereby certify that the bearer hereof a Negro Woman, named Juliet Lear, who applies for her certificate of freedom is free - having been manumitted in the year 1825 by Casper W. Wever, as will more fully appear by reference to Deed of Manumission recorded in Liber H.H. folios 512 & 513, one of the Land Records of said County. The said Juliet is a Dark Mulatto, five feet high, about 23 years of age & has no perceptible marks about her.
Test   Otho H. Williams Clerk March 24th 1842

B40c   State of Maryland, Washington County, Towit:
I Otho H. Williams Clerk of Washington County Court, do hereby certify that the bearer hereof, a negro woman, named Priscilla Pindell, who applies for her certificate of Freedom, is free - having been manumitted by Isaac Kane, as will more fully appear by reference to a Deed of Manumission recorded the 10 day of March, 1842 in Liber ZZ, one of the Land Records of Washington County. The said Priscilla Pindell is a dark Mulatto, five feet three inches high, about 35 years of age, & has no perceptable marks about her. The said Priscilla has a Daughter, two years old, named Henny, who is likewise manumitted with her.   Test Otho H. Williams Clerk May 30 1842

B41a   State of Maryland, Washington County, Towit:
I Otho H. Williams Clerk of Washington County Court, do hereby certify that the bearer hereof, a negro man, named William Henry Ridout, who applies for his certificate of Freedom, was manumitted by Samuel Young of said County and State, on the 6th day of September 1828, (as will more fully appear by reference to a Deed of Manumission recorded in Liber

African American Manumissions

K.K. folio 256 etc. one of the Land Records of said County) on the following terms and conditions, to wit: The said William Henry being of the age of 8 years and 10 Months on the date of said Deed, "shall go to the State of Pennsylvania with James O. Carson of the Town of Mercersburg in said State and well and faithfully serve the said Carson until he shall arrive at the age of 28 years - and further, that on the removal of the said William Henry into the State of Pennsylvania, he shall execute to the said Carson a Deed of Indenture, binding himself to serve the said Carson his heirs etc. until he shall attain the age of 28 years - which Indenture shall be executed agreeably to the laws of Pennsylvania in such case made and provided. And further, that is the said William Henry shall fail to comply with the above conditions, then every thing herein contained shall be absolutely null and void any thing herein contained to the contrary notwithstanding."

The said William Henry is a dark Mulatto, five feet five 3/4 inches high, will be 23 years old on the 6th day of Novr.. next, and has a scar on the left eyebrow, occasioned by a cut.
Test   Otho H. Williams Clerk July 13. 1842

B41b   State of Maryland, Washington County, Towit:
I Otho H. Williams Clerk of Washington County Court, do hereby certify that the bearer hereof a Negro Woman, named Letty Peters, who applies for her certificate of Freedom, is free - said Letty was purchased of Charles Rice, of Williamsport, Maryland, by Arthur Johnson, Esquire, of Hagerstown, County and State aforesaid, on the 25th day of September 1833 to serve said Johnson until the 25th day of Septr 1841 and then to be free as has been, by said Johnson, fully and satisfactorily proven to me. The said Letty is a bright Mulatto, with long black hair, about 26 years of age, 5 feet 4 ins. high, and has no perceptible marks about her.
Test   Otho H. Williams Clerk Septr. 28th, 1842

B42a   State of Maryland, Washington County, Towit:
I Otho H. Williams Clerk of Washington County Court, do hereby certify that the bearer hereof a negro woman named Mary Holmes who applies for her certificate of Freedom, was manumitted by Samuel M. Hitt, of the County and state aforesaid, on the 28 day of February 1829; as will appear by reference being had to Liber KK, folios 745 and 756 one of the

of Washington County, Maryland

land records of said County. Said Mary Holmes is 5 feet 2 inches high, about 40 years of age, of a tolerable dark complexion, and has a small scar on her forehead.
Test   Otho H. Williams Clerk Nov. 4, 1842

B42b   State of
Maryland, Washington County, Towit:
I Otho H. Williams Clerk of Washington County Court, hereby certify to all whom it doth or may concern, that Martha Linnette Brown (the daughter of Lucy Brown (who is recorded herein, see folio 27) as is satisfactorily proven to me, is free. The said Martha is a bright mulatto, four feet, ten 1/2 inches high, twelve years of age, and has no visible marks about her.
Test   Otho H. Williams Clerk Novr. 16th 1842

B42c   State of Maryland, Washington County, Towit:
I Otho H. Williams Clerk of Washington County Court, hereby certify to all whom it doth or may concern, that the bearer hereof, Lucinda Handy, from satisfactory evidence to me given, is free. That she is the daughter of Nelly Handy who was free born. The said Lucinda is about eighteen years of age, five feet six 1/2 inches high, a dark Mulatto, and has a scar on her right leg which was produced by a scald.
Test   Othó H. Williams Clerk January 10th. 1843

B42d   State of Maryland, Washington County, Towit:
I Otho H. Williams Clerk of Washington County Court do hereby certify that it has been satisfactorily proven to me, that the bearer hereof a negro woman named Ann Rebecca Matthews is free being the daughter of of [sic] Frank & Emma Matthews who were regularly manumitted by their respective masters, and has ever since resided in the County aforesaid. The said Ann Rebecca is 4 feet 9 inches high, 21 years of age, has no perceptible marks about her, & of a dark complexion.
Test   Otho H. Williams Clerk May 26th. 1843.

B43a   State of Maryland, Washington County, Towit:
I Otho H. Williams Clerk of Washington County Court do hereby certify to all whom it doth or may concern, that the bearer hereof, William Riley (a negro) from satisfactory evidence to me given, is free, - having been born of a free woman. The said William is now in the 21st year of his age, is five feet 9 3/4 inches

African American Manumissions

high, and has two scars one just above the left corner of the mouth, and the other across the left eye brow; is tolerably black, and has a pleasant countenance.
Test   Otho H. Williams Clerk June 15, 1843

B43b   State of Maryland, Washington County, Towit:
I Otho H. Williams Clerk of Washington County Court, do hereby certify to all whom it may or doth concern that the bearer hereof a negro man named Somerset Ballard, as has been satisfactorily proven to me, is free. The said Somerset is a bright Mulatto square built, five feet seven and 3/4 inches high, about fifty one years of age, and has no visible scars about him.
Test   Otho H. Williams Clerk July 22. 1843

B43c   State of Maryland, Washington County, Towit:
I Otho H. Williams Clerk of Washington County Court, do hereby certify that it hath been satisfactorily proven to me that the bearer hereof, Henry Williamson was born free. He is five feet six inches high, about 22 years of age, of a tolerable dark complexion, and has two small scars - one in the middle of his forehead, the other near the upper joint of his left forefinger; and has a pleasant countenance.
Test   Otho H. Williams Clerk Sept. 5th. 1843

B44a   State of Maryland, Washington County, Towit:
I hereby certify that it appears from a deed of Manumission recorded in my office that the bearer hereof a mulatto woman named Susan Ann Jenkins was manumitted and set free by Col. Frisby Tilghman of Washington County aforesaid, on the Twenty seventh day of July 1829. The said Susan Ann is about 23 years of age, five feet, 3/4 of an inch in height: she is a bright mulatto, and has no perceptible marks about her.
Test   Otho H. Williams Clerk Sept 25th. 1843.

B44b   State of Maryland, Washington County, Towit:
I Otho H. Williams Clerk of Washington County Court, hereby certify that Lavinia Susan Gruber who applies for her certificate of Freedom, was born free as it hath been to me satisfactorily proven. The said Lavinia is a bright Mulatto girl, four feet eleven inches high, stout made, is somewhat freckled, and is in the twenty first year of her age; without any perceptable marks

about her: she has a child four years old in August last, who is also a bright mulatto, and is named James Cheston Cline.
In Test. V&c
Test   Otho H. Williams Clerk October 16. 1843

B44c   State of Maryland, Washington County, Towit:
Mary Ann Hattan, who applies for her Certificate of Freedom, I hereby certify was born free, being the the [sic] Daughter of David & Margaret Hattan - said David being recorded in Liber A. folio No. 50, one of the Records for recording Free negroes, as will fully appear. Said Mary Ann is a bright & likely Mulatto, five feet three inches high, will be 18 years old on the 10th January next, and has no visible marks about her.
Test   Otho H. Williams Clerk Novr. 15th. 1843.

B45a   State of Maryland, Washington County, Towit:
I Otho H. Williams Clerk of Washington County Court do hereby certify that it appears from the records of my office that the bearer hereof named Charles Smith is free. The said Charles Smith was manumitted and set free by deed of Manumission on the 9th day of February 1843 and recorded in Liber Z.Z. folio 744. He is a very bright mulato. Five & a half feet high, with a scar just above the right eye, aged 28 years, & has a pleasing countenancé.
Test   Otho H. Williams Clerk Dec. 4th 1843.

B45b   State of Maryland, Washington County, Towit:
I Otho H. Williams Clerk of Washington County Court hereby certify, that to all whom it doth or may concern, that it appears by the Records of Washington County aforesaid that a certain Charles A. Darby of said County by his Deed of Manumission bearing date on the 4th day of April 1844, did liberate, manumit, set free and discharge form slavery (the bearer hereof) a negro woman named Maria Richardson.
And I further certify that the said Maria was 33 years of age on the 8th day of November last, is about 5 feet 2 1/2 inches high, of a tolerably dark complexion, and has no marks perceptible.
Test   Otho H. Williams Clerk April 6th 1844.

B45c   State of Maryland, Washington County, Towit:
I Otho H. Williams Clerk of Washington County Court, do hereby certify that the bearer hereof, John Wagoner, a negro Boy,

African American Manumissions

who applies for his certificate of Freedom, is free, having been born free, which is proven to me by satisfactory evidence. The said John will be 19 years of age the 29th day of November next, is a bright mulatto, 5 feet 5 1/2 inches high, has a scar just above the left eye, and one in the middle of the forehead, with a mole over the right eye.
Test   Otho H. Williams Clerk April 6th 1844.

B46a   State of Maryland, Washington County, Towit:
I Otho H. Williams Clerk of Washington County Court hereby certify that it has been satisfactorily proven to me, that the bearer hereof, Henrietta Barnes, a negro woman, who applies for Certificate of Freedom, is free, having been born free. The said Henrietta, was 20 years of age on the 11th day of September last, is a very bright mulatto, 5 feet 2 1/2 inches high, with a mole on her right cheek near the jaw and has an intelligent countenance.
Test   Otho H. Williams Clerk April 6th 1844

B46b   State of Maryland, Washington County, Towit:
I Otho H. Williams Clerk of Washington County Court, hereby certify, to all whom it may or doth concern, that it appears from the Records of Washington County Court aforesaid, that a certain John Reel of said County, by his deed of manumission, bearing date the 7th day of May 1844, did liberate, manumit and set free, and discharge from slavery, his negro man named John Keyser, being of the age of 32 years, is five feet eight inches high, and has a small scar under his right eye, and the middle finger of his left hand is stiff from the middle joint. He has a pleasant countenance.
Test   Otho H. Williams Clerk May 7 1844

B46c   State of Maryland, Washington County, Towit:
I Otho H. Williams Clerk of Washington County Court, hereby certify to all whom it doth or may concern, that it appears by the records of Washington County that the bearer hereof, Sandy Tatterson a colored man is free, having been manumitted & set free by a certain George I. Harry Trustee of John Reynolds, by Deed of Manumission, dated the 8th day of May, A.D. 1844. The said Sandy Tatterson is 25 years of age, 5 feet 7 1/2 inches high, with a scar on the right side of his chin & one on the right Thumb.   Test   Otho H. Williams Clerk May 8th. 1844

of Washington County, Maryland

B47a State of Maryland, Washington County, Towit:
I Otho H. Williams Clerk of Washington County Court, hereby certify to all whom it may or doth concern, that the bearer hereof, Frances Cole, a colored woman, is free, which has been proven to me by satisfactory testimony. The said Frances Cole was 27 years of age on the 3d day of February last, is of a tolerably dark complexion, 4 feet 9 inches high, has a pleasant countenance and delicate form, and has no marks visable about her.
In Testy. etc. Test   Otho H. Williams Clerk July 9th 1844

B47b State of Maryland, Washington County, Towit:
I Otho H. Williams Clerk of Washington County Court, hereby certify to all whom it may or doth concern, that it appears from the records of my Office, that the bearer hereof, David Gray, a man of color, is free, having been manumitted & set free by Paul Summers, by Deed of Manumission, bearing date the 20th day of January 1844, & recorded in Liber O.H.W. No. 2 folio 273. The said David is about 41 years of age, stout built, dark complexion, 6 feet 1 inch high, has 6 teeth out in front: 3 above, and 3 below and no marks perceptible about him.
Test   Otho H. Williams Clerk July 12th 1844

B47c State of Maryland, Washington County, Towit:
I O. H. Williams Clerk of Washington County Court, do hereby certify to all whom it may or doth concern, that it appears from the Records of my office, that the bearer hereof, William Hess, a man of color, is free; he having been manumitted and set free by a certain Margaret Hedrick by Deed of Manumission bearing date the 29th day of July 1844, and recorded in Liber OHW. No. 2, folio 347. The said Williams is now forty four years of age, five feet four inches high; a small scar on the forehead above the right eye; a front tooth out of the upper jaw; and the point of his nose slightly disfigured from a bite.
Test   Otho H. Williams Clerk July 30th 1844

B48a State of Maryland, Washington County, Towit:
I hereby certify to all whom it may or doth concern that the bearer hereof, Mary Ridout, a colored woman, is free, as has been satisfactorily proven to me by a competent witness. The said Mary is five feet two inches high, and about twenty years of

African American Manumissions

age, of a dark complexion and pleasant countenance, and has two children, Rachael Ann aged 3 years & Louisa aged one year.
Test   Otho H. Williams Clerk   August 20, 1844

B48b   State of Maryland, Washington County, Towit:
I Otho H. Williams Clerk of Washington County Court, do hereby certify that the bearer hereof, a colored woman named Dorcas, is free, as has been proven to me by satisfactory testimony. The said Dorcas is about 45 years of age, 5 feet 3 1/2 inches high, dark complexion, with a scar on the left side of her forehead, and a small black mark on her nose.
Test   Otho H. Williams Clerk   August 24th 1844
[In the margin is written, "Dorcas Norris"]

B48c   State of Maryland, Washington County, Towit:
I Otho H. Williams Clerk of Washington County Court, hereby certify to all whom it may or doth concern, that the bearer hereof, a colored woman named Elizabeth Ross, is free; having been born free, which is proven to me by satisfactory testimony. The said Elizabeth is about 39 years of age, 5 feet 7 inches high, tolerably dark complexion, with a scar on the upper part of the wrist of her right hand. She is of very slender form, and has a very pleasant countenance.
Test   Otho H. Williams Clk   Augt. 27th 1844

B49a   State of Maryland, Washington County, Towit:
I Otho H. Williams Clerk of Washington County Court, hereby certify to all whom it doth or may concern, that the bearer hereof, Elijah Chew, was duly manumitted and set free by a certain Frederick Snyder, by deed of manumission bearing date the 30th day of May 1844, and recorded in Liber OHW No. 2, folio 273, one of the Land Records of Washington County. The said Elijah Chew is a mulatto five feet six inches and a half high, about 32 years of age, and has a small scar on his right hand above the thumb, and has a good countenance.
Test   Otho H. Williams Clk   October 7, 1844.

B49b   State of Maryland, Washington County, Towit:
I Otho H. Williams Clerk of Washington County Court, hereby certify to all whom it may or doth concern, that the bearer hereof, Henry Miles, a negro man, who applies for his certificate of freedom, was born free, as it hath been satisfactorily proven to

of Washington County, Maryland

me. The said Henry is about 23 yearas of age, is five feet eight inches high, of a dark or black complexion, and of good countenance. No marks perceivable.
Test   Otho H. Williams Clk   October 7, 1844

B49c   State of Maryland, Washington County, Towit:
I Otho H. Williams Clerk of Washington County Court, hereby certify to all whom it may or doth concern, that the bearer hereof Mahala Douglas, a negro woman, who now here, applies for her Certificate of Freedom, is free, having been born free, which is proven by testimony to me satisfactory. The said Mahala Douglass was 21 years of age the 12th of February last, is 5 feet 2 1/2 inches high, a light mulatto thick set & has a mark on the first joint of the first finger of the left hand.
Test   Otho H. Williams Clk   Oct. 23d 1844.

B50a   State of Maryland, Washington County, Towit:
I Otho H. Williams Clerk of Washington County Court, hereby certify to all whom it may concern, that the bearer hereof, a negro man named Solomon James is free, having been manumitted and set free by George Beard by Deed of Manumission, bearing date the 2d day of November A.D. 1844, which will fully appear by reference to the Land Records of Washington County. The said Solomon is about 40 years of age, 5 feet 6 inches high, is of a tolerably light complexion, and has no perceptable marks about him.
Test   Otho H. Williams Clk   Nov. 2d 1844.

B50b   State of Maryland, Washington County, Towit:
I hereby certify to all whom it may concern, that the bearer hereof Matilda James, a negro woman, is free, which appears from the records of my office. The said Matilda was manumitted by John Oswalt on the 27th of April 1831 to take affect when she arrived at the age of Twenty years; she then being 6 years old. The said Matilda is about 20 years of age, 5 feet 1 inch high, tolerablly dark complected, and has no visable marks about her.
Test   Otho H. Williams Clk   Nov. 12th. 1844.

B50c   State of Maryland, Washington County, Towit:
I Otho H. Williams Clerk of Washington County Court, do hereby certify that the bearer hereof, a negro man named Peter Truman, is free, which is proven to me by satisfactory evidence.

African American Manumissions

The said Peter is about 24 years of age, 5 feet 10 inches high, thick set, his 1st finger of the left hand is crooked caused by being broke.
Test   Otho H. Williams Clk   Nov. 13th 1844.

B51a   State of Maryland, Washington County, Towit:
I Otho H. Williams Clerk of Washington County County Court, hereby certify to all whom it may or doth concern, that the bearer hereof, a negro man, named Samuel Williams, is free, having been manumitted by Catharine Sharer on the 27th day of March, 1826, by Deed of Manumission which is recorded in Liber H.H. folio 891, one of the Records of my office. The said Samuel is 58 years of age, 6 feet 2 inches high, has a scar ont he left cheekbone, and tolerably dark complected.
Test   Otho H. Williams Clk   Dec. 18th 1844.

B51b   State of Maryland, Washington County, Towit:
I O. H. Williams Clerk of Washington County Court, hereby certify to all whom it may concern, that it appears from the records of Washington County Court, that the bearer hereof William R. Norris is a freeman, having been manumitted by a certain Andrew Newcomer, by deed of Manumission dated the day of the date hereof, and duly recorded in Liber O.H.W. No. 2, one of the Land Records of said County. The said William, is a negro, of the age of twenty six years on the first day of March next, is five feet seven inches high, and of rather a light complexion.
Test   Otho H. Williams Clk   December 31st. 1844

B51c   State of Maryland, Washington County, Towit:
I, Isaac Nesbitt Clerk of Washington County Court, do hereby certify that it has been satisfactorily proven to me, that the bearer hereof, Samuel Overton Stewart, was born free, and that he now applies for his certificate of Freedom. The said Samuel Overton Stewart is now about Twenty years of age, five feet four inches high; has a small red spot on his upper lip, and is of a light complexion, and by profession a Blacksmith
Test   Isaac Nesbitt, Clk   March 3, 1845.

B52a   State of Maryland, Washington County, Towit:
I, Isaac Nesbitt, clerk of Washington County Court, hereby certify to all whom it may concern, that it appears from the

of Washington County, Maryland

Records of my office that the bearer hereof, Ann C. Jenkins, a negro woman, is free, having been manumitted by Frisby Tilghman, on the 27th day of July 1829. The said Ann C. Jenkins is about 17 years of age, 5 feet 1 inch high, bright complexion and rather a good looking girl, and has a scar above her right eye.   Test   Isaac Nesbitt, Clk   July 8th. 1845

B52b   State of Maryland, Washington County, Towit:
I Isaac Nesbitt, Clerk of Washington County Court, do hereby certify to all whom it may or doth concern that it appears from the Records of my office that the bearer hereof, a Negro Man, named William Turner, who applies for his certificate of Freedom, was this day manumitted by Jacob Turner, by Deed of Manumission, duly executed, and now of Record in my said office: The said William is about 25 years of age, is five feet eight inches high, has a scar on the back of his neck, caused by an issue for the cure of weak eyes, and is of a very dark complexion.
Test   Isaac Nesbitt, Clk   August 4th 1845

B52c   State of Maryland, Washington County, Towit:
I, Isaac Nesbitt, Clerk of Washington County Court, hereby certify to all whom it may or doth concern that it appears from testimony of Thomas Bateler, Esq. that the bearer hereof, Alfred Ducket, a negro man, is free. The said Alfred was 22 years of age last January, is 6 feet high, has a scar on the back of his right hand over the first finger, and another in his right eye brow; and also a small mole near the right, dark complexion & good countenance.   Test Isaac Nesbitt, Clk   Aug. 28th 1845.

B53a   State of Maryland, Washington County, Towit:
I, Isaac Nesbitt, Clerk of Washington County Court, hereby certify to all whom it may or doth concern that it appears from testimony of Lewis Fletcher, Esq. that the bearer hereof, John Williams Shorter, who applies for a certificate of his freedom, is entitled to the same, he having been born free. The said Jn. William shorter, is five feet five and an half inches high, is about 21 years of age, and has three distinguishing marks, to wit: a small scar over the right eye; a scar on the left wrist at the junction of the hand; & the stump or growth of a second thumb [the word "thumb" is underlined] on the right hand. He is of a light complexion, and pleasant countenance.
Test   Isaac Nesbitt, Clk   Sept. 2, 1845

African American Manumissions

B53b State of Maryland, Washington County, Towit:
I, Isaac Nesbitt, Clerk of Washington County Court, do hereby certify to all whom it may or doth concern that it appears from the Records of said County, that the bearer hereof, Aaron Williams, is free, having been manumitted by Deed bearing date the 12 Dec. 1826, by Cath. Sharer, & recorded in Liber II folios 294 & 295, one of the said Records. The said Aaron Williams is aged about 27 years, 5 feet 9 inches high, has a small scar on the forehead near the hair, and of rather light complexion.
Test   Isaac Nesbitt, Clk   Dec. 20 1845

B54a State of Maryland, Washington County, Towit:
I, Isaac Nesbitt, Clerk of Washington County Court, do hereby to all whom it doth or may concern, that it hath satisfactorily shewn to me upon the testimony of Michael P. Smith, that the bearer hereof, Henry Moody, a Negro man, is entitled to his Freedom, having been heretofore sold for a Term of years, which has fully expired: The said Henry Moody is now 32 years of age, five feet four and 1/2 inches high, very black, but of good countenance, without any perceivable marks, and tolerably stout in body.
In Test   Test: Isaac Nesbitt, Clk Jany. 26. 1846.

B54b State of Maryland, Washington County, Towit:
I, Isaac Nesbitt, Clk. of Washington County Court, do hereby certify to all whom it may or doth concern, that it has been satisfactorily proven to me upon the testimony of Michael P. Smith, that the bearer hereof William Moody, a negro man, is entitled to his Freedom, having been heretofore sold for a Term of years, which has fully expired: The said William Moody is now 31 years of age, 5 feet 3 3/4 inches high, very black, but of good countenance without any perceivable marks, and small of body.   In Testy &c   Test: Isaac Nesbitt, Clk Jany. 26 1846

B55a State of Maryland, Washington County, Towit:
I, Isaac Nesbitt, Clerk of Washington County Court, do hereby certify to all whom it may or doth concern that it has been satisfactorily proven to me upon the testimony of Michael P. Smith, that the bearer hereof, Mary Moody, a negro woman is entitled to her Freedom, having heretofore been sold for a term of years, which has fully expired: The said Mary Moore is now 28 years of age, is 4 feet 11 inches high, dark complexion, and of good countenance, without any perceivable marks.

of Washington County, Maryland

In Testy, etc.y   Test: Isaac Nesbitt, Clk   Jany. 26 1846

B55b   State of Maryland, Washington County, Towit:
I Isaac Nesbitt, Clerk of Washington County Court, do hereby certify to all whom it may or doth concern that it appears from the Records of my office that the bearer hereof, Elisha Caution, a negro man is free, having been set free & manumitted on the 28th day of Jany. 1846, by a certain Henry Williams of the State of Pennsylvania by Deed of manumission. The said Elisha is 26 years of age, five feet 5 inches high, very dark complexion & of good countenance, with a scar between the left eye & ear.
In Testy etc.   Test Isaac Nesbitt, Clk   Jany. 30th 1845

B56a   State of Maryland, Washington County, Towit:
I Isaac Nesbitt, Clerk of Washington County Court, do hereby certify to all whom it may or doth concern that it appears from the Records of my office that the bearer hereof, Regis Galloway, a Negro Man, is free; having been duly manumitted by deed duly executed by John McClaughlin, and others, and recorded in Liber I.N. No. 1, folios 454 & 455, one of the Land Records of said office. The said Regis is 40 years of age, 5 feet 5 1/4 inches high, has a scar on his forehead, high up, and a small scar on the right cheek, and one under the left eye; and is quite black.
In Test. etc.   Isaac Nesbitt, Clk   Jany. 31st. 1846

B56b   State of Maryland, Washington County, Towit:
I, Isaac Nesbitt, Clerk of Washington County Court, do hereby certify to all whom it may or doth concern that it appears from the Records of said County, that the bearer hereof, a negro man, named Stephen Brooks, is free, having been manumitted and set free, by a certain Alexander Reeder, by Deed of Manumission bearing date the 23d day of April 1842, and duly recorded in Liber Z.Z. folios 223 & 4 one of the Records of my office. The said Stephan is about 37 years of age, 5 feet 7 1/2 inches high, dark complexion, and has a scar on the left side of the nose, near the left eye, good countenance and of slender form.
In Testy etc.   Isaac Nesbitt, Clk   Feby 13. 1846.

B57a   State of Maryland, Washington County, Towit:
I, Isaac Nesbitt, Clerk of Washington County Court hereby certify to all who it may or doth concern that it appears from the Records in my office that the bearer hereof, a negro man, named

African American Manumissions

Samuel Miller, is free, having been manumitted and set free by a certain Susan Middlekauff by Deed of Manumission dated the 25 day of February 1845, and recorded in Liber I.N. one of the Land Records of said office. The said Samuel is about 28 years of age, 5 feet 5 inches high, of rather light complexion, thickset, with a scar on the right side of the forehead, and has a good countenance.
In Testy, etc.   Test   Isaac Nesbitt, Clk   13 Feby. 1846

B57b   State of Maryland, Washington County, Towit:
I, Isaac Nesbitt, Clerk of Washington County Court hereby certify to all whom it may or doth concern that it appears from the Records in my office that the bearer hereof, a negro woman, named Fanny Johnson, is free, she having been sold by a certain Philip Reeder to Benj. Yoe, in the year 1823 for a term of years, which has fully expired. The said Fanny was 38 years of age in January last, 5 feet 3 inches high, has a scar on the left hand near the wrist, and has a very freckled face.
In Testy. etc.   Isaac Nesbitt, Clk   5th March 1846.

B57c   State of Maryland, Washington County, Towit:
I, Isaac Nesbitt, Clerk of Washington County Court hereby certify to all whom it may or doth concern that it appears from the Records in my office that the bearer hereof, a negro man, named Caesar Peters, is free, he having been manumitted by John Van Lear, Jr. Ext. of Mary Van Lear, decd. by Deed of manumission, bearing date the 31st day of Dec. 1844. The said Caesar is 45 years of age, 6 feet 1 1/4 inch high, very dark complexion, no marks perceptible, and has a good countenance.
In Tes. &   Isaac Nesbitt, Clk   Mar. 11 1846

B58a   State of Maryland, Washington County, Towit:
I Isaac Nesbitt, Clerk of Washington County Court, do hereby certify to all whom it may or doth concern that it is satisfactorily proven to me by the certificate of Freedom of her mother, and other testimony, that the bearer hereof Sealy Watts, alias Sealy Lee is a free woman of color. The said Sealy is 5 feet 4 1/2 inches high, born the 31st day of August 1817; has a scar on her right wrist, good countenance, and of a very black complexion. She has also four children - Henry Long, born the 11th day of July 1832; William Lee, born the 14 day of March 1838; Joshua Lee,

of Washington County, Maryland

born on the 5 day of March, 1840, and Catharine Lee, born on the 24 day of December 1841.
In Testimony & C.   Isaac Nesbitt, Clk   March 20. 1846

B58b   State of Maryland, Washington County, Towit:
I, Isaac Nesbitt, Clerk of Washington County Court do hereby certify to all whom it may or doth concern, that it is satisfactorily proven to me by Mr. Samuel Middlekauff, that the bearer hereof James Miller, who now applies for her certificate of freedom, was born free. The said James Miller is now Nineteen years of age, five feet eight and an half inches high, has a scar on his left cheek caused by a scratch of a pin, and is of a rather light complexion.
In Testimony & Isaac Nesbitt, Clk   April 2nd. 1846

B58c   State of Maryland, Washington County, Towit:
I, Isaac Nesbitt, Clerk of Washington County Court, do hereby certify to all whom it doth or may concern that it appears from the records of said Court, that the bearer hereof, a negro Man, named Nathan Williams, who applies for a certificate of Freedom was duly manumitted by a certain Catharine Sharer, as by reference to the said records it will fully and at large appear. The said Nathan is five feet eleven & 1/4 inches high, has a scar on the left hand near the junction of the thumb and is of a light or copper complexion.
In Testimony & C.   Isaac Nesbitt, Clk   April 7, 1846

B59a   State of Maryland, Washington County, Towit:
I, Isaac Nesbitt, Clerk of Washington County Court hereby certify to all whom it may or doth concern that it appears from the Records of Washington County Court that the bearer hereof, a negro man, named Isaac Crawford, is free, he having been manumitted and set free by Saml. Ringgold, on the 2d day of Dec. 1818. The said Isaac will be 47 years of age on the 18 day of Dec. next, and is five feet nine & one half inches high, stout built, and of very dark complexion. And I further certify, that the said Isaac is the father of the following children, who it is satisfactorily proven to me, were free, and whose respective names and ages are as follows, to wit: Jesse, born 22d August 1833; Maria, born January, 1835; James, born Sept. 13 1837; Mary, born November 1839; and Isaac, born May 23d 1842.
In Testy. etc.   Isaac Nesbitt, Clk   23d April 1846

African American Manumissions

B59b   Washington County to wit:
I, Isaac Nesbitt, Clerk of Washington County Court, hereby certify to all whom it may or doth concern, that the bearer hereof a negro man, named Henry Goings, is free, having been manumitted by Jonathan Rowland by Deed of Manumission dated the 10 day of March, 1846, and recorded in the Records of my office. The said Henry is about 35 years of age, five feet 9 3/4 inches high, has a scar on the left side of his forehead, rather light complexion, and has a good countenance.
In Testy, etc.   Isaac Nesbitt, Clk   May 1st 1846

B60a   State of Maryland, Washington County, Towit:
I, Isaac Nesbitt, Clerk of Washington County Court, hereby certify that the bearer hereof, a negro woman, named Priscilla Concy, is free, having been manumitted and set free by a certain Leonard H. Johns, on the 7th day of February, 1846, as will appear by reference to a Deed of Manumission, recorded in Liber I.N. No. 1 one of the Land Records of my office. The said Priscilla is 26 years of age, 5 feet 2 inches high, has a large scar on the back of her left hand, caused from a burn when a child, and is thick set & of very dark complexion.
In Testy. & C.   Test:; Isaac Nesbitt, Clk   May 16 1846

B60b   State of Maryland, Washington County, Towit:
I, Isaac Nesbitt, Clerk of Washington County Court, hereby certify to all whom it may or doth concern, that the bearer hereof, a negro man named Samuel Bean, is free, he having been manumitted and set free by a certain Danl. P. Miller, by Deed of Manumission bearing date 31st day of March, 1846, by reference to which recorded in Liber I.N. No. 1, folio 682 one of the Records of my office, will more fully appear. The said Samuel is 22 years of age, 5 feet 6 1/2 inches high, has a small scar on the right side of his forehead, and of very dark complexion.
August 1st 1846.   In Testy etc.Test: Isaac Nesbitt, Clk

B61a   State of Maryland, Washington County, Towit:
I, Isaac Nesbitt, Clerk of Washington County Court, hereby certify to all whom it may or doth concern, that Henry Craig, the bearer hereof, a negro man, is free, - having been duly manumitted by George Snyder, by deed of manumission bearing date the 12 day of December, in the year of our Lord 1840, and duly executed and acknowledged according to law, and

of Washington County, Maryland

recorded in Liber Y.Y. folio 66, one of the Land Records of Washington County. The said Henry is now 31 years of age, is 5 feet 9 inches high, with a scar on the back of each hand, and is of a light or yellow complexion.
In Testimony etc.   Isaac Nesbitt, Clk   August 1st. 1846

B61b   State of Maryland, Washington County, Towit:
I, Isaac Nesbitt, Clerk of Washington County Court, hereby certify to all whom it may or doth concern, that the bearer hereof, Emanuel Rollings, a negro man, is free, which has been proven to me by satisfactory evidence. The said Emauel is 22 years of age, 5 feet 7 inches high, tolerably dark complexion, and has no marks perceptible about him.
In Testy, etc.   Test: Isaac Nesbitt, Clk Aug. 15. 1846

B61c   State of Maryland, Washington County, Towit:
I, Isaac Nesbitt, Clerk of Washington County Court, hereby certify to all whom it may or doth concern that the bearer hereof, a negro man, named Jacob Washington, is free, which has been satisfactorily proven to me. The said Jacob is 23 years of age, 5 feet 8 1/2 inches high, has a scar between the two last fingers of his left hand, and of tolerably dark complexion.
In Testy. etc.   Test: Isaac Nesbitt, Clk Aug. 15 1846

B62a   State of Maryland, Washington County, Towit:
I, Isaac Nesbitt, Clerk of Washington County Court, hereby certify to all whom it may or doth concern that the bearer hereof, a negro man, named James Washington is free, which has been satisfactorily proven to me. The said James is 33 years of age, 5 feet 7 1/2 inches high, and tolerably dark complexion.
In Testy. etc.   Test: Isaac Nesbitt, Clk Augt. 15, 1846

B62b   State of Maryland, Washington County, Towit:
I, Isaac Nesbitt, Clerk of Washington County Court, hereby certify to all whom it may or doth concern that the bearer hereof, a negro woman, named Susan Keller, is free, which has been satisfactorily proven to me. The said Susan is now 27 years of age, 5 feet 3 1/2 inches high, has a scar on the 2d finger of the left hand and dark complexion.
In Testy. etc.   Test: Isaac Nesbitt, Clk Aug. 15 1846

African American Manumissions

B62c State of Maryland, Washington County, Towit:
I, Isaac Nesbitt, Clerk of Washington County Court, hereby certify to all whom it may or doth concern that the bearer hereof, a negro woman, named Henrietta Gasper, is free, having been manumitted and set free by Susan Lynch by Deed of Manumission bearing date the 18 day of August 1846, and duly recorded among the Land Records of Washington County. The said Henrietta is 28 years of age, 5 feet 4 3/4 inches high, of slender form, her complexion rather light and has no mark perceptible about her.
In Testy etc.   Test: Isaac Nesbitt, Clk Aug. 18. 1846

B63a Washington County to wit:
I, Isaac Nesbitt, Clerk of Washington County Court, hereby certify to all whom it may or doth concern that the bearer hereof, a mulatto woman, named Sarah Reeder is free, having been manumitted and set free by a certain Philip Reeder by Deed of Manumission bearing date the 11 day of February, A.D. 1828, and recorded in Liber I.I. folio 834 & 835, one of the Land Records of Washington County Court. The said Sarah is about 20 years of age, 5 feet 5 inches high, slender form, pleasing countenance and of very light complexion, and no marks perceptible about her.
In Testy. etc.   Test: Isaac Nesbitt, Clk Sept. 11 1846

B63b State of Maryland, Washington County, Towit:
I, Isaac Nesbitt, Clerk of Washington County Court, hereby certify to all whom it may or doth concern that the bearer hereof, a negro man, named Henry Mitchell, who now applies for his certificate of Freedom, is free, which is Known to me from my personal Knowledge. The said Henry is about 22 years of age, five feet 8 inches high, dark complexion, has a scar under the right eye and also two others, on his right hand - one on the side near the root of the thumb - the other on the back below the 2d finger and has no other marks perceptible.
In Testy, etc.   Test: Isaac Nesbitt, Clk Sept. 28 1846

B64a State of Maryland, Washington County, Towit:
I, Isaac Nesbitt, Clerk of Washington County Court, hereby certify to all whom it may or doth concern that the bearer hereof, a negro man, named Erasmus Taylor, is free, having been manumitted and set free by a certain Anthony Varner by Deed of

of Washington County, Maryland

Manumission bearing date the 10th day of October, 1846, and recorded among the Land Records of Washington County C., reference to which will more fully appear. The said Erasmus is about 35 years of age, 6 feet one half inch high, dark complexion, and has a scar on the ball of the first finger of each hand, caused by the cut of a sickle.
In Testy, etc.   Test: Isaac Nesbitt, Clk Oct. 16 1846

B64b   State of Maryland, Washington County, Towit:
I, Isaac Nesbitt, Clerk of Washington County Court, hereby certify to all whom it may or doth concern that the bearer hereof, a negro woman, named Henrietta Snyder is free, which has been proven to me by satisfactory evidence. The said Henrietta is about 22 years of age, 5 feet 2 inches & 1/4 high, has a scar on the elbow of the left arm, has a good countenance and tolerably dark complexion. She has also one mulatto child named Mary Ann Eliza, who is 5 years of age.
In Testimony, etc.   Test: Isaac Nesbitt, Clk Oct. 21st 1846

B64c   State of Maryland, Washington County, Towit:
I hereby certify to all whom it may or doth concern, that the bearer hereof, a negro woman named Maria Sims, is free, which has been proven to me by Wm. H. Fitzhugh, Esq. with whom she served her time as an indented servant. The said Maria is about 24 years of age, five feet 4 1/2 inches high, has a scar on the left side of her forehead, of dark complexion, & a pleasing countenance.
In Testy. etc.   Test: Isaac Nesbitt, Clk Nov. 3d. 1846   [In the margin is written "Maria Simms"]

B65a   State of Maryland, Washington County, Towit:
I hereby certify to all whom it doth or may concern, that the bearer hereof a negro man, named Thomas Clements, is free, ["which has been" crossed out] having been manumitted and set free by a certain John Van Lear Jr. by Deed of Manumission bearing date the 14th day of November 1846, and recorded among the Land Records of Washington County by reference to which, will more fully appear. The said Thomas is about 35 years of age 5 feet six inches high, dark complexion, and has a scar on his left hip, breast and one on his left hand, caused by the cut of a knife.   In Testy   Test
Isaac Nesbitt, Clk   Nov. 18th 1846

African American Manumissions

B65b   State of Maryland, Washington County, Towit:
I hereby certify to all whom it doth or may concern, that the bearer hereof, a negro woman, named Charity Clements is free having been manumitted and set free, by a certain Eleanor Friend by Deed of Manumission bearing date the 16. day of November 1846, and recorded among the Land Records of Washington County, by reference to which will more fully appear. The said Charity Clements is about thirty seven years of age 5 feet 3 inches high, not very dark complexion; and her five children, viz Charles aged 10 years, Mary aged eight years, Eliza aged six, George Henry aged three years, and Susannah Emma Ramsey, aged one year.
In Test Test. Isaac Nesbitt   Nov. 18th 1846

B66a   State of Maryland, Washington County, Towit:
I, Isaac Nesbitt, Clerk of Washington County Court, hereby certify to all whom it may or doth concern that the bearer hereof, a negro woman, named Mary Cooney, is free, having been manumitted by a certain Joseph Martin, Jr., by Deed of Manumission bearing date the 16 day of March 1832, & recorded in Liber M.M. folio 914, one of the Records of Washington Co. The said Mary is about 57 years of age, 5 feet 2 1/2 inches high, dark complexion, stout built and has no marks perceptible about her.   In Testy. etc.   Test: Isaac Nesbitt, Clk   Oct. 13. 1846

B66b   State of Maryland, Washington County, Towit:
I, Isaac Nesbitt, Clerk of Washington County Court, hereby certify to all whom it may or doth concern that the bearer hereof, a negro woman, named Lucy Byram who applies for her certificate of Freedom is free, having been sold for a term of years, which term ended on the 17 day of January 1834, as will more fully appear by reference to Liber G.G. folio 969 etc., one of the Land Records of Washington County. The said Lucy is about 39 years of age, 5 feet 3 3/4 inches high, very dark complexion; has a scar on the end of the 1st finger of the right hand, caused from a felon. She has a good countenance.
In Testy. etc.   Test: Isaac Nesbitt, Clk   Dec. 11. 1846.

B67a   State of Maryland, Washington County, Towit:
I, Isaac Nesbitt, Clerk of Washington County Court, hereby certify to all whom it may or doth concern that the bearer hereof, a negro man, named Thomas Kane, is free, having been

of Washington County, Maryland

manumitted and set free, by Maria E. Reynolds, by Deed of Manumission, dated the 23d December 1846, and recorded among, the Records of Washington County. The said Thomas is about 40 years of age, five feet six & a quarter inches high, dark complexion, the first finger of the right hand is crooked, caused from a cut, and has a good countenance.
In Testy. etc. Test: Isaac Nesbitt, Clk Dec. 28. 1846

B67b State of Maryland, Washington County, Towit:
I hereby certify to all whom it doth or may concern, that the bearer hereof, a mulatto man, named Robert Henry Gruber, is free, as it hath been to me satisfactorily proven. The said Robert Henry is 20 years of age, 5 feet 6 inches high, stout built is somewhat freckled, has a scar on the right cheek just below the bone, - no other marks perceptible about him.
In Testy. etc. Test: Isaac Nesbitt, Clk Jany. 5. 1847

B68a State of Maryland, Washington County, Towit:
I, Isaac Nesbitt, Clerk of Washington County Court, hereby certify to all whom it may or doth concern that the bearer hereof, a negro man, named James Ding, who now here applies for his certificate of Freedom, is free, having been manumitted and set free by a certain Henson Jones by Deed of manumission dated the 6 day of March 1847 & recorded in Liber I.N. No.2, one of the Records of my office. The said James Ding is about 43 years of age, 5 feet 5 inches high, the upper part of his face rather lighter than the lower; has a scar on the forehead.
In Testy, etc. Test: Isaac Nesbitt, Clk April 3d. 1847.

B68b State of Maryland, Washington County, Towit:
I, Isaac Nesbitt, Clerk of Washington County Court, hereby certify to all whom it may or doth concern that the bearer hereof, a negro man, named, Samuel W. Jones, who applies for his cert. of Freedom, is free, as appears from the testimony of Edward W. Beathy, and other satisfactory evidence to me given. The said Samuel W. is about 33 years of age, 5 feet 10 1/4 inches high; very dark complexion; stout built, and has a small scar on the left side of the upper lip.
In Testy. etc. Isaac Nesbitt, Clk   Apl 21st 1847.

African American Manumissions

B68c State of Maryland, Washington County, Towit:
I, Isaac Nesbitt, Clerk of Washington County Court, hereby certify to all whom it may or doth concern that the bearer hereof, a negro woman, named Margaret Snyder, who applies for a cert. of her Freedom, is free, she being the daughter of a certain Betsy Snyder, who was set free by the Will of Richard Barnes, decd. which will more fully appear by reference to the Records of the Register of Wills of Washington County aforesaid. The said Margaret is about 19 years of age, 5 feet 2 1/2 inches high; not very dark complected, slightly built and has no marks perceptible about her.
In Testy. etc.　　Isaac Nesbitt, Clk　　　　May 15. 1847

B69a State of Maryland, Washington County, Towit:
I, Isaac Nesbitt, Clerk of Washington County Court, hereby certify to all whom it may or doth concern that the bearer hereof, a negro man, named John Gruber, who applies for his certificate of Freedom, is free, which has been to me satisfactorily proven. The said John is about 22 years of age, 5 feet 5 1/2 inches high, dark complexion; stout built, and has a scar on the corner of the right eye.　　　In Testy. etc.　　Isaac Nesbitt, Clk　May 15. 1847

B69b State of Maryland, Washington County, Towit:
I, Isaac Nesbitt, Clerk of Washington County Court, hereby certify to all whom it may or doth concern that the bearer hereof, a dark mulatto woman, named Mary Jane Snyder, who applies for a certificate of Freedom, is free, being the daughter of a certain Betsy Snyder, who was set free by the Will of Richd. Barnes, decd. & which is proven to me by satisfactory testimony. The said Mary Jane is aged about 28 years; 5 feet high; has a scar on the forehead, and a wart near the right ear; stout built and pleasant countenance.
In Testimony etc.　　　Isaac Nesbitt, Clk　　　　July 14 1847

B69c State of Maryland, Washington County, Towit:
I, Isaac Nesbitt, Clerk of Washington County Court, hereby certify to all whom it may or doth concern that the bearer hereof, a negro woman, is free as appears from a Deed of Manumission to Agnes Robinson from John Witmer on Record in my office. The said Agnes is about 18 years of age, 5 feet 3 inches high, black complexion, has a scar on the right hand caused from a

burn, stout built, cross eyed or slightly affected with strabismus and no other marks perceptible.
In Testimony, etc.   Test: Isaac Nesbitt, Clk July 23d, 1847

B70a   State of Maryland, Washington County, Towit:
I, Isaac Nesbitt, Clerk of Washington County Court, hereby certify to all whom it may or doth concern that the bearer hereof, a negro man, named John Brown, who applies for his certificate of Freedom, is free, he having been manumitted and set free by a certain Henry Firey by Deed of Manumission recorded in Liber I.N. No. 2 one of the Records of Washington County Court. The said John is about 42 years of age, 5 feet 11 inches high, the third finger of the right hand is stiff, has a tolerably dark complexion, is slightly built, has a good countenance, and is a Blacksmith by profession. In Testy. etc. Test: Isaac Nesbitt, Clk July 28, 1847

B70b   State of Maryland, Washington County, Towit:
I, Isaac Nesbitt, Clerk of Washington County Court, hereby certify to all whom it may or doth concern that the bearer hereof, a mulatto woman, named Eveline Snively, who applies for her Certificate of Freedom, is free, being the daughter of a certain Rebecca Compton (formerly Rebecca Minor) who was set free by the Will of a certain Richard Barnes, late of Washington County, decd. which to me is satisfactorily proven by the certo. of the Register of Wills of the County aforesaid, & other proof. The said Eveline, is about 28 years of age, 5 feet 1 3/4 inches high, very light mulatto and of delicate form, and rather comely in appearance.
In Testy. etc.   Test: Isaac Nesbitt, Clk Augt. 6, 1847

B70c   State of Maryland, Washington County, Towit:
I, Isaac Nesbitt, Clerk of Washington County Court, hereby certify to all whom it may or doth concern that the bearer hereof, a negro woman, who applies for her certificate of Freedom, is free, she being the daughter of Rebecca Compton (formerly Rebecca Minor) to whom was given her Freedom by the Will of a certain Richard Barnes, late of Washington County, decd., which to me is satisfactorily proven, by the Cert. of the Register of Wills for said County, and other proof. The said woman is named Margaret Shorter, 5 feet 3 inches high, very dark complexion, thick set, and no marks perceptible about her.
In Testy., etc.   Test: Isaac Nesbitt, Clk Aug. 6, 1847

African American Manumissions

B71a State of Maryland, Washington County, Towit:
I, Isaac Nesbitt, Clerk of Washington County Court, hereby certify to all whom it may or doth concern that the bearer hereof, a negro woman, named Eliza Compton, who applies for her certificate of Freedom, is free, she being the daughter of Rebecca Compton (formerly Rebecca Minor) to whom was given her Freedom by the last Will and Testament of the late Richard Barnes, decd., which is to me satisfactorily proven by the cert. of the Register of Wills for the said County, and other proof. The said Eliza is about 19 years of age, 5 feet 3 inches high, very dark complexion as dark as you generally find the children of Ethiopia, and stout built, with a mole on the forehead near the root of the nose.
In Testy. etc.   Test: Isaac Nesbitt, Clk Augt. 6 1847

B71b State of Maryland, Washington County, Towit:
I, Isaac Nesbitt, Clerk of Washington County Court, hereby certify to all whom it may or doth concern that the bearer hereof, a negro woman named Martha Snyder, who applies for her certificate of Freedom, is free, she being the daughter of Betsy Snyder, who was manumitted and set free by the Will of the late Richard Barnes, decd. which is proven to me by the Cert. of the Register of Wills of Washington County; and that she is the daughter as aforesaid by sufficient proof. The said Martha is about 17 years of age, 5 feet 2 3/4 inches high, rather light complexion, delicate form & has a scar on the left side of her forehead near the hair.
In Testy. etc.   Test: Isaac Nesbitt, Clk Aug. 9. 1847

B71c State of Maryland, Washington County, Towit:
I, Isaac Nesbitt, Clerk of Washington County Court, hereby certify to all whom it may or doth concern that the bearer hereof, a negro man, named Loyd Miles, is free, having been manumitted and set free by Michl. Swingley by Deed of Manumission dated the 19 day of July 1847, & Recorded in Liber I.N. No. 2, one of the Land Records of Washington County, by reference to which will more fully appear. The said Loyd is about 32 years of age, 5 feet 9 inches high, very dark, stout made, and pleasant countenance & has no marks perceptible about him.
In Testimony etc.   Test: Isaac Nesbitt, Clk August   17. 184B7

of Washington County, Maryland

B72a State of Maryland, Washington County, Towit:
I, Isaac Nesbitt, Clerk of Washington County Court, hereby certify to all whom it may or doth concern that the bearer hereof, Frances Ann Lewis, is a free woman, - she having produced an affidavit to me, sworn to by a respectable white citizen, that she was born free. The said Frances Ann is a Mulatto, of the age of twenty-eight years, five feet high, stout built, has a scar on the left arm; with the little finger of the left hand crooked, and has a pleasant countenance.
In Testimony etc.   Test: Isaac Nesbitt, Clk
    August 18, 1847.

B72b State of Maryland, Washington County, Towit:
I, Isaac Nesbitt, Clerk of Washington County Court, hereby certify to all whom it may or doth concern that the bearer hereof, Elizabeth Gates, (formerly Elizth Moody) is a free woman, she being the daughter of Lucy Moody (now Lucy Blakes) whose mother & future issue was manumitted [one unreadable word and "children" crossed out] by a certain Ann Tarvin of Charles County, by Deed bearing date the 21st day of September 1784, as appears by the certificate of the Clerk of said County; and by sufficient testimony that the said Elizabeth is the daughter of the said Lucy. The said Elizabeth is about 30 years of age, 5 feet 3 inches high, stout made, dark complexion, and has no marks perceptible about her.
In Testy. etc.   Test: Isaac Nesbitt, Clk
August 31st. 1847

B72c State of Maryland, Washington County, Towit:
I, Isaac Nesbitt, Clerk of Washington County Court, hereby certify to all whom it may or doth concern that the bearer hereof, a negro woman, named Mary Ann Dunham, (formerly Mary Ann Moody) is free, she being the daughter of Lucy Moody (now Lucy Blake) whose mother & her future issue was manumitted by Ann Tarvin, of Charles County, by Deed dated the 21st day of September 1784, which appears by a certificate of the Clerk of said County; and I further certify that I am satisfied from respectable testimony that the said Mary Ann is the daughter of said Lucy. The said Mary Ann is 29 years of age, 5 feet 3 1/2 inches high, dark color, has a scar behind the left ear, and has scars on all the fingers of the left hand, caused from a burn.
In. Testy. etc.   Test: Isaac Nesbitt, Clk Aug. 31s. 1847

African American Manumissions

B73a State of Maryland, Washington County, Towit:
I, Isaac Nesbitt, Clerk of Washington County Court, hereby certify to all whom it may or doth concern that the bearer hereof, a negro woman, named Barbara Goins, (formerly Barbara Moody) is free, she being the daughter of Lucy Moody, (now Lucy Blake) whose mother, and her future issue was manumitted by Ann Tarvin by Deed dated the 21st day of September 1784, which appears by a certificate of the Clerk of said County, and I further certify that I am satisfied from respectable testimony that the said Barbara is the daughter of the said Lucy. The said Barbara is the daughter of the said Lucy. The said Barbara is about 29 years of age, 5 feet 5 1/2 inches high, dark complexion, face marked by small pox, has a scar on the right hand near the root of the thumb & first finger, & slender form.
In Testimony, etc.   Test: Isaac Nesbitt, Clk Aug. 31st 1847.

B73b State of Maryland, Washington County, Towit:
I, Isaac Nesbitt, Clerk of Washington County Court, hereby certify to all whom it may or doth concern that the bearer hereof, a negro woman, named Sarah Ann Adley, is free, having been manumitted and set free by a certain Thomas Edwards, by Deed dated the 4 day of March 1817 & recorded in Liber B.B. folio 784, one of the Records of my office by reference to which will more fully appear. The said Sarah Ann is about 30 years of age, 5 feet 6 inches high, of slender form, light complexion, comely in appearance, with no marks perceptible; and her two children named John Henry aged 8 years; and Henrietta aged 2 years.
In Testimony, etc.   Test: Isaac Nesbitt, Clk Sept. 1st. 1847.

B74a State of Maryland, Washington County, Towit:
I, Isaac Nesbitt, Clerk of Washington County Court, hereby certify to all whom it may or doth concern that the bearer hereof, a negro woman, named Catharine Davis, formerly Catharine Barnes, is free, she being the daughter of Negro Winnie, who was set free by the will of the late Richard Barnes, decd.; all which is satisfactorily proven to me. The said Catharine is about 45 years of age, 5 feet 5 inches high, dark complexion, slender form and has no perctible [sic] marks about her.
In Testy. etc.   Test: Isaac Nesbitt, Clk Sept. 3d. 1847

of Washington County, Maryland

B74b   State of Maryland, Washington County, Towit:
I, Isaac Nesbitt, Clerk of Washington County Court, hereby certify to all whom it may or doth concern that the bearer hereof, a negro man, named Charles Gates, is a free man, who was born free, which is proven to ["by" crossed out] me by respectable and satisfactory testimony. The said Charles is about 50 years of age, 6 feet 1/2 inch high, complexion dark, slender made, and has a mark on the back and fingers of the left hand, and inclined to baldness.
In Testimony, etc. Test: Isaac Nesbitt, Clk   Sept. 4. 1847

B74c   State of Maryland, Washington County, Towit:
I, Isaac Nesbitt, Clerk of Washington County Court, hereby certify to all whom it may or doth concern that the bearer hereof, a negro man, named Richard Gates, is free; having been born free, which is proven to me by satisfactory testimony. The said Richard is about 47 years of age, 5 feet 11 1/2 inches high, not very dark complected, has received an injury in the left eye, & has a good countenance.
In Testimony, etc.   Isaac Nesbitt, Clk   Sept. 4 1847

B75a   State of Maryland, Washington County, Towit:
I, Isaac Nesbitt, Clerk of Washington County Court, hereby certify to all whom it may or doth concern that the bearer hereof, a negro man, named Jacob Chesley, is a free man, which has been satisfactorily proven to me by competent testimony. The said Jacob is about 44 years of age, 5 feet 10 3/4 inches high, of slender form, very dark complexion; has a scar on the 2d joint of the first finger of the left hand.
In Testy. etc.   Test: Isaac Nesbitt, Clk Sep. 21st. 1847

B75b   State of Maryland, Washington County, Towit:
I, Isaac Nesbitt, Clerk of Washington County Court, hereby certify to all whom it may or doth concern that the bearer hereof, a negro woman, named Nancy Cooper, is free, which is satisfactorily proven to me by respectable testimony. The said Nancy is about 48 years of age, 5 feet 2 1/2 inches high, dark complexion, slenderly made, has a scar in the hollow of the nose, and has a very good countenance.
In Testy. etc.   Test: Isaac Nesbitt, Clk Sep. 21st 1857

African American Manumissions

B75c   State of Maryland, Washington County, Towit:
I, Isaac Nesbitt, Clerk of Washington County Court, hereby certify to all whom it may or doth concern that the bearer hereof Letitia James, who applies for her Certificate of Freedom, was manumitted by John Oswald, as appears from the records of this office, to serve until she should attain to the age of sixteen years, which time has now fully expired. Said Letitia is 5 feet 2 inches high, of very dark or black complexion; stout built, with no distinguishing marks, except that her mouth is drawn somewhat down on the left side.
In Testimony etc. Test: Isaac Nesbitt, Clk Sept. 23d. 1847.

B76a   State of Maryland, Washington County, Towit:
I, Isaac Nesbitt, Clerk of Washington County Court, hereby certify to all whom it may or doth concern that the bearer hereof named Betsey Mingo, is a free colored woman, as appears to my satisfaction from respectable testimony. The said Betsy is about 24 years of age, 5 feet 1 1/2 inches high, of rather light complexion, has a mole near the side of her mouth, and has a good countenance.
In Testy. etc.   Test: Isaac Nesbitt, Clk Sep. 25, 1847

B76b   State of Maryland, Washington County, Towit:
I, Isaac Nesbitt, Clerk of Washington County Court, hereby certify to all whom it may or doth concern that the bearer hereof, a negro woman, named Jane N. Blake, is free, as is made to appear to my satisfaction from respectable testimony. The said Jane is about 29 years of age, 5 feet 1 1/2 inches high, of dark complexion, has no distinguishing mark about , except that there are 3 of her upper front teeth out, and delicately made.
In Testy. etc.   Test: Isaac Nesbitt, Clk Sep. 25. 1847

B76c   State of Maryland, Washington County, Towit:
I, Isaac Nesbitt, Clerk of Washington County Court, hereby certify to all whom it may or doth concern that the bearer hereof, a negro woman, named Sophia Thompson (formerly Jones) is free, which is proven to my satisfaction by respectable testimony. The said Sophia is about 25 years of age, 5 feet 4 3/4 inches high, tolerably dark complexion, and has a scar over the right eye near the brow.
In Testy. etc.   Test: Isaac Nesbitt, Clk   Sept. 25th 1847

of Washington County, Maryland

B77a State of Maryland, Washington County, Towit:
I, Isaac Nesbitt, Clerk of Washington County Court, hereby certify to all whom it may or doth concern that the bearer hereof, a negro woman, named Sarah Jones (formerly Cooper) is free, which is satisfactorily proven to me by respectable testimony. The said Sarah is about 29 years of age, 5 feet 1/2 inch high, dark complexion, has a scar on the brow near the left eye, and onther [sic] on the back of the thumb of the left hand.
In Testy. etc.   Test: Isaac Nesbitt, Clk Sep. 25. 1847

B77b State of Maryland, Washington County, Towit:
I, Isaac Nesbitt, Clerk of Washington County Court, hereby certify to all whom it may or doth concern that the bearer hereof, a negro man, named Robert Jones, is free which is proven to my satisfaction by respectable testimony. The said Robert is about 27 years of age 6 feet high, of very dark or black complexion, of slender form and has no distinguishing marks about him.
In Testy. etc.   Test: Isaac Nesbitt, Clk Sep. 25. 1847

B77c State of Maryland, Washington County, Towit:
I, Isaac Nesbitt, Clerk of Washington County Court, hereby certify to all whom it may or doth concern that the bearer hereof, a negro man, named William Camfield Cooper, is free, which is proven to my satisfaction by respectable testimony. The said William is about 22 years of age, 5 feet 11 inches high, very dark or black, & has a scar on ridge of the nose.
In Testy. etc.   Test: Isaac Nesbitt, Clk Sep. 25. 1847

B78a State of Maryland, Washington County, Towit:
I, Isaac Nesbitt, Clerk of Washington County Court, hereby certify to all whom it may or doth concern that the bearer hereof, a negro man, named Henry Briscoe, is free, he having been manumitted by a certain Samuel H. Briscoe, by Will recorded among the Records of Baltimore County by reference to which will more fully appear; and which has been fully proven to my satisfaction by respectable and competent testimony. The said Henry is about 38 years of age, 5 feet 8 1/4 inches high, rather dark complexion; the end of the little finger of the left hand is off to the 1st joint; has a scar on the back of wrist of the right hand, and bald.
In Testy. etc.   Test: In TestimonycSep. 27. 1847

African American Manumissions

B78b   State of Maryland, Washington County, Towit:
I, Isaac Nesbitt, Clerk of Washington County Court, hereby certify to all whom it may or doth concern that the bearer hereof, a negro man, named John Briscoe, is free, he having been manumitted by the Will of a certain Samuel H. Briscoe, which is recorded among the Records of Baltimore County, by reference to which will more fully appear, and which has been fully proven to me by respectable testimony. The said John is about 35 years of age, 6 feet 1 1/2 inches high, dark complexion, stout built, the third finger of his left hand is crooked, & has a scar on the back of the same hand.
In Testy etc.   Test: Isaac Nesbitt, Clk Sep. 27. 1847

B78c   State of Maryland, Washington County, Towit:
I, Isaac Nesbitt, Clerk of Washington County Court, hereby certify to all whom it may or doth concern that the bearer hereof, a negro woman, named Terry Cooper Briscoe, is free, she having been manumitted by the Will of the late Samuel H. Briscoe, which has been fully proven to my satisfaction by respectable testimony. The said Terry Cooper is about 45 years of age, 5 feet 3 3/4 inches high; tolerably dark complexion; and has no distinguishing marks about her.
In Testy, etc.   Test: Isaac Nesbitt, Clk Sep. 27. 1847

B79a   State of Maryland, Washington County, Towit:
I, Isaac Nesbitt, Clerk of Washington County Court, do hereby certify that it appears from the records of my office, that the bearer hereof, Henry Brown Jenkins, was duly manumitted by Col. Frisby Tilghman, on the 27th day of July 1829; at which time the said Henry was of the age of three years. The said Henry Brown Jenkins is a Mulatto, five feet seven inches high, slender built, with a scar on the left cheek bone, occasioned by a scratch, and has also a scar, scarcely visible, in the left eye brow.
In Testy etc.   Test: Isaac Nesbitt, Clk Oct. 1st. 1847.

B79b   State of Maryland, Washington County, Towit:
I, Isaac Nesbitt, Clerk of Washington County Court, hereby certify to all whom it may or doth concern that the bearer hereof, a negro woman, named Nancy Reeder, (formerly Jones) is a free woman, which is satisfactorily proven to me by respectable testimony. The said Nancy is about 36 years of age, 5 feet 7 3/4 inches high, dark complexion, slender form, has a scar on the

of Washington County, Maryland

upper lip, and has a good countenance. She has two children, named James Henry, aged 19 years; Eliza Ellen aged 16 years.
In Testy. etc.   Isaac Nesbitt, Clk   Nov. 1st. 1847.

B79c   State of Maryland, Washington County, Towit:
I, Isaac Nesbitt, Clerk of Washington County Court, hereby certify to all whom it may or doth concern that the bearer hereof, a negro man named John Moody, is entitled to his freedom, of which I am fully satisfied from the testimony of Upton Powell, a creditable citizen of the county aforesaid, having been heretofore sold to him the said Powell for a term of years, which has fully expired. The said John Moody was born on the 16 day of June 1819, and is five feet four inches high, very black, and has a deep indentation on the forehead, occasioned by the operation of trepanning.
In Test etc.   Isaac Nesbitt, Clk   Nov. 16 1847.

B80a   State of Maryland, Washington County, Towit:
I, Isaac Nesbitt, Clerk of Washington County Court, hereby certify to all whom it may or doth concern that the bearer hereof, a negro man named George Harrison, is free, having been manumitted and set free by Samuel Middlekauff by Deed of Manumission dated the 18th day of November 1847 and recorded in Liber I.N. No.2, one of the Land Records of Washington County, by reference to which will more fully appear. The said George is about 28 years of age, 5 feet 10 3/4 inches high, dark complexion, with two small scars on his right eye brow, of a good countenance.
In Testy. etc.   Test: Isaac Nesbitt, Clk   Nov. 18th, 1847.

B80b   State of Maryland, Washington County, Towit:
I, Isaac Nesbitt, Clerk of Washington County Court, hereby certify to all whom it may or doth concern that the bearer hereof named Catharine Jenifer, is a free coloured woman, as appears to my satisfaction upon the testimony of Captn. Samuel Clagett. The said Catharine is about 26 years of age, of dark complexion, has a mole on the upper lip, about five feet, seven inches high, and has a good countenance.
In Testimony etc.   Test: Isaac Nesbitt, Clk Decr. 1st. 1847.

African American Manumissions

B80c State of Maryland, Washington County, Towit:
I, Isaac Nesbitt, Clerk of Washington County Court, hereby certify to all whom it may or doth concern that the bearer hereof named Rozetta Washington, is a free coloured woman, as appears to my satisfaction upon the testimony of Capt. Samuel Clagett. The said Rozetta is about 22 years of age, of dark complexion, has a scar above the right eye, five feet, five & a quarter inches, and has a good countenance.
In Testimony etc.   Test; Isaac Nesbitt, Clk   Dec. 1st 1847.

B81a State of Maryland, Washington County, Towit:
I, Isaac Nesbitt, Clerk of Washington County Court, hereby certify to all whom it may or doth concern that the bearer hereof named Ellen Young, is a free coloured woman as appears to my satisfaction upon the testimony of Capt. Samuel Clagett. The said Ellen is about 24 years of age, of dark complexion, has a scar on the left wrist, five feet, five & a half inches high, of a good countenance.
In Testimony etc. Tst: Isaac Nesbitt, Clk December 1st. 1847

B81b State of Maryland, Washington County, Towit:
I, Isaac Nesbitt, Clerk of Washington County Court, hereby certify to all whom it may or doth concern that the bearer hereof named Eliza Ellen Slifer, is a free coloured girl, as appears to my satisfaction upon the testimony of Capt. Samuel Clagett. The said Ellen is about 16 years of age, of a light complexion, has a scar on the right eye & cheek, five feet, three & a half inches high.   In Testimony etc.   Test: Isaac Nesbitt, Clk
December 1st. 1847

B81c State of Maryland, Washington County, Towit:
I, Isaac Nesbitt, Clerk of Washington County Court, hereby certify to all whom it may or doth concern that the bearer hereof named Henry Williams, is a free coloured man as appears to my satisfaction upon the testimony of Isaac Nesbitt. The said Henry is about 21 years of age, a very bright Mulatto, five feet, three inches high, has a scar on the left arm, near the wrist, & a small one, on the left cheek, caused from the burn of a Segar, and has a good countenance.   In Testimony etc.   Test.   Isaac Nesbitt, Clk   December 3[or 5?]. 1847.

B82a State of Maryland, Washington County, Towit:

of Washington County, Maryland

I, Isaac Nesbitt, Clerk of Washington County Court, do hereby certify that it appears from the records of my office, that the bearer hereof Thomas James, a negro man, was manumitted by John Oswald by deed of manumission dated the 29th April, 1831, and duly recorded in Liber M.M. folio 387, to serve until he should arrive at the age of 21 years, which time has fully expired. Said negro is 5 feet 6 inches high, tolerably stout, with a scar on the little finger of the left hand, and a scar or mark on the forehead above the left eye, and is of a yellowish complexion.
In Testimony whereof etc.   Isaac Nesbitt, Clk
December 13, 1847.

B82b   State of Maryland, Washington County, Towit:
I, Isaac Nesbitt, Clerk of Washington County Court, hereby certify to all whom it may or doth concern that the bearer hereof, a negro man, named Thomas Bonhom, was this day manumitted from slavery, and set free by Josiah Davis, of said county, by Deed of Manumission duly executed and acknowledged. Said negro man is five feet eleven and a half inches high, rather slender made of a yellow or copper color, with a small scar on the forehead, over the right eye, aged thirty three years.
In Testimony etc. Isaac Nesbitt, Clk   December 28th 1847.

B83a   State of Maryland, Washington County, Towit:
I, Isaac Nesbitt, Clerk of Washington County Court, hereby certify to all whom it may or doth concern that the bearer hereof, a negro man, named John William Bell, who applies for a Certificate of his Freedom, is free, as has been satisfactorily proven to me on the testimony of Thos. Boteler, a competent witness. The said John is about 24 years of age, 5 feet 9 inches high, has a heavy scar under the lower lip occasioned by the Kick of a horse, and tolerably black or copper colored.
In Testy. etc.   Isaac Nesbitt, Clk   Febry. 17. 1848

B83b   State of Maryland, Washington County, Towit:
I, Isaac Nesbitt, Clerk of Washington County Court, do hereby certify to all whom it doth or may concern, that, it appears from the testimony of Edmund H. Turner, the bearer hereof, George Dorsey, who applies for a certificate of his freedom, is entitled to the same, having been born free. The said George Dorsey is five feet five inches high, stout made, with a scar on his left wrist; is about twenty-three years of age, and quite dark.
In Testimony etc.   Isaac Nesbitt, Clk   March 15th. 1848.

African American Manumissions

B83c State of Maryland, Washington County, Towit:
I, Isaac Nesbitt, Clerk of Washington County Court, hereby certify to all whom it may or doth concern that the bearer hereof, a negro man, named Henry Cooper, who applies for his certificate of freedom, has satisfactorily proven to me, by the affidavit of James Neal, a respectable white citizen, that said Henry was born free. The said Henry is five Feet five & a half inches high; stout made; has a scar on the ball of the left hand; is 23 years of age; and of a tolerably dark complexion.
In Testimony etc.   Isaac Nesbitt, Clk   March 17th. 1848

B84a State of Maryland, Washington County, Towit:
I, Isaac Nesbitt, Clerk of Washington County Court, hereby certify to all whom it may or doth concern that the bearer hereof, William Shorter, a negro man, who applies for a certificate of his freedom, has proven to my satisfaction, by the oath of Mr. James Neal, a respectable white citizen of said county, that he the said William was born free. The said William Shorter is 5 feet 3 1/2 inches high; 30 years of age; has a scar on the back of the left hand occasioned by a burn; and the end of the forefinger of the left hand has been injured and is a little stiff, and of a light copper complexion.
In Testimony etc.   Isaac Nesbitt, Clk   March 17th. 1848.

B84b State of Maryland, Washington County, Towit:
I, Isaac Nesbitt, Clerk of Washington County Court, hereby certify to all whom it may or doth concern that the bearer hereof, a negro man, named Samuel Benjamin Cooper, who applies for a certificate of his freedom, has satisfactorily proven to me, by the oath of James Neal, a respectable white citizen of said County, that he the said Samuel Benjamin Cooper, was born free. He, the said Samuel, is five feet eight & 1/2 inches high; with a scar between the eye brows; ["has" crossed out] the little finger of the right hand is somewhat crooked; is 21 years of age, stout made with a tolerably black complexion.
In Testimony etc.   Isaac Nesbitt, Clk   March 17, 1848.

B84c Maryland, Washington County
I, Isaac Nesbitt, Clerk of Washington County Court, hereby certify to all whom it may or doth concern that the bearer hereof, a negro woman, named Mary F. Williams, who applies for a Certificate of her freedom was manumitted on the 11th day of

of Washington County, Maryland

March 1848 by Benjamin Ingram, of said County by Deed of Manumission duly executed and acknowledged; said negro woman is five feet one & an half inches high; thick set, of a yellow or copper color, with a scar on the right side of her forehead, aged about twenty eight years.
In Testimony etc.   Isaac Nesbitt, Clk   April 4, 1848.

B85a   State of Maryland, Washington County, Towit:
I, Isaac Nesbitt, Clerk of Washington County Court, hereby certify to all whom it may or doth concern that the bearer hereof, John Butler, a negro man, who applies for a certificate of his freedom, has proven to my satisfaction by respectable white testimony that he was born free. The said John is 5 feet 7 3/4 inches high, about 22 years of age; has a small scar in the hollow of his nose and of a very dark complexion.
In Testimony whereof, etc. Test: Isaac Nesbitt, Clk May 17. 1848.

B85b   State of Maryland, Washington County, Towit:
I, Isaac Nesbitt, Clerk of Washington County Court, hereby certify to all whom it may or doth concern that the bearer hereof, a negro man, named Leonard Butler, has satisfied me upon the testimony of a respectable white person, that he was born free. The said Leonard is 5 feet 7 1/2 inches high, about 19 years of age; has a scar on the left ear caused by the Kick of a horse and of a very dark complexion.
In Testimony etc.   Isaac Nesbitt, Clk   May 17. 1848

B85c   State of Maryland, Washington County, Towit:
I, Isaac Nesbitt, Clerk of Washington County Court, hereby certify to all whom it may or doth concern that the bearer hereof, a negro man, named George Bayley, was duly manumitted & set free on the 1st day of June A.D. 1848, by a certain Lewis R. Martin, of Washington County & State of Maryland aforesaid, as appears from the Records of my office, in Liber I.N. No. 3 folios 229 & 230; the said negro having been sold under the law of 1839 ch. 3200 for coming into this State contrary to the provisions of said Law.
In Testy. etc.   Isaac Nesbitt, Clk   June 1st 1848

B86a   State of Maryland, Washington County, Towit:
I, Isaac Nesbitt, Clerk of Washington County Court, hereby certify to all whom it may or doth concern that the bearer hereof,

African American Manumissions

named Comfort Stewart, is free, which is proven to me by satisfactory testimony. The said Comfort Stewart is about 20 years of age, 5 feet 3 3/4 inches high; very light mulatto; has a good countenance and no marks perceptible about her.
In Testy. etc.   Isaac Nesbitt, Clk   June 6, 1848

B86b   State of Maryland, Washington County, Towit:
I, Isaac Nesbitt, Clerk of Washington County Court, hereby certify to all whom it may or doth concern that the bearer hereof, a negro man, named Henry Hill, is free, having been manumitted and set free by a certain Joseph Long, by Deed bearing date the 15 day of August, 1848, and recorded in Liber I.N. No.3, one of the Land Records of Washington County. The said Henry is 43 years of age; five feet 8 inches high; of a very dark complexion; has no perceptible marks about him, and walks a little lame from the effects of Rhumatism.
In Testy. etc.   Isaac Nesbitt, Clk   [no date - probably done on the same day as the following entry because there was no line drawn between them]

B86c   State of Maryland, Washington County, Towit:
I, Isaac Nesbitt, Clerk of Washington County Court, hereby certify to all whom it may or doth concern that the bearer hereof, a negro man, named William Hanson, is free, having been manumitted and set free by a certain Solomon James by Deed of Manumission, dated the 2d day of September 1848, and recorded in I.N. No.3, one of the Land Records of Washington County. The said William is about 44 years of age; 5 feet 9 inches high; of a very dark complexion, and has no marks perceptible about him.   In Testy. etc.   Isaac Nesbitt, Clk   Sept. 5. 1848

B87a   State of Maryland, Washington County, Towit:
I, Isaac Nesbitt, Clerk of Washington County Court, hereby certify to all whom it may or doth concern that the bearer hereof a negro woman, named Mary Ann Washington, is free, which is satisfactorily proven to me by the testimony of R. Fowler a respectable citizen of said County. The said Mary Ann is about 37 years of age; 5 feet 1/2 inch high; hair is very straight for a daughter of Ethiopia; comely in appearance and has no perceptible marks about her. The said Mary Ann has six children whose names and ages are as follow: Alfred, aged 14 years;; Louisa, aged 12 years; Joseph, aged 8 years; Mary Ellen,

aged 7 years; Laura, aged 3 years; Manjelic, aged 1 year & 5 months. In Testy., etc. Test: Isaac Nesbitt, Clk Oct. 11. 1848.

B87b State of Maryland, Washington County, Towit:
I, Isaac Nesbitt, Clerk of Washington County Court, hereby certify to all whom it may or doth concern that the bearer hereof, a negro woman, named Maria Matthews, is free, having been set free and manumitted by a certain Elizabeth Lawrence by Deed of Manumission bearing date the 13 day of August 1847, and recorded in Liber I.N. No. 2 folio 73 one of the Land Records of Washington County, to which reference is hereby made. The said Maria is about 33 years of age, 5 feet 8 1/4 inches high, dark complexion..
And her 5 children whose names and ages are as follow: Edward, aged 18 years; Susan Rebecca, aged 16 years; Alfred, aged 10 years; Samuel S. aged 9 years; and Mary Ann, aged 6 years. In Testy. etc.   Isaac Nesbitt, Clk   Nove. 1st. 1848.

B88a State of Maryland, Washington County, Towit:
I, Isaac Nesbitt, Clerk of Washington County Court, hereby certify to all whom it may or doth concern that the bearer hereof, a negro man, named, George Wagoner, is free, as has been proven to me by satisfactory testimony. The said George is about 24 years of age, 5 feet 6 inches high, has a scar on the left side of the forehead near the parting, of the hair; complexion a bright mulatta color, and his appearance comely.
In Testy. etc.   Isaac Nesbitt, Clk   Nov. 1st. 1848.

B88b State of Maryland, Washington County, Towit:
I, Isaac Nesbitt, Clerk of Washington County Court, hereby certify to all whom it may or doth concern that the bearer hereof, a negro woman, named Susanna Campbell is free, as has been satisfactorily proven to me by respectable testimony. The said Susanna Campbell is 26 years of age; 5 feet 7 3/4 inches high; has a small scar on the lower part of her right wrist, complexion bright mulatto, and in appearance rather likely. She has 3 children, whose names and ages are as follow: Thos. Franklin, aged 7 years; Mary Isabella, aged 6 years and Ann Eliza, aged 8 months.In Testy. etc.   Isaac Nesbitt, Clk   Nov. 1st. 1848.

African American Manumissions

B89a   State of Maryland, Washington County, Towit:
I, Isaac Nesbitt, Clerk of Washington County Court, do hereby certify to all whom it may or doth concern, that the bearer hereof, a negro woman, named Adelia Jones, is free, of which I am satisfied from respectable testimony. The said Adelia is 28 years of age; 5 feet 3 inches high, light mulatto; has a small scar under the lower lip, caused by a burn when a child; and is thick set and rather likely. She has 4 children to wit: Mary Sophia, aged 9 yrs.; Christopher, aged 7 yrs.; Chas. Edwd., aged 4 yrs. & Cynthia Ellen aged 3 yrs.
In Testy. etc.   Isaac Nesbitt, Clk   Nov. 2, 1848.

B89b   State of Maryland, Washington County, Towit:
I, Isaac Nesbitt, Clerk of Washington County Court, do hereby certify to all whom it may or doth concern, that the bearer hereof, a negro woman, named Rosa Ann Dorsey, is entitled to her Freedom, of which I am fully satisfied from the testimony of Miss Eliza Schnebly, a respectable citizen of said County. The said Rosa Ann Dorsey is about 17 years of age; 5 feet 2 3/4 inches high; has a small scar lengthwise on her right thumb, dark complexion and of small stature.
In Testy., etc.   Isaac Nesbitt, Clk   Nov. 18. 1848.

B89c   State of Maryland, Washington County, Towit:
I, Isaac Nesbitt, Clerk of Washington County Court, do hereby certify to all whom it may or doth concern, that the bearer hereof, a negro man, named Robert Johnson, was manumitted and set free by a certain Elizabeth Meredith, by Deed of Manumission, dated the 24 day of January 1848, and recorded in Liber I.N. No. 3, folio 133, one of the Land Records of Washington County, to which reference is hereby made. The said Robert is about 21 years of age, 5 feet 10 1/2 inches high, of a tolerable dark complexion and has no marks perceptible about him.   In Testy. etc.   Isaac Nesbitt, Clk   Jany. 9. 1849

B90a   State of Maryland, Washington County, Towit:
I hereby certify to all whom it doth or may concern, that the bearer hereof, a negro man named Samuel Pye who applies for his certificate of Freedom, is entitled to the same as has been satisfactorily proven to me. The said Samuel is about 23 years and 6 months of age, 6 feet 2 inches high, has two small scars on the forehead and one on the left hand near the junction of the

of Washington County, Maryland

thumb and fore finger, of light brown complexion and rather slender form.
In Testy. etc.   Test: Isaac Nesbitt, Clk March 9. 1849

B90b   State of Maryland, Washington County, Towit:
I, Isaac Nesbitt, Clerk of Washington County Court, do hereby certify to all whom it may or doth concern, that the bearer hereof, a negro man named John Rozier was manumitted and set free by Elie Stake & Willoughby S.G. McCardell, by deed of Manumission dated the 4th day of April 1849, and recorded in Liber I.N. No. 4, folios [blank] one of the Land Records of Washington County, to which reference is hereby made. The said John is about 26 years of age, 5 feet 8 1/4 inches high, of a light copper complexion, has a scar on the upper lip & forehead, and one on the left breast.
In Testy. etc.   Test: Isaac Nesbitt, Clk April 5th. 1849.
[Note: Liber I.N. 4, folio 141 lists this transaction.]

B90c   State of Maryland, Washington County, Towit:
I, Isaac Nesbitt, Clerk of Washington County Court, do hereby certify to all whom it may or doth concern, that the bearer hereof, a negro man named Yorick Ambush was manumitted and set free by Miss Virginia Mason, by deed of Manumission dated the 3d day of April 1849, and recorded in Liber I.N. No. 4, folio [blank] one of the Land Records of Washington County, to which reference is hereby made. The said Yorick Ambush is about 44 years of age, 5 feet 6 inches high, no marks perceptible, black complexion.
In Testy. etc.   Test: Isaac Nesbitt, Clk   April 9th. 1849.

B91a   State of Maryland, Washington County, Towit:
I, Isaac Nesbitt, Clerk of Washington County Court, do hereby certify to all whom it may or doth concern, that the bearer hereof a negro woman named Polly Ambush was manumitted and set free by Miss Virginia Mason by deed of Manumission dated the 3d day of April 1849, and recorded in Liber I.N. No. 4, folio [blank line drawn] one of the Land Records of Washington County, to which reference is hereby made. The said Polly is about 35 years of age, 5 feet 3/4 of an inch high, cross eyed, Dark complexion.
In Testy. etc.   Test: Isaac Nesbitt, Clk   April 9th. 1849.

African American Manumissions

B91b State of Maryland, Washington County, Towit:
I, Isaac Nesbitt, Clerk of Washington County Court, do hereby certify to all whom it may or doth concern, that the bearer hereof a negro man, named Arnold Summers, was manumitted and set free by John Shafer. Jr, by Deed of Manumission bearing date the 4 day of May 1849, and recorded in Liber I.N. No. 4 folio
 [blank] one of the Land Records of Washington County, to which reference is hereby made. The said Arnold is aged 39 years; 5 feet 5 1/2 inches high, very dark complexion, stout built and has two scars, one on the forehead & one on the ridge of his nose. In Testy. etc. Test: Isaac Nesbitt, Clk May 7. 1849.

B92a State of Maryland, Washington County, Towit:
I, Isaac Nesbitt, Clerk of Washington County Court, do hereby certify to all whom it may or doth concern, that the bearer hereof, a negro man, named Jim Shorter, was manumitted and set free by a certain V.W. Mason, by Deed of Manumission dated 3d day of April 1849, and recorded in Liber I.N. No. 4, folio
 [blank] one of the Land Records of Washington County, to which reference is hereby made. The said Jim is about 45 years of age; 5 feet 5 3/4 inches high; has an enlargement of the wrist bone of the right hand; also a small scar above the right eye; and of dark complexion.
In Testy., etc.   Test: Isaac Nesbitt, Clk May 28, 1849.

B92b State of Maryland, Washington County, Towit:
I, Isaac Nesbitt, Clerk of Washington County Court, do hereby certify to all whom it may or doth concern, that the bearer hereof, a negro woman named Eliza Shorter was manumitted and set free by a certain Virginia W. Mason, by Deed of Manumission dated the 3d day of April 1849, and recorded in Liber I.N. No. 4, folio   [blank] one of the Land Records of Washington County, to which reference is hereby made. The said Eliza is about   [blank] years of age; 5 feet 3 inches high; of very dark complexion; has a comely appearance and no marks perceptible about her.
In Testy., etc.   Test: Isaac Nesbitt, Clk May 28. 1849.

B92c State of Maryland, Washington County, Towit:
I, Isaac Nesbitt, clerk of Washington County Court, do hereby certify that it hath been satisfactorily proven to me that the bearer hereof, Milly Graham is a free woman, having served a

of Washington County, Maryland

term of years for which she had been sold to John T. Edwards, Esq., of Cumberland. She is a likely woman, complexion tolerably dark, five feet one inch high, and has a scar on the back of the left wrist. Age about 34.
In Testy etc.   Isaac Nesbitt, Clk   June 1st, 1849.

B93a   State of Maryland, Washington County, Towit:
I, Isaac Nesbitt, Clerk of Washington County Court, do hereby certify to all whom it may or doth concern, that the bearer hereof, a mulatto man, named Thomas Jones, was heretofore manumitted and set free by a certain Elizabeth Lawrence by Deed of Manumission dated the 30th day of August 1847, and recorded in Liber I.N. No. 2 folio 735, one of the Land Records of Washington County, to which reference is hereby made. The said Thomas Jones is about 23 years of age; 5 feet 8 inches high; complexion tolerably light mulatto color, and has a scar on the first finger of the left hand.
In Testy. etc.   Test: Isaac Nesbitt, Clk [no date]

B93b   State of Maryland, Washington County, Towit:
I, Isaac Nesbitt, Clerk of Washington County Court, do hereby certify to all whom it may or doth concern, that the bearer hereof, a negro man, named Thomas Sanders, was duly manumitted and set free by a certain Daniel Winters, by Deed of Manumission dated the 4 day of August, 1849, and recorded in Liber I.N. No. 4 one of the Record Books of Washington County, to which reference is hereby made. The said Thomas is about 42 years of age, 5 feet 6 1/4 inches high, of very dark complexion, and has a scar on the lower lip caused from a fall.
In Testy, etc.   Test: Isaac Nesbitt, Clk Aug. 7, 1849.

B94a   State of Maryland, Washington County, Towit:
I hereby certify, as Clerk of Washington County Court, that the bearer hereof, a negro man, named Richard Hill, was heretofore duly manumitted and set free, by a certain David Nikirk by Deed of Manumission dated the 7 day of August 1849, and recorded in Liber I.N. No. 4, one of the Record Books of Washington County, to which reference is hereby made. The said Richard is about 43 years of age, 5 feet 7 1/2 inches high, of very dark complexion, and has a scar on the 2d finger of the left hand, & rather slender form. In Testy, etc.   Test: Isaac Nesbitt, Clk [no date]

African American Manumissions

B94b State of Maryland, Washington County, Towit:
I, Isaac Nesbitt, Clerk of Washington County Court, do hereby certify to all whom it may or doth concern, that the bearer hereof, a negro man, named, Joshua Anderson was heretofore duly manumitted and set free by a certain Susan Harry & Jacob I. Harry, Exts. of Geo. I. Harry, and others by Deed of Manumission dated the 15 day of December 1847, and recorded in Liber I.N. No. 4, one of the Record Books of Washington County, to which reference is hereby made. The said Joshua is about 40 years of age, 5 feet 5 1/2 inches high, tolerably dark complexion and has a scar on the 1st finger of the left hand.
In Testy. etc. Test: Isaac Nesbitt, Clk Aug. 7, 1849.

B95a State of Maryland, Washington County, Towit:
I hereby as Clerk of Washington County Court, to all whom it may or doth concern that the bearer hereof, a negro man, named John Brown, was heretofore manumitted and set free by a certain Warford Mann, Ext. of John H. Mann, decd by Deed of Manumission, dated the 1st day of June 1849, and recorded in Liber I.N. No. 4, one of the Land Records of Washington County, to which reference is hereby made. The said John is about 40 years of age, 5 feet 11 inches high of a dark complexion, has a scar on the back of the head, and of a slender form.
In Testimony etc. Test: Isaac Nesbitt, Clk August 24, 1849.

B95b State of Maryland, Washington County, Towit:
I, Isaac Nesbitt, Clerk of Washington County Court, do hereby certify to all whom it may or doth concern, that the bearer hereof, a negro woman, named Susan Brown, was manumitted and set free, by a certain Nathaniel Summers, by deed of Manumission dated the 5th day of May 1829, and recorded in in [sic] Liber K.K. folio 739, one of the Land Records of Washington County, to which reference is hereby made. The said Susan is about 35 years of age, 5 feet 5 inches high, tolerably light complexion, has a good countenance and no marks perceptible about her. In Testimony whereof etc. Test: Isaac Nesbitt, Clk August 24 1849.

B96a State of Maryland, Washington County, Towit:
I, Isaac Nesbitt, Clerk of Washington County Court, do hereby certify to all whom it may or doth concern, that the bearer hereof, a negro woman, named Valise Key, is free, which has

of Washington County, Maryland

been to me satisfactorily proven. The said Valise is about 22 years of age, 5 feet 1/2 inch high, of a dark complexion, stout built and has no marks perceptible about her.
In Testy. etc.   Test: Isaac Nesbitt, Clk Sept. 5. 1849.

B96b   State of Maryland, Washington County, Towit:
I, Isaac Nesbitt, Clerk of Washington County Court, do hereby certify to all whom it may or doth concern, that the bearer hereof named Marie Van Ear a negro woman who applies for her Certificate of Freedom, was duly manumitted and set free by a certain John Reel by Deed of Manumission dated September 3d. 1849, and recorded in Liber IN. No. 4 folios 353 & 354, one of the Land Records of Washington County, to which reference is hereby made. The said Marie is about 31 years of age, 5 feet 2 1/4 inches high, has a scar on the neck from a burn, very dark complexion, and slender form.
In Testy. etc.   Test: Isaac Nesbitt, Clk [no date]

B96c   State of Maryland, Washington County, Towit:
I, Isaac Nesbitt, Clerk of Washington County Court, do hereby certify to all whom it may or doth concern, that the bearer hereof, Daniel Barnes, a Negro man, was duly manumitted by Jacob Firey, of said County, as it appears by a deed of manumission duly executed, acknowledged, and recorded in the Clerk's office of said County. the said Daniel is about thirty years of age, 5 feet 6 3/4 inches high, tolerably black, with a scar on the back of his right hand, and also a scar below the right ear, on the neck.
In Testimony etc.   Isaac Nesbitt, Clk   Oct. 10 1849.

B97a   State of Maryland, Washington County, Towit:
I, Isaac Nesbitt, Clerk of Washington County Court, do hereby certify to all whom it may or doth concern, that the bearer hereof, a colored man named Jefferson Martin, was born free, as it hath been made to appear to me, on sufficient proof. Said Jefferson is 5 feet 7 inches high, with a light or yellow complexion, about 24 years of age, and has some small scars on the back part of both his hands.
In Testimony etc. Isaac Nesbitt, Clk   November 6th. 1849.

African American Manumissions

B97b State of Maryland, Washington County, Towit:
I, Isaac Nesbitt, Clerk of Washington County Court, do hereby certify to all whom it may or doth concern, that the bearer hereof, a colored woman named Susan Ellen Dorsey, is free, having been manumitted and set free by a certain John Cook by Deed of Manumission dated the 21st day of January 1850, and recorded in Liber I.N. No. 4, one of the Land Records of Washington County, to which reference is hereby made. The said Susan Ellen is about 20 years of age, 5 feet 1/2 inch high; dark mulatto color, and has a scar running transversely across the forehead.
In Testimony, etc.   Test: Isaac Nesbitt, Clk   Jany. 22d. 1850.

B98a State of Maryland, Washington County, Towit:
I, Isaac Nesbitt, Clerk of Washington County Court, do hereby certify to all whom it may or doth concern, that the bearer hereof Richard Pindle, a negro man, was manumitted and set free by Deed of Manumission from a certain Isaac Cane, on the 13 day of March 1850, and which is recorded the same day in Liber I.N. No. 4, one of the Land Records of Washington County, to which reference is hereby made. The said Richd. is 35 years of age, 5 feet 10 1/4 inches high, having the little finger of the left hand deformed, and has two moles one upon the right side of his forehead the other on the right cheek, rather light complexion, on the order of the mulatto.
In Testy. etc.   Test: Isaac Nesbitt, Clk   March 13. 1850.

B98b State of Maryland, Washington County, Towit:
I, Isaac Nesbitt, Clerk of Washington County Court, do hereby certify to all whom it may or doth concern, that the bearer hereof a negro woman, named Henrietta Jones, is free, which is satisfactorily proven to me by the testimony of Samuel Clagett, a citizen of said County. The said Henrietta is about 17 years of age, 5 feet 4 1/4 inches high, of very dark complexion and has no scars perceptible about her.
In Testy. etc.   Test: Isaac Nesbitt, Clk   April 23d. 1850.

B99a State of Maryland, Washington County, Towit:
I, Isaac Nesbitt, Clerk of Washington County Court, do hereby certify to all whom it may or doth concern, that the bearer hereof, a negro woman, named Ann Matilda Jones, is free, which is satisfactorily proven to me on the testimony of Capt. Saml.

of Washington County, Maryland

Clagett, a citizen of said County. The said Ann Matilda is about 19 years of age, 5 feet 5 1/2 inches high, of dark complexion and has no scars perceptible about her.
In Testy. etc.   Test: Isaac Nesbitt, Clk   April 23d. 1850.

B99b   State of Maryland, Washington County, Towit:
I, Isaac Nesbitt, Clerk of Washington County Court, do hereby certify to all whom it may or doth concern, that the bearer hereof, a negro man, named John Dawson Jones, is free, which is to me satisfactorily proven on the testimony of Capt. Saml. Clagett, a citizen of said County. The said John Dawson is about 21 years of age, 5 feet 11 1/2 inches high, of dark complexion and has a scar on the right wrist.
In Testy. etc.   Test: Isaac Nesbitt, Clk   April 23d. 1850.

B100a   State of Maryland, Washington County, Towit:
I, Isaac Nesbitt, Clerk of Washington County Court, do hereby certify to all whom it may or doth concern, that the bearer hereof a negro man, named Jackson Lee, is free, having been manumitted & set free by a certain J. Thompson Mason, by Deed of Manumission dated the 21st December 1846 & recorded in Liber I.N. No. 2. folios 245 & 246, one of the Land Records of Washington County Court. The said Jackson is about 31 years of age, 5 feet 2 3/4 inches high, very dark complexion and no marks perceptible about him.
In Testimony etc.   Test: Isaac Nesbitt, Clk   May 27. 1850

B100b   State of Maryland, Washington County, Towit:
I, Isaac Nesbitt, Clerk of Washington County Court, do hereby certify to all whom it may or doth concern, that the bearer hereof, a negro girl, named Cecelia Blake, is free, which is to me satisfactorily proven on the testimony of Wm. M.K. Keppler Esquire, a Citizen of said County. The said Cecelia Blake is about 22 years of age, 5 feet 1 1/2 inches high, of dark complexion has a scar near the 3d joint of the first finger of the left hand.
In Testimony etc.   Test: Isaac Nesbitt, Clk   June 5th, 1850.

B101a   State of Maryland, Washington County, Towit:
I, Isaac Nesbitt, Clerk of Washington County Court, do hereby certify to all whom it may or doth concern, that the bearer hereof, a negro man, named Thomas B. Duckett, is free, which is

African American Manumissions

satisfactorily proven to me by respectable testimony. The said Thomas B. Duckett is about 21 years of age; 5 feet 8 3/4 inches high, has a scar on his forehead, running towards the left eye, and one on the left wrist below the little finger, is of very dark complexion & well built.
In Testy. etc.   Test: Isaac Nesbitt, Clk July 20. 1850.

B101b   State of Maryland, Washington County, Towit:
I, Isaac Nesbitt, Clerk of Washington County Court, do hereby certify to all whom it may or doth concern, that the bearer hereof, a negro woman, named, Mary Phenix was manumitted & set free by a certain Benjamin Witmer by Deed of Manumission, dated the 16 day of January 1850, & recorded in Liber I.N. No. 5. The said Mary is about 34 years of age, 5 feet 3 inches high, has a scar on the left hand below the thumb, near the palm, and has very dark complexion.
In Testy. etc.   Test: Isaac Nesbitt, Clk July 27. 1850.

B102a   State of Maryland, Washington County, Towit:
I hereby certify, as Clerk of Washington County Court, to all whom it may or doth concern, that the bearer hereof, a negro woman, named Harriet Smith, (formerly Hariet Rozier) was manumitted and set free by James A. Magruder by Deed of Manumission bearing date the 10 day of June 1850, & recorded in Liber I.N. No. 5, one of the Land Records of Washington County. The said Harriet is about 28 years of age, 5 feet 1 1/2 inches high, has a scar on the left hand below the first finger, & another over the right eye, and of dark complexion.
In Testy. etc.   Test: Isaac Nesbitt, Clk July 30. 1850.

B102b   State of Maryland, Washington County, Towit:
I, Isaac Nesbitt, Clerk of Washington County Court, do hereby certify to all whom it may or doth concern, that the bearer hereof, a negro man, named William Brown, is free, having been manumitted & set free by a certain Sally Troup by Deed of Manumission, bearing date the 24 day of June 1850, & recorded in Liber I.N. No. 5, one of the Land Records of Washington County. The said William about 50 years of age, 5 feet 8 3/4 inches high, has a scar on the last joint of the little finger of his left hand, and the same finger has been injured at its point, is of very dark complexion and stoutly built.
In Testy. etc.   Test: Isaac Nesbitt, Clk   August 6. 1850.

B103a State of Maryland, Washington County, Towit:
I, Isaac Nesbitt, Clerk of Washington County Court, do hereby certify to all whom it may or doth concern, that the bearer hereof, a negro woman named Sarah Ellen Matthews, is free, having been born free as has been satisfactorily proven to me by respectable testimony. The said Sarah Ellen is about 24 years of age, 4 feet 11 inches high, has a scar in the centre of her forehead and of very dark complexion.
In Testimony, etc.   Test: Isaac Nesbitt, Clk August   24. 1850.

B103b State of Maryland, Washington County, Towit:
I, Isaac Nesbitt, Clerk of Washington County Court, do hereby certify to all whom it may or doth concern, that the bearer hereof, a negro man, named Robert Lee, is free, having been manumitted & set free by John T. Mason by Deed of Manumission dated the 21st day of December 1846, and recorded in Liber I.N. No. 2, folios 245 & 246, one of the Land Records of Washington County. The said Robert is about 37 years of age, 5 feet 7 inches high, is of very dark complexion, has a good countenance and no marks perceptible about him.
In Testimony, etc. Test: Isaac Nesbitt, Clk   Sept. 10. 1850

B104a State of Maryland, Washington County, Towit:
I, Isaac Nesbitt, Clerk of Washington County Court, do hereby certify to all whom it may or doth concern, that the bearer hereof, a negro woman, named Levina Dunmore, is free, having been manumitted and set free by Deed of Manumission, bearing date the 24 day of August 1822, and recorded in Liber F.F. folio 882, one of the Land Records of Washington County. The said Levinia is about 30 years of age, 5 feet 1 3/4 inches high, of yellow complexion, & has a scar on the back of the left hand.
In Testy. etc.   Test: Isaac Nesbitt, Clk Sept. 14. 1850
[margin reads "Lavinia"]

B104b State of Maryland, Washington County, Towit:
I, Isaac Nesbitt, Clerk of Washington County Court, do hereby certify to all whom it may or doth concern, that the bearer hereof, a negro woman, named Frances Kane, is free, having been manumitted and set free by a certain Sarah Ann Price, by Deed of Manumission dated 9 September 1850, and recorded in Liber I.N. No. 5, folio 310, one of the Land Records of

African American Manumissions

Washington County. The said Frances is about 22 years of age, 5 feet 5 1/2 inches high, has a scar below the right eye, and one near the chin on the right side of the jaw bone, caused by the Kings evil, and of very dark complexion.
In Testy., etc.   Test, Isaac Nesbitt, Clk   Oct. 8. 1850.

B105a   State of Maryland, Washington County, Towit:
I, Isaac Nesbitt, Clerk of Washington County Court, do hereby certify to all whom it may or doth concern, that the bearer hereof, a negro man, named Lymus Lynch, was manumitted & set free by a certain Ann E. Cushwa, by deed of Manumission dated the 10 day of July 1850, and recorded in Liber I.N. No. 5, folio 291, etc. one of the Land Records of Washington County. The said Lymus is about 43 years of age, 5 feet 6 inches high, has both eye teeth out, and of very dark complexion, with no other marks perceptible about him.
In Testy. etc.   Test: Isaac Nesbitt, Clk Oct. 21st 1850.

B105b   State of Maryland, Washington County, Towit:
I, Isaac Nesbitt, Clerk of Washington County Court, do hereby certify to all whom it may or doth concern, that the bearer hereof, a negro woman, named Jane Duckett, is free, which is satisfactorily proven to me by respectable testimony. The said Jane is about 23 years of age, 5 feet 7 inches high, has a mole on the upper lip and a scar in the palm of the left hand.
In Testy, etc.   Test: Isaac Nesbitt, Clk Nov. 1. 1850

B106a   State of Maryland, Washington County, Towit:
I, Isaac Nesbitt, Clerk of Washington County Court, do hereby certify to all whom it may or doth concern, that the bearer hereof, a negro woman, named Sarah Whiting, is free, which is satisfactorily proven to me. The said Sarah is about 33 years of age, 5 feet 5 inches high, has a scar in the center of the forehead and another near the hair at the top of the forehead.
In Testy. etc.   Test: Isaac Nesbitt, Clk Nov. 1. 1850

B106b   State of Maryland, Washington County, Towit:
I, Isaac Nesbitt, Clerk of Washington County Court, do hereby certify to all whom it may or doth concern, that the bearer hereof, a negro man, named Levi Hall, is free, which is satisfactorily proven to me. The said Levi is about 33 years of

of Washington County, Maryland

age, 6 feet high, has a scar on the left arm near the wrist, and no other marks perceptible about him.
In Testy. etc.   Test: Isaac Nesbitt, Clk Nov. 1st. 1850

B106c State of Maryland, Washington County, Towit:
I, Isaac Nesbitt, Clerk of Washington County Court, do hereby certify to all whom it may or doth concern, that the bearer hereof, a negro woman, named Sarah Wagoner, formerly Sarah Harrison, is free, which is satisfactorily proven to me. The said Sarah is about 22 years of age, 5 feet 5 1/2 inches high, has a mole on the left cheek & a red mark on the left hand, of a bright mulatto In Testy. etc. Isaac Nesbitt, Clk [no date]

B107a State of Maryland, Washington County, Towit:
I, Isaac Nesbitt, Clerk of Washington County Court, do hereby certify to all whom it may or doth concern, that the bearer hereof a negro woman, named Jane Cosey, was manumitted & set free by a certain Samuel W. Jones by deed of Manumission dated the 21st day of December 1850, recorded in Liber I.N. No. 5, one of the Land Records of Washington County. The said Jane is about 35 years of age, 5 feet 2 1/2 inches high, has a mole on the left cheek and of very dark complexion.
In Testimony etc. Test: Isaac Nesbitt, Clk Dec. 21st. 1850.

B107b State of Maryland, Washington County, Towit:
I, Isaac Nesbitt, Clerk of Washington County Court, do hereby certify to all whom it may or doth concern, that the bearer hereof, a negro woman, named Ann Maria Smith, was manumitted and set free by a certain Sarah Ann Price by Deed of Manumission dated the 9 day of September 1850, and recorded in Liber I.N. No. 5 folio 310, one of the Land Records of Washington County. The said Ann Maria is about 27 years of age, 5 feet 7 1/2 inches high, has a scar on the forehead above the right eye, and very dark complexion.
In Testy. & d.   Test: Isaac Nesbitt, Clk May 6, 1851.

B108a State of Maryland, Washington County, Towit:
I, Isaac Nesbitt, Clerk of Washington County Court, do hereby certify to all whom it may or doth concern, that the bearer hereof, a negro man, named Lewis Mills was manumitted & set free by a certain Mary Schnebly by Deed of Manumission, dated the 13 day of May 1851, & recorded in Liber I.N. No. 5, one of

African American Manumissions

the Land Records of Washington County, to which refer.. The said Lewis is about 28 years of age, 5 feet 9 inches high, has a large wart on the first finger of the right hand, and walks lame from a dislocation of the right hip joint, and of a tawney or copper complexion.
In Testimony, etc.   Test: Isaac Nesbitt, Clk   May 20, 1851

B108b   State of Maryland, Washington County, Towit:
I, Isaac Nesbitt, Clerk of Washington County Court, do hereby certify to all whom it may or doth concern, that the bearer hereof, a negro man, named Henry J. Butler, is free, having been born free, as has been satisfactorily proven tome. The said Henry J. Butler is about 23 years of age, 5 feet 9 3/4 inches high, has a cut on the top of the right ear, and a scar on the back of the right hand, and of a dark complexion.
In Testimony, etc. Test: Isaac Nesbitt, Clk   July 29. 1851

B109a   State of Maryland, Washington County, Towit:
I, Isaac Nesbitt, Clerk of Washington County Court, do hereby certify to all whom it may or doth concern, that the bearer hereof, a negro man, named Michael Watts, is free, having been manumitted & set free by a certain Wm. Dellinger and wife by Deed of Manumission dated Aug. 7, 1851, and recorded in Liber I.N. No. 6, one of the Land Records of the County aforesaid. The said Michael is about 40 years of age, 5 feet 6 inches high, has a scar on the forehead above the left eye, and one on the left hand between the thumb & forefinger, and of a perfectly black complexion.
In Testy. etc.   Test:; Isaac Nesbitt, Clk Aug. 18. 1851.

B109b   State of Maryland, Washington County, Towit:
I, Isaac Nesbitt, Clerk of Washington County Court, do hereby certify to all whom it may or doth concern, that the bearer hereof, a negro woman, named Sarah Watts, is free, having been manumitted & set free by a certain Joseph P. Mong and Wm. Dellinger by Deed of Manumission dated the 19 day of August 1851, and recorded in Liber I.N. No. 6 one of the Land Records of Washington County County [sic]. The said Sarah is about 39 years of age, 5 feet 1 inch high, of a dark complexion, has a pleasant countenance and no visable marks about her.
Test: Isaac Nesbitt, Clk Aug. 19. 1851.

of Washington County, Maryland

B110a State of Maryland, Washington County, Towit:
I, Isaac Nesbitt, Clerk of Washington County Court, do hereby certify to all whom it may or doth concern, that the bearer hereof, a negro man, named John Stewart, is free, having been manumitted by a certain Samuel M. Hitt, who purchased the said John from a certain Mr. E. Miller she having sold him to serve until he arrived at the age of twenty eight years, which term has since expired, as by reference to Liber G.G. folio 728, will more fully appear. The said John is about 31 years of age, 5 feet eight inches high, has a scar under the left eye, and under the chin, is somewhat marked with small pox in the face, has a good countenance, and of tolerably dark complexion.
Test: Isaac Nesbitt, Clk   Sept. 2d. 1851.

B110b State of Maryland, Washington County, Towit:
I, Isaac Nesbitt, Clerk of the Circuit Court for Washington County, do hereby certify to all whom it may concern, that the bearer hereof a negro woman, named Rosanna Washington, hath satisfactorily proven to me, upon competent testimony, that she was born free. The said Rosanna was born on the 30th day of August, 1830, is five feet high, stout built, and has a scar on the back of the right hand, above the third and fourth fingers, a dark yellowish complexion, and has considerable space between her upper front teeth.
Test: Isaac Nesbitt, Clk December 6th. 1851.

B111a State of Maryland, Washington County, Towit:
I, Isaac Nesbitt, Clerk of the Circuit Court for Washington County, do hereby certify to all whom it may concern, that the bearer hereof a negro man, named Thomas Briscoe, has been proved to me upon satisfactorily testimony, that he is free. The said Thomas is about 24 years of age, five feet en inches high; has a small scar on the first finger of the right hand, and is of very dark complexion.
Test: Isaac Nesbitt, Clk Feby. 17 1852

B111b State of Maryland, Washington County, Towit:
I, Isaac Nesbitt, Clerk of the Circuit Court for Washington County, do hereby certify to all whom it may concern, that the bearer hereof, a negro man, named Bartley Conn, is free, having been born free, which is proven to my satisfaction by competent testimony. The said Bartley was 24 years of age on the 25 of last

African American Manumissions

April, is five feet 9 inches high, has a scar on the end of the 2d finger of the left hand, and a mole over the left eye, and of a copper colored complexion.
Test: Isaac Nesbitt, Clk   Feby. 24. 1852

B112a   State of Maryland, Washington County, Towit:
I, Isaac Nesbitt, Clerk of the Circuit Court for Washington County, do hereby certify to all whom it may concern, that the bearer hereof, a negro man, named Joshua Washington, was born free, which has been satisfactorily proven to me by competent testimony. The said Joshua was 21 years of age on the 20 July 1851, is five feet & 6 inches high, has a small black mole under the chin on the left side, and a scar on the back of the neck; stout built and of a copper complexion.
Test: Isaac Nesbitt, Clk   March 19. 1852

B112b   State of Maryland, Washington County, Towit:
I, Isaac Nesbitt, Clerk of the Circuit Court for Washington County, do hereby certify, to all whom it may or doth concern, that the bearer hereof, a colored man, named Edward Mathews, is free; having been duly manumitted and set free by Elizabeth Lawrence, by deed duly executed, and recorded among the Land Records of said County. The said Edward Mathews is now about 22 years of age, five feet 8 inches high, of a light complexion and somewhat freckled; has a scar on the right ear, a slight scar under the left eye, and also one on the inside of the right hand.
In Testimony etc.   Isaac Nesbitt, Clk   April 3d. 1852.

B113a   State of Maryland, Washington County, Towit:
I, Isaac Nesbitt, Clerk of the Circuit Court for Washington County, do hereby certify, to all whom it may or doth concern, that the bearer hereof, a negro woman named Mary Dunward, is free, having been duly manumitted and set free by David H. Keedy, by deed bearing date on the 3d day of May 1852, duly executed & recorded in the Land Records of Washington County aforesaid. the said Mary is about 30 years of age, 5 feet 4 1/2 inches high; both of her little fingers are crooked or bent, and is of a dark complexion.
Test: Isaac Nesbitt, Clk   May 4. 1852

of Washington County, Maryland

B113b State of Maryland, Washington County, Towit:
I, Isaac Nesbitt, Clerk of the Circuit Court for Washington County, do hereby certify, to all whom it may or doth concern, that the bearer hereof, a negro man, named Peter Stephens, is free, having been duly manumitted & set free by Elie Woltz & Martin Startzman, by deed dated the 31st day of May 1852, duly executed & recorded in the Land Records of the County aforesaid. The said Peter is about 31 years of age, five feet ten & a half inches high, has a large scar on his upper lip extending to the right eye, and of very dark complexion.
Test: Isaac Nesbitt, Clk   May 31st 1852

B114a State of Maryland, Washington County, Towit:
I, Isaac Nesbitt, Clerk of the Circuit Court for said county, do hereby certify, that it hath been satisfactorily proven to me, on the affidavit of John Stemple, a creditable white citizen of said county, that the bearer hereof, James Gruber, was born free. He is now about twenty one years of age; five feet four inches high; has two scars on the back of his right hand, also a scar on his right cheek bone; of rather a light complexion, and slightly built.
   In Testimony whereof etc.   August 14th. 1852.

B114b State of Maryland, Washington County, Towit:
I, Isaac Nesbitt, Clerk of the Circuit Court for said county, do hereby certify that it is satisfactorily proven from the Records of my office, that the bearer hereof, Margaret Collins, (wife of William Collins) was born free. she is now about 26 years of age; five feet four inches and a half high; of a yellow complexion, and has a scar on the back of the left hand, and the hair on her head rather thin. She has at this time two children, one named Joseph Hanson Green, born October 7, 1843; the other named Benjamin Edward Green, born in September, 1846.
In Testimony whereof etc.   August 24th. 1852.

B114c State of Maryland, Washington County, Towit:
I, Isaac Nesbitt, Clerk of the Circuit Court for Washington County, do hereby certify, to all whom it may or doth concern, that the bearer hereof Catharine Phenix, a colored woman, was manumitted by Catharine Sharer, by deed of manumission, duly executed and acknowledged, and recorded in Liber II, folios 295 & 296, one of the Land Records of said county. The said Catharine Phenix is forty two years of age; five feet, five and a

African American Manumissions

half inches high; stout built; tolerably black; has a scar on the middle finger of the left hand, and a small scar above the elbow of the right arm.
In Testimony whereof etc.   August 30, 1852.

B115a   State of Maryland, Washington County, Towit:
I, Isaac Nesbitt, Clerk of the Circuit Court for said county, do hereby certify to all whom it doth or may concern that the bearer hereof, a negro man, named George Porter, was duly manumitted by Samuel Mason, by deed of manumission dated the first day of September, 1852, and recorded in my office. The said George is five feet eight & a half inches high, has a small scar on the back of his right hand, above the forefinger; is tolerably stout, and now in the 27 year of his age. complexion pretty black.   In Testimony etc.   September 1st, 1852.

B115b   State of Maryland, Washington County, Towit:
I, Isaac Nesbitt, Clerk of the Circuit Court for said county, do hereby certify to all whom it doth or may concern, that it hath been satisfactorily proven tom e upon the oath of Mary Ann Feeby, a white person, that the bearer hereof, Maria Diggs, was born free. the said Maria is now in the nineteenth year of her age; is five feet, one and a half inches high; and a bright mulatto. No perceivable marks.
In Testimony whereof etc.   Sept. 4 1852.

B115c   State of Maryland, Washington County, Towit:
I, Isaac Nesbitt, Clerk of the Circuit Court for said County, do hereby certify to all whom it doth or may concern, that it hath been satisfactorily proven to me upon the Oath of Daniel Thomas & Jacob Speilman, two white persons, of respectable character, that Corban Adley, a Negro man is free having been born free. The said Corban is about twenty two years of age - five feet 5 inches high, has a scar under the Chin, and the little finger of the right hand crooked, and no other marks perceptible.
In Testimony whereof etc.   Test: Isaac Nesbitt, Clk October 9th, 1852.

B116a   State of Maryland, Washington County, Towit:
I, Isaac Nesbitt, Clerk of the Circuit Court for said County, do hereby certify to all whom it doth or may concern, that the bearer hereof, Mahala Garner, a Mulatto Girl, was born free; - it having

of Washington County, Maryland

been satisfactorily proven to me on the Oath of the Mother of said girl, who is a white woman. The said Mahala is about twenty years of age, five feet two Inches high; and has a small Mole on the left side of her nose.   In Testimony whereof etc.   Test: Isaac Nesbitt, Clk Nov. 10th, 1852.

B116b State of Maryland, Washington County, Towit:
I, Isaac Nesbitt, Clerk of the Circuit Court for Washington County, do hereby certify, to all whom it may or doth concern, that the bearer hereof, Sarah Garner, a Mulatto girl, was born free; - it having been proven to me satisfactorily on the Oath of the Mother of said Girl, who is a white woman. The said Sarah is about seventeen years old, five feet high without any perceptible Marks.
In Testimony whereof etc.   Test: Isaac Nesbitt, Clk
    November 10th, 1852

B116c State of Maryland, Washington County, Towit:
I, Isaac Nesbitt, Clerk of the Circuit Court for Washington County, do hereby certify, to all whom it doth or may concern, that it hath been satisfactorily proven to me that the bearer hereof, Elizabeth Williams, a negro woman, was born free; she is now about 34 years of age, 5 feet 5 3/4 inches high, rather slender, tolerably black, with no perceivable marks about the face. She has five children, viz; Mayberry, aged 13; Amanda, aged 12; Henry, aged 6; John, aged 5; and Jane, aged 4.
In Testimony whereof etc.   Test: Isaac Nesbitt, Clk
    December 14th, 1852.

B117a State of Maryland, Washington County, Towit:
I, Isaac Nesbitt, Clerk of the Circuit Court for Washington County, do hereby certify to all whom it may or doth concern, that satisfactory proof hath been adduced before me, and also of my own knowledge, that the bearer hereof Matilda Watts, a Negro woman, was born free. She is now about 31 years of age, 5 feet 2 3/4 inches high, well formed, with both small fingers a little crooked, and front teeth considerably decayed. She has six children namely, David Henry, aged 14 years; Sarah Elizabeth, aged 13 years; Josiah, aged 12 years; John Dorsey, aged 10 years, Lewis Calvin, aged 6 years; and Thomas Gohean, aged 4 years.
In Testimony whereof etc.   Test: Isaac Nesbitt, Clk
    December 14th, 1852.

African American Manumissions

B117b State of Maryland, Washington County, Towit:
I, Isaac Nesbitt, Clerk of the Circuit Court for Washington County, do hereby certify, to all whom it may or doth concern, that satisfactory proof hath been adduced before me, that the bearer hereof, Elizabeth Ann Lyles, a negro girl, was born free. She is now about 22 years of age, 5 feet 1 3/4 inches high, a bright mulatto, with no perceivable marks, about the face.
In Testimony whereof etc.   Test: Isaac Nesbitt, Clk
            December 21st 1852.

B117c State of Maryland, Washington County, Towit:
I, Isaac Nesbitt, Clerk of the Circuit Court for Washington County, do hereby certify to all whom it may or doth concern that it hath been satisfactorily proven to me, on competent testimony that the bear hereof, a negro man, named Isaiah Henry [margin reads "Jsaiah Henry"] was born free. He will be 23 years of age in March next: is 5 feet 11 3/4 inches high. has a large scar on the forehead caused by a burn, and also a scar on the chin, & one on the back of each hand complexion tolerably black.
In testimony whereof etc.   Test: Isaac Nesbitt, Clk January 3 1853.

B118a State of Maryland, Washington County, Towit:
I, Isaac Nesbitt, Clerk of the Circuit Court for said county, do hereby certify that the bearer hereof, Hilliary Adley, hath satisfactorily proven tome, upon the oath of John Snyder, a white person that he was born free. He is now 23 years of age, 5 feet 4 1/2 inches high; stout made; has a mole on the left cheek; and is of a copper color, with pleasant countenance.
In Testimony, etc. Isaac Nesbitt, Clk   January, 18 1853.

B118b State of Maryland, Washington County, Towit:
I. Isaac Nesbitt, Clerk of the Circuit Court for said County, do hereby certify that the bearer hereof Mary Jane Younker, hath satisfactorily proven to me by respectable testimony, that she was born free. She is now 25 years of age; five feet, one inch high, a small scar on the wrist of the left hand, and of tolerably dark complexion, with a pleasant countenance.
Isaac Nesbitt, Clk   March 11th. 1853

of Washington County, Maryland

B118c   State of Maryland, Washington County, Towit:
I, Isaac Nesbitt, clerk of the Circuit Court for said county, do hereby certify to all whom it doth or may concern, that the bearer hereof, Delia Johnson, was this day regularly manumitted by Frederick Bryan of said County, by deed of manumission duly executed, acknowledged, and recorded. The said Delia is a bright mulatto, aged about 20 years; has red hair; and is five feet one inch high.
In Testimony etc. Isaac Nesbitt, Clk   March 18, 1853.

B119a   State of Maryland, Washington County, Towit:
I, Isaac Nesbitt, Clerk of the Circuit Court for said County, do hereby certify, that the bearer hereof, a mulatto man named Benjamin Reeder, hath satisfactorily proven to me that he is the identical person who was manumitted by deed of manumission, bearing date the 11 day of February 1828, by a certain Philip Reeder and recorded in Liber I.I. folio 834, one of the Land Records of said County. The said Benjamin is about 34 years of age, 6 feet high, of light complexion, having his right knee stiff by white swelling.
In Testimony etc. Isaac Nesbitt, Clk   Mar. 19. 1853

B119b   State of Maryland, Washington County, Towit:
I, Isaac Nesbitt, Cldrk of the Circuit Court for said county, do hereby certify, that the bearer hereof, a mulatto man, named Charles Reeder, hath satisfactorily proven to me, that he is the identical person, who was manumitted by deed of manumission, bearing date the 11th day of February 1828, by a certain Philip Reeder and recorded in Liber I.I. folio 834 one of the Land Records of said County. The said Charles is about 33 years of age, 5 feet, 10 inches high, of light complexion, two scar on his right leg caused by the kick of a horse.
In Testimony etc. Isaac Nesbitt, Clk   Mar. 21st. 1853.

B119c   State of Maryland, Washington County, Towit:
I, Isaac Nesbitt, Clerk of the Circuit Court for said County, do hereby certify to all whom it doth or may concern, that the bearer hereof, William Lee, was duly manumitted by John Thomson Mason, by Deed of Manumission dated the 21st day of December, 1846 and recorded in Liber I.N. No. 2 folios 245 & 246, one of the Land Records of said County, as by reference thereto will more fully and at large appear. Said William is no

African American Manumissions

about 31 years of age, is 5 feet 4 1/2 inches high with a scar in the right eye brow, and also one over the left eye brow, and has a mark on the left side of the neck; is stoutly built and is tolerably black.
In Testimony etc. Isaac Nesbitt, Clk   April 21st, 1853

B120a State of Maryland, Washington County, Towit:
I, Isaac Nesbitt, clerk of the Circuit Court for said County, do hereby certify to all whom it may or doth concern, that the bearer hereof, a negro man, named John Henry Arms, has been proven to me by satisfactory testimony to be free. The said John Henry is now about 23 years of age, 6 feet 2 inches high, slender form, has a small scar on the left side of his forehead, a front upper tooth out, and his right arm stiff at the elbow, and not very black.
In Testy etc.   Test: Isaac Nesbitt, Clk   April 26, 1853.

B120b State of Maryland, Washington County, Towit:
I, Isaac Nesbitt, Clerk of the Circuit Court for said County, do hereby certify to all whom it may or doth concern, that the bearer hereof, a negro boy, named Levi Twine, was manumitted & set free by Saml. Zeller, by Deed dated the 1st day of April 1853, and recorded in Liber I.N. No. 7, one of the Land Records of Washington County, to which reference is made. The said Levi is about 36 years of age, 5 feet 9 inches high, has a scar on the left cheek and a small one near the eye, and very black.
Test: Isaac Nesbitt, Clk May 3, 1853.

B121a State of Maryland, Washington County, Towit:
I, Isaac Nesbitt, Clerk of the Circuit Court for said County, do hereby certify to all whom it doth or may concern, that the bearer hereof, Catharine Simms, a colored woman, was born free; it being satisfactorily proven to me that she is the daughter of Hannah Vernor, who was manumitted by Dr. Zachariah Clagett by deed of manumission duly executed and recorded in this office, in Liber GG, folio 513. The said Catharine Simms is now 23 years of age; five feet one inch high, (scant;) the little finger of the left hand, was injured form a cut; has a small mark on the forehead from a burn. She has a child named Mary Louisa, who will be two years old in July next.
In Testimony etc.   Isaac Nesbitt, Clk   May 19, 1853.

of Washington County, Maryland

B121b State of Maryland, Washington County, Towit:
I, Isaac Nesbitt, Clerk of the Circuit Court for said County, do hereby certify to all whom it doth or may concern, that the bearer hereof, a colored woman, named Catharine Campbell, was duly manumitted on the 21st instant, by Samuel Williams, by Deed of Manumission duly executed and recorded among the records of my office. The said Catharine Campbell is now about 29 years of age, is five feet two and a quarter inches high; without any perceptible marks, of light complexion, well formed, and likely. She has a son now five months old, whom she calls Wm. Campbell Lake, and who is also manumitted in the same deed.
In Testimony whereof etc.   Isaac Nesbitt, Clk   May 23d. 1853

B121c State of Maryland, Washington County, Towit:
I, Isaac Nesbitt, Clerk of the Circuit Court for said County, do hereby certify to all whom it doth or may concern, that the bearer hereof, a negro woman, named Lucy, alias Louisa Blake, was duly manumitted by Eve Moudy, by Deed of Manumission duly executed and acknowledged, and this day filed in my office for record. Said Louisa is about 28 or 30 years of age; five feet four & a half inches high; has a small scar on the little finger of the left hand, and a scar on the right wrist; complexion quite black. She has also a son named James Robert Blake, about ten years old, also manumitted in the same deed of manumission, who has a scar over the left eye brow.
In Testimony etc. Isaac Nesbitt, Clk   June 14th. 1853.

B122a State of Maryland, Washington County, Towit:
I, Isaac Nesbitt, Clerk of the Circuit Court for said County, do hereby certify to all whom it doth or may concern, that the bearer hereof, Gitty Lake, was duly manumitted by her husband, Thomas Lake, by deed duly executed, acknowledged, and recorded in my office on the 10th day of February, A.D. 1849. The said Gitty is now in the 50th year of her age, is five feet three and 1/4 inches high, has a scar between here eyes, and of a light or yellow complexion. She has five children of the following names and ages: Samuel Lake, born July 26th. 1826; Mary Elender Lake, born April 6th. 1831; Thomas E. Lake, born February 10th. 1836; Elizabeth I.[? - not a "J"] Lake, born July 19th. 1841; and Wesley Lake, born May 8th. 1846.
In Testimony etc. Isaac Nesbitt, Clk   July 23d. 1853

African American Manumissions

B122b State of Maryland, Washington County, Towit:
I, Isaac Nesbitt, Clerk of the Circuit Court for said County, do hereby certify to all whom it doth or may concern, that the bearer hereof, Jeremiah Colbert, a negro man, was born free, as it hath been satisfactorily proven to me. The said Jeremiah Colbert, is now in the 22d. year of his age; is five feet, six and a half inches high; has a scar on the left side of the forehead, and complexion tolerably black. In Testimony whereof etc.   Isaac   Nesbitt, Clk   July 29th. 1853.

B123a State of Maryland, Washington County, Towit:
I, Isaac Nesbitt, Clerk of the Circuit Court for said County, do hereby certify to all whom it doth or may concern, that it hath been satisfactorily proven to me, that the bearer hereof, a negro woman, named Ann Thompson, was born free. She is now about 34 years of age; is five feet and one fourth of an inch high; has a scar on the right arm, and complexion quite black.
In Testimony whereof etc. Isaac Nesbitt, Clk   July 29 1853.

B123b State of Maryland, Washington County, Towit:
I, Isaac Nesbitt, Clerk of the Circuit Court for said County, do hereby certify to all whom it doth or may concern, that it hath been satisfactorily proven to me, that the bearer hereof, a negro woman, named Rachael Gates, was born free. Her age is now about 26 years; is five feet four inches in height; has a scar on the right hand above the thumb; complexion tolerably black, or rather of a dark copper color.   In Testimony whereof etc.
Isaac Nesbitt, Clk   July 29th. 1853.
She has a child named Ann Elizabeth in her 5th year.

B123c State of Maryland, Washington County, Towit:
I, Isaac Nesbitt, Clerk of the Circuit Court for said County, do hereby certify to all whom it doth or may concern, that it hath been satisfactorily proven to me, that the bearer hereof, a negro girl named Catharine Colbert, was born free. She is now about eighteen years of age; is four feet ten inches high; has a scar on the right arm, with a tolerably black complexion.
In Testimony etc. Isaac Nesbitt, Clk   July 29th 1853.

B124a State of Maryland, Washington County, Towit:
I, Isaac Nesbitt, Clerk of the Circuit Court for said County, do hereby certify to all whom it doth or may concern, that the bearer

of Washington County, Maryland

hereof, James Edward Verner, was born free, as hath been satisfactorily proven to me by competent testimony; he being the son of Hannah Verner, who was manumitted by Z. Clagett, as is show by reference to Liber GG, folio 513, one of the Land Records of my office. The said James Edward Verner is now 26 years of age; is six feet two inches high; has a long scar on his forehead, and also one on his right arm near to the wrist. His complexion is yellow, or light copper, and is well formed.
In Testimony whereof etc. Isaac Nesbitt, Clk   August   9th. 1853.

B124b State of Maryland, Washington County, Towit:
I, Isaac Nesbitt, Clerk of the Circuit Court for said County, do hereby certify to all whom it doth or may concern, that the bearer hereof, Mary Ellen Winkley, a negro woman, was born free, as has been satisfactorily proven to me by proper evidence; she being the daughter of Mary Winkley who was manumitted by Philip Reeder [sic] on the 6 June 1826, as by reference to the Land Records of my office will appear. The said Mary Ellen, will be 20 years of age on the 14 of Sept. 1853, 4 feet 11 1/2 inches high, has a good countenance, stout built, dark complexion with no marks perceptible about her.
In Testy. etc. Isaac Nesbitt, Clk August 31st. 1853.

B125a State of Maryland, Washington County, Towit:
I, Isaac Nesbitt, Clerk of the Circuit Court for said County, do hereby certify to all whom it doth or may concern, that the bearer hereof, a negro woman named Mary Bell, was sold and conveyed by a certain William Wellmore, of Baltimore County, to a certain Joseph Crowl, to serve as a slave until the 30th day of May, 1851, as will appear by a Bill of sale duly acknowledged and recorded in Liber K.K. folios 506 and 507, one of the Land Records of my office, and that she is now free. The said Mary Bell is now 32 years of age, 4 feet 11 inches high; has a mark on her right wrist, and one on the left temple; is stout built, and tolerably black. She has at this time 3 children: Lucretia, in the 8th year of her age; Eliza Jane, born December 9th. 1848; and Isabella, born October 6th. 1852; - the two former to be slaves until they respectively arrive at the age of thirty years, according to the terms of the deed aforesaid.
In Testimony etc. Isaac Nesbitt, Clk   August 31, 1853.

African American Manumissions

B125b State of Maryland, Washington County, Towit:
I, Isaac Nesbitt, Clerk of the Circuit Court for said County, do hereby certify to all whom it doth or may concern, that the bearer hereof, a negro woman, named Nancy Peterson was manumitted & set free by Hannah Porterfield by deed of manumission, dated the 19 day of August 1853, and recorded in Liber I.N. No. 7, folio [blank] one of the Land Records of said County. The said Nancy is about 43 years of age, 5 feet 1 1/2 inches high, has a scar on the left hand and of dark complexion.
In Testimony etc. Isaac Nesbitt, Clk   Sept. 2. 1853.

B126a State of Maryland, Washington County, Towit:
I, Isaac Nesbitt, Clerk of the Circuit Court for said County, do hereby certify to all whom it doth or may concern, that the bearer hereof, a mulatto man, named Isaac Pattengall, was manumitted & set free by Susan Leasure, by deed of Manumission dated the 6 day of September, 1853, recorded in Liber I.N. No. 7 folio [blank]. The said Isaac is about 25 years of age, five feet 4 inches high, has a scar under the left eye, a cut on the second finger of the right hand, the little finger of his right hand crooked, and of a bright mulatto color.
In Testimony whereof etc. Isaac Nesbitt, Clk   September 17th. 1853.

B126b State of Maryland, Washington County, Towit:
I, Isaac Nesbitt, Clerk of the Circuit Court for said County, do hereby certify to all whom it doth or may concern, that the bearer hereof, Thomas Asbury Proctor was born free, as hath been satisfactorily proven to me by competent testimony; he being the son of Edward Proctor. The said Thomas Asbury Proctor is now in his twenty first year; is five feet, three inches high, has a scar on the instep of his right foot; of a dark complexion.   In Testimony whereof etc. Isaac Nesbitt, Clk   September 29th 1853.

B126c State of Maryland, Washington County, Towit:
I, Isaac Nesbitt, Clerk of the Circuit Court for said County, do hereby certify to all whom it doth or may concern, that the bearer hereof, a negro woman, named Chloe Chase, was duly manumitted by Susan Middlekauff, by Deed of Manumission dated July 26, 1850, and recorded in my office, in Liber I.N. No. 5, folio 271, one of the Land Records of said county. The said

of Washington County, Maryland

Chloe Chase is 4 feet, 10 inches high; has a scar on the back of the right hand, and quite black; age now about thirty three years. In Testimony whereof etc.   Isaac Nesbitt, Clk   October 1st. 1853.

B127a   State of Maryland, Washington County, Towit:
I, Isaac Nesbitt, Clerk of the Circuit Court for said County, do hereby certify to all whom it doth or may concern, that the bearer hereof, a negro man named Jeremiah Pye was born free, as has been proven to me by satisfactory testimony. The said Jeremiah is about 25 years of age, 6 feet 1/4 inch high, has a scar on the left cheek, of rather light complexion, good countenance, and slim[?] make.
In Testimony etc.,   Test: Isaac Nesbitt, Clk   Oct. 11. 1853.

B127b   State of Maryland, Washington County, Towit:
I hereby certify, as Clerk of the Circuit Court for said County, that the bearer hereof, a negro man, named Jonathan Hager Pye was born free, as has been satisfactorily proven to me. The said Jonathan Hager is about 23 years of age, 5 feet 8 1/4 inches high, has a mole on the left side of his neck, light copper complexion, well made and a good countenance.
In Testimony etc. Test: Isaac Nesbitt, Clk   Oct. 11. 1853.

B128a   State of Maryland, Washington County, Towit:
I, Isaac Nesbitt, Clerk of the Circuit Court for said County, do hereby certify to all whom it doth or may concern, that the bearer hereof, a negro woman named Mary Ellen Harper was manumitted & set free on the 14. day of October 1853 by Samuel Craig, by deed of Manumission recorded in Liber I.N. No. [blank] one of the Land Records of said County, to which reference is made. The said Mary Ellen is now about 24 years of age, 5 feet 2 inches high, has a scar on the back of the left hand, stout built and of tolerably black complexion.
In Testimony, etc. Isaac Nesbitt, Clk   Oct. 14. 1853.

B128b   State of Maryland, Washington County, Towit:
I, Isaac Nesbitt, Clerk of the Circuit Court for said County, do hereby certify to all whom it doth or may concern, that the bearer hereof, a negro boy, named David B. Sammons, was manumitted & set free on the 20 day of October 1853, by Benjamin Sammons, by deed of Manumission recorded in Liber I.N. No. 8   [blank space where folio should be] one of the Land Records of said

African American Manumissions

County, to which reference is made. The said David B. Sammons is now about 21 years of age, 5 feet 7 1/4 inches high, has a mole on his right hip, stout built, and of a light complexion. In Testimiony, etc. Isaac Nesbitt, Clk   October 20th, 1853

B129a   State of Maryland, Washington County, Towit:
I, Isaac Nesbitt, Clerk of the Circuit Court for said County, do hereby certify to all whom it doth or may concern, that the bearer hereof, a negro man named Peter Sophus was manumitted and set free by Mrs. Catharine Ridenour by Deed dated the 1st day of April 1854, and recorded in Liber I.N. No. 8, one of the Land Records of said County, reference thereto being had will more fully appear. The said Peter is now 27 years of age, five feet 7 1/2 inches high, has a scar on the back of the right hand and dark complexion.
Test: Isaac Nesbitt, Clk April 3d. 1854.

B129b   State of Maryland, Washington County, Towit:
I, Isaac Nesbitt, Clerk of the Circuit Court for said County, do hereby certify to all whom it doth or may concern, that the bearer hereof, a negro man, named Samuel Williams, was manumitted and set free by John Ingram by Deed dated the 6th. day of April 1854, and recorded in Liber I.N. No. 8, one of the Land Records of said County, reference thereto being had will more fully appear. The said Samuel is now thirty five years of age, five feet, five inches high, has scars under[?] each[?] Jaw and dark complexion.
In Testimony etc.   Test: Isaac Nesbitt, Clk   [no date]

B129c   State of Maryland, Washington County, Towit:
I, Isaac Nesbitt, Clerk of the Circuit Court for said County, do hereby certify to all whom it doth or may concern, that the bearer hereof, a negro man, named William Turner, was manumitted and set free by a certain Jacob Turner by Deed of Manumission dated the fourth day of August 1845, and recorded in Liber I.N. No. 1, folio 255 & 256, one of the Land Records of said County, reference to which is hereby made. The said William is about 33 years of age, five feet eight inches high, a little cross-eyed, has a scar on the right arm above the wrist, caused by a scald and is very black.
Test: Isaac Nesbitt, Clk April 24. 1854.

of Washington County, Maryland

B130a State of Maryland, Washington County, Towit:
I, Isaac Nesbitt, Clerk of the Circuit Court for said County, do hereby certify to all whom it doth or may concern, that the bearer hereof, a negro woman, named Milly Winkly, was manumitted and set free by a certain Philip Reeder by Deed of Manumission dated the 4th day of March 1837, and recorded in Liber I.I folio, 582 one of the Land Records of said county, reference to which is hereby made. The said Milly is about sixty four years of age, five feet 5 1/8 inches high, of a light colour.
In Testimony etc.   Test: Isaac Nesbitt, Clk
    April 29th. 1854

B130b State of Maryland, Washington County, Towit:
I, Isaac Nesbitt, Clerk of the Circuit Court for said County, do hereby certify to all whom it doth or may concern, that it hath been satisfactorily proven to me, that the bearer hereof, a colored girl, named Margaret Goings, was born free. She is now about twenty one years of age; is five feet five inches high; well formed; has a scar on her right arm, below the elbow; another scar on the left arm above the wrist; another scar on the forefinger of the left hand; and also one on the forehead, above the right eye of a dark copper complexion.
In Testimony etc. Isaac Nesbitt, Clk   May 1st. 1854.

B130c State of Maryland, Washington County, Towit:
I, Isaac Nesbitt, Clerk of the Circuit Court for said County, do hereby certify to all whom it doth or may concern, that the bearer hereof, a negro woman named Jennie Goens was manumitted and set free by Mrs. Susan Rench, by Deed dated the 29. day of May 1854, and recorded in Liber I.N. No. 8, one of the Land Records of said County, to which reference is hereby made. The said Jennie is about 43 years of age, 5 feet 1 1/2 inches high, of delicate form, has a small scar on the right side of her forehead, and of very dark complexion.
In Testy. etc.   Test: Isaac Nesbitt, Clk May 29. 1854

B131a State of Maryland, Washington County, Towit:
I, Isaac Nesbitt, Clerk of the Circuit Court for said County, do hereby certify to all whom it doth or may concern, that the bearer hereof, a negro woman, named Harriet Nimmy, is entitled to her freedom, - she having been manumitted by a certain John Hershey, as appears by the Records of my office. Said Harriet is

African American Manumissions

now 28 years of age; is four feet eleven inches high, (scant;) has a scar on the knuckle of the forefinger of the right hand, slight in person, with a very dark or black complexion.
In Testimony etc. Isaac Nesbitt, Clk   May 29th. 1854.

B131b   State of Maryland, Washington County, Towit:
I, Isaac Nesbitt, Clerk of the Circuit Court for said County, do hereby certify to all whom it doth or may concern, that the bearer hereof, a negro woman, named Emily Marshall, was manumitted an set free by James Tenant by Deed of Manumission, dated the 2nd. day of June 1854, and recorded in Liber I.N. No. 8, one of the Land Records of said County, to which reference is hereby made. The said Emily is about 31 years of age, five feet 1/2 an inch high has a front tooth out of the upper jaw, and projecting a little over the lower teeth when she laughs, and is of very dark complexion.
In Testimony etc. Isaac Nesbitt, Clk   June 2. 1854.

B132a   State of Maryland, Washington County, Towit:
I, Isaac Nesbitt, Clerk of the Circuit Court for said County, do hereby certify to all whom it doth or may concern, that the bearer hereof, a negro man, named Mark Marshall, was manumitted & set free by James Tenant by Deed of Manumission dated the 11th day of November 1850, and recorded in Liber I.N. No. 8, one of the Land Records of said County, to which reference is made. The said Mark is about 33 years of age, 5 feet 7 1/2 inches high, has a scar on the left hand near the thumb, and is of very dark complexion.
In Testimony etc. Isaac Nesbitt, Clk   June 2. 1854.

B132b   State of Maryland, Washington County, Towit:
I, Isaac Nesbitt, Clerk of the Circuit Court for said County, do hereby certify to all whom it doth or may concern, that the bearer hereof, a negro man named George Harrison was duly manumitted by Richard Harrison, on the 21st day of October, 1853, as it doth appear by reference to Liber I.N. No. 8, folio 199, one of the Land records of said county. The said George is five feet six inches high; has a small scar between the eye-brows; has suffered the loss of a small piece of the forefinger of his left hand; is in person thin, or spare, and complexion quite black.
In Testimony etc. Isaac Nesbitt, Clk   June 3d. 1854.

of Washington County, Maryland

B132c State of Maryland, Washington County, Towit:
I, Isaac Nesbitt, Clerk of the Circuit Court for said County, do hereby certify to all whom it doth or may concern, that the bearer hereof, a negro woman named Charlotte Chesley, formerly Charlotte Blake, was duly manumitted by Mrs. Eve Moudy by Deed of Manumission dated the 12th. day of February 1838, and recorded in Liber F.F. folio 266, one of the Land Records of said County, to which reference is hereby made. The said Charlotte Chesley is five feet, one & a quarter inches high, very dark complexion.
In Testimony etc. Isaac Nesbitt, Clk [no date]

B133a State of Maryland, Washington County, Towit:
I, Isaac Nesbitt, Clerk of the Circuit Court for said County, do hereby certify to all whom it doth or may concern, that the bearer hereof, a negro woman, named Lucinda Jones is free, having been born free as has been satisfactorily proven tome. The said Lucinda is about 22 years of age, five feet three & one half inches high, has a scar on the right cheek, and on the same side under the jaw bone, and very dark complexion.
Test: Isaac Nesbitt, Clk Sept. 4. 1854.

B133b State of Maryland, Washington County, Towit:
I, Isaac Nesbitt, Clerk of the Circuit Court for said County, do hereby certify to all whom it doth or may concern, that the bearer hereof, a negro woman, named Louisa Davis, formerly Louisa Carn [or Caru?], is free as has been proven to me on the oath of Thomas Watkins & other testimony satisfactory. The said Louisa has 5 children, whose names & ages are as follow: Margaret Rebecca aged 12 years; Catharine Jane, aged 10 years; Mary Louisa, aged 9 years; Columbus, aged 6 years; and Ellen Lavinia, aged 11 months & 26 days. The said Louisa is about 29 years of age, 5 feet 5 1/2 inches high, has a scar on the back of her right hand, and of rather dark complexion.
Test: Isaac Nesbitt, Clk Sept. 26, 1854

B134a State of Maryland, Washington County, Towit:
I, Isaac Nesbitt, Clerk of the Circuit Court for said County, do hereby certify to all whom it doth or may concern, that the bearer hereof, a negro man named Joseph Young Boyer, is a free man, having been born free, as it hath been satisfactorily proven to me. He is now in the 22d. year of his age; is five feet four inches high;

African American Manumissions

stout built; has two scars on the back of the left hand; and is of a dark copper or yellowish complexion.
In Testimony etc. Isaac Nesbitt, Clk   October 11th. 1854.

B134b   State of Maryland, Washington County, Towit:
Circuit Court it hath been satisfactorily proven to me that the bearer hereof, a negro man named John Robert Henry, was born free. He is twenty four years of age; five feet seven inches high; has a scar over the left eyebrow; and tolerably high cheek bones, and complexion quite black.
In Testimony whereof I hereunto subscribe my name, and affix the seal of said Court this 13th. day of October, A.D. 1854.
     Isaac Nesbitt, Clk

B134c   State of Maryland, Washington County, Towit:
I, Isaac Nesbitt, Clerk of the Circuit Court for said County, do hereby certify to all whom it doth or may concern, that the bearer hereof, Joseph H. Cole, a negro man, who applies for a certificate of his freedom, was born free, as it that been satisfactorily proven to me on the oath of Samuel Brumbaugh. The said Joseph is now twenty our years of age; is five feet nine inches high; has a small scar on the right cheek, about 1 1/2 inches from the eye; also a small scar near the right corner of the mouth; and another over the left eye brow. She is tolerably black and has a good countenance.
In Testimony whereof, I hereunto subscribe my name, and affix the seal of said Circuit Court this 16th day of October A.D. 1854.
     Isaac Nesbitt, Clk

B135a   State of Maryland, Washington County, Towit:
I, Isaac Nesbitt, Clerk of the Circuit Court for said County, do hereby certify to all whom it doth or may concern, that it hath been satisfactorily proven to me, that the bearer hereof, a negro girl named Mary Colbert, was born free. She is [blank] of age; four feet, eleven inches high; has a scar on the right side of her upper lip, and of a dark mulatto complexion.
In Testimony etc. Isaac Nesbitt, Clk   November 29th. 1854

B135b   State of Maryland, Washington County, Towit:
I, Isaac Nesbitt, Clerk of the Circuit Court, for said County, do hereby certify, to all whom it doth or may concern, that it hath been satisfactorily proven to me by Milton M. Claggett, that the

FOR SALE,

A NEGRO WOMAN about 22 years of age—and her two children. Price $300. Enquire at this Office.

January 20   13-6w

Hagerstown Newspapers

Washington County Manumission

State of Maryland, Washington County to wit

I hereby certify that Sarah Butler hath taken me by her own oath that Celia Butler the bearer hereof who applies for this Certificate, is free born and of free condition, that she was born in St Mary's County in the State of Maryland, and hath resided in Washington County about fourteen years, said Celia Butler is about four feet two inches high, about twenty four years of age, of a dark complexion, no noted marks.

Certificate given the 13th day of August 1806

Test   A H Williams

Isaac Nesbitt 1845-1865

Otho H. Williams, Jr., Clerk of the Court 1800 - 1845

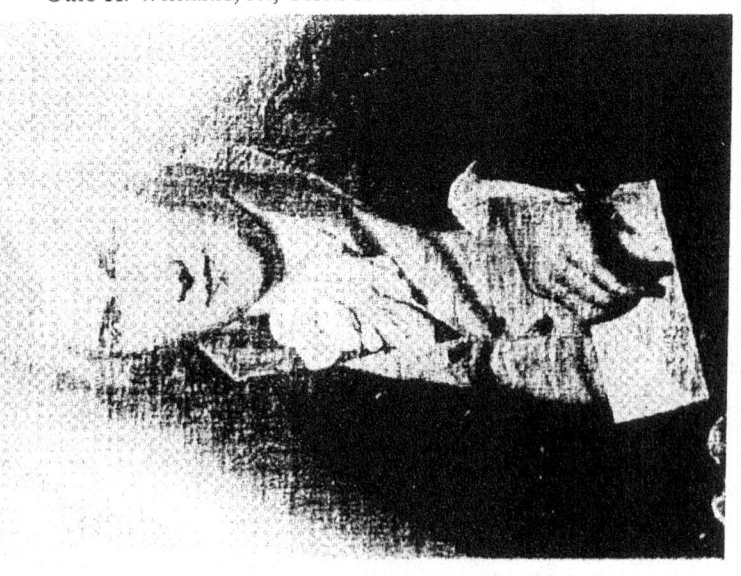

of Washington County, Maryland

bearer hereof, a negro man named John Henry Duckett, was born free, he is 22 years of age, five feet, ten inches high; of a dark complexion. Has a scar on the nose.
In Testimony etc. Isaac Nesbitt, Clk March [no day or year]

B135c State of Maryland, Washington County, Towit:
[This entire entry has been crossed out.]
I, Isaac Nesbitt, Clerk of the Circuit Court for said County, do hereby certify to all whom it doth or may concern, that the bearer hereof, a negro man named Madison Goings, was duly manumitted by Mrs. Susan E. Rench, on the 29th day of March, 1856. The said Madison is five feet six inches high, has a scar on the back of the right hand & on the third finger of

B136a State of Maryland, Washington County, Towit:
I, Isaac Nesbitt, Clerk of the Circuit Court for said County, do hereby certify to all whom it doth or may concern, that the bearer hereof, a mulatto woman named Frances Wagoner, (formerly Frances Paca,) was duly manumitted by Stephen Paca, her Grand Father, by whom she was purchased from the mother of Richard T. Holliday, as appears by his certificate. The said Deed of Manumission was duly executed and recorded the day of the date hereof. The said Frances is 5 feet 2 inches high, aged about 19 years; and is a bright mulatto, and has a scar or mark of a burn on the right arm above the elbow.
In Testimony whereof etc.   Isaac Nesbitt, Clk
April 23d. 1855.

B136b State of Maryland, Washington County, Towit:
I, Isaac Nesbitt, Clerk of the Circuit Court for said county do hereby certify that the bearer hereof, Isabella Jackson, a negro woman, was sold by George Feidt to Tobias Johnson for a term of years which has now expired, as will appear by a deed of bargain and sale, duly executed and recorded in Liber I.N. No. 9, folio 303, one of the Land Records of said county; and the said Johnson is willing that a certificate of freedom shall issue according to law, to the said Isabella Jackson. Therefore I hereby certify that said Isabella Jackson is a free woman; she is five feet two and a half inches high, and has two small moles or spots near the right eye, in the region of the temple; complexion brown or copper color.   In Testimony whereof etc.   Isaac Nesbitt, Clk   May 28th. 1855.

African American Manumissions

B137a
[The following entry has been crossed out]
I, Isaac Nesbitt, Clerk of the Circuit Court for said county, do hereby certify that it appears from a Deed of Manumission duly executed and filed in my office this day for record, that

B137b State of Maryland, Washington County, Towit:
I, Isaac Nesbitt, Clerk of the Circuit Court for said county, do hereby certify that the bearer hereof, Mahala Crew, a negro woman, is free, - she having been duly manumitted by deed bearing even date with these presents, and executed by a certain Isaac B. Rowland, and now of file in my office for record. The said Mahala Crew being about the age of thirty two years, is five feet four inches high; tolerably black, with temples very much sunken.
       In Testimony whereof I hereunto subscribe my name etc.
Isaac Nesbitt, Clk   August 20. 1855.

B137c State of Maryland, Washington County, Towit:
I, Isaac Nesbitt, Clerk of the Circuit Court for said County, do hereby certify, that the bearer hereof, Matthias Hanson, a negro man, was duly manumitted by Esther Brisco, his mother, by her purchased from Joel Newcomer, as appears by a Bill of Sale duly recorded. The said Deed of Manumission was duly executed and recorded the day of the date thereof. The said Matthias Hanson being about the age of thirty one years, is five feet, seven and an half inches high, tolerably black, a scar on the left arm near the wrist.
In Testimony whereof, I hereunto subscribe my name etc. Isaac Nesbitt, Clk   September 11th. 1855.

B138a State of Maryland, Washington County, Towit:
I, Isaac Nesbitt, Clerk of the Circuit Court for said County, do hereby certify, to all whom it doth or may concern, that the bearer hereof, a negro girl, named Ann Maria Henson, was duly manumitted by Henrietta Gaither, by deed dated May 23d. 1853, and recorded in my office, September 26th. 1853. The said Ann Maria is about 21 years of age; 5 feet and 2 inches high; complexion quite black; with scars on the left arm.
In Testimony etc. Isaac Nesbitt, Clk   Oct. 5th. 1855.

of Washington County, Maryland

B138b State of Maryland, Washington County, Towit:
I, Isaac Nesbitt, Clerk of the Circuit Court for said County, do hereby certify to all whom it doth or may concern, that it hath been satisfactorily proven to me, by competent testimony that the bearer hereof, a negro man, named John William Thompson, was born free, and is therefore entitled to this his certificate of Freedom. the said John is five feet three inches high; has a black spot on the right arm above the elbow; complexion quite black; and aged about twenty two years.
In Testimony etc. Isaac Nesbitt, Clk   Oct. 15th. 1855.

B139a State of Maryland, Washington County, Towit:
I, Isaac Nesbitt, Clerk of the Circuit Court for Washington County, hereby certify to all whom it doth or may concern, that it appears from the records of Washington County Court that the bearer hereof, a negro man, named, John White, was duly manumitted and released form slavery, by Deed of manumission dated November 6, 1855, and duly executed and acknowledged by Jacob Dellinger, of said county. The said negro man John is five feet seven and three quarter inches high, and is blind in the left eye.
In Testimony etc. Isaac Nesbitt, Clk [no date]

B139b State of Maryland, Washington County, Towit:
I, Isaac Nesbitt, clerk of the Circuit Court for Washington County, do hereby Certify, to all whom it doth or may concern, that it appears from the records of my office, that the bearer hereof, a negro man named Joseph Blake, was duly manumitted and released from slavery, by Deed of Manumission, dated 11 March 1856, and duly executed and acknowledge by Rev. John Campbell White, of the City of Baltimore, State aforesaid. The said negro man Joseph is five feet nine inches high, has 2 scars on the right hip, Scar over the left eye, and a scar on 3d finger of left hand, of a dark complexion.
In Testimony etc. Isaac Nesbitt, Clk [no date]

B140a State of Maryland, Washington County, Towit:
I, Isaac Nesbitt, Clerk of the Circuit Court for said County, do hereby certify to all whom it doth or may concern, that the bearer hereof, a negro man named Madison Goings, was duly manumitted by Mrs. Susan E. Rench, by deed dated March 29th 1856, and recorded in my Office. The said Madison Goings is

African American Manumissions

about 43 years of age; 5 feet and 6 inches high; complexion quite dark has a scar on the back of the right hand, one on the third finger of the left hand & one above the left eye, with a pleasant countenance.
In Testimony etc. Isaac Nesbitt, Clk   March 29th. 1856

B140b   State of Maryland, Washington County, Towit:
I, Isaac Nesbitt, Clerk of the Circuit Court for said County, do hereby certify to all whom it doth or may concern, that the bearer hereof, a negro man named Jacob Jeffreys, was duly manumitted by Jacob Arms, by deed dated September 4, 1855, and recorded in Liber I.N. No. 9. The said Jacob Jeffreys is about 40 years of age - 5 feet and 6 inches high, complexion quite dark, has a scar on the third finger of his right hand.
In Testimony etc. Isaac Nesbitt, Clk   April 5th. 1856

B141a   State of Maryland, Washington County, Towit:
I, Isaac Nesbitt, Clerk of the Circuit Court for said county of Washington, do hereby certify to all whom it doth or may concern, that it hath been satisfactorily proven to me upon the oath of William Cramer, a white citizen of credibility of said county, that the bearer hereof, named Frisby T. Jenkins, was born free. He is a bright Mulatto, now about 24 years of age; is 5 feet 6 inches in height; ["complexion a bright" crossed out] and has two small scars on the back of his neck, and a large one on the left leg below the knee. He is stout built and likely.
In Testimony whereof etc. Isaac Nesbitt, Clk   May 29th. 1856

B141b   State of Maryland, Washington County, Towit:
I, Isaac Nesbitt, Clerk of the Circuit Court for said County of Washington, do hereby certify, that the bearer hereof, a negro man named John Fletcher was duly manumitted by Mrs. Martha Huyett, Sarah & Julianna Gaither, by Deed of Manumission, dated 20 June 1856, and recorded in my Office. The said John Fletcher is about fifty three years of age, 5 feet, 9 1/2 inches high; complexion quite dark, has a scar on the second joint of the thumb on right hand, little finger of the right hand crooked.
In Testimony whereof etc. Isaac Nesbitt, Clk   June 21th 185 [full year not given]

B141c   State of Maryland, Washington County, Towit:

of Washington County, Maryland

I, Isaac Nesbitt, Clerk of the Circuit Court for said County of Washington, do hereby certify, that the bearer hereof, a negro woman named Mary Dickerson, was duly manumitted by Mrs. Martha Huyett, Sarah & Juliann Gaither, by Deed of Manumission, dated 7th day of June 1856, and recorded in my Office. The said Mary Dickerson is about forty three years of age, 5 feet, 6 inches in height, of a dark complexion, has a scar on her breast.
In Testimony whereof etc. Isaac Nesbitt, Clk   June 21st, 1856

B142a   State of Maryland, Washington County, Towit:
I, Isaac Nesbitt, Clerk of the Circuit Court for said County, do hereby certify to all whom it doth or may concern, that the bearer hereof, a negro woman named Lucy Young, was duly manumitted by Samuel Mumma, by Deed of Manumission dated 23. day of September A.D. 1856. The said Lucy Young is about 28 years of age, five feet, 5 inches high, complexion dark, blind in the right eye, and has a wart in the palm of her left hand.
In Testimony whereof etc. Isaac Nesbitt, Clk   October   7th. 1856.

B142b   State of Maryland, Washington County, Towit:
I, Isaac Nesbitt, Clerk of the Circuit Court for said County, do hereby certify to all whom it doth or may concern, that the bearer hereof, a negro man, named John Henry Goens, hath been satisfactorily proved to me upon the testimony of Doct. Clagett Dorsey, a white citizen of credibility of said County, that the bearer hereof, was born free. He is a bright mulatto, now about 22 years of age, five feet, 6 3/4 inches in height, and has a scar on the left hand, & end of first finger bent on same hand.
In Testimony whereof etc. Isaac Nesbitt, Clk   October   7th 1856

B143a   State of Maryland, Washington County, Towit:
I, Isaac Nesbitt, Clerk of the Circuit Court for said County, do hereby certify to all whom it doth or may concern, that the bearer hereof, a negro man named Samuel Williams, was duly manumitted by Miss Catharine Shearer, by Deed of Manumission dated 12 day of December 1826, & recorded in Liber I.I. folios 294 & 295, and recorded in my Office. The said Samuel Williams is about 42 years of age, 5 feet, 7 inches in

height, complexion dark, has a scar on the right leg below the knee, and one on the left leg above the knee, walks a little lame.
In Testimony whereof etc. Isaac Nesbitt, Clk   December 10th. 1856.

B143b I, Isaac Nesbitt, Clerk of the Circuit Court for said County, do hereby certify to all whom it doth or may concern, that it hath been satisfactorily proven to me, that the bearer hereof Catharine Washington, a negro woman, was born free. She is four feet eight inches in hight;[sic] aged 22 years on the 3d day of October last; has several small scars on the forehead, and one on the right cheek bone; complexion a yellow or light brown. She has a mulatto child whom she calls Mary Catharine, born December 20th, 1855.
In Testimony whereof etc. Isaac Nesbitt, Clk   January   2nd 1857

B143c State of Maryland, Washington County, Towit:
I, Isaac Nesbitt, Clerk of the Circuit Court for said County, do hereby certify to all whom it doth or may concern, that the bearer hereof, a negro man named Abraham Howard, was duly manumitted by James A. Magruder, by deed dated this 17th day of February, 1857, and same day recorded in my Office. The said Abrahm is about 44 years of age, five feet, nine inches high, and complexion quite black; with two scars on the knuckles of his left hand.
In Testimony, etc. Isaac Nesbitt, Clk   February, 17th 1857.

B144a State of Maryland, Washington County, Towit:
I, Isaac Nesbitt, Clerk of the Circuit Court in and for said county, do hereby certify to all whom it doth or may concern, that the bearer hereof, a negro man, named Stephen Anderson, was duly manumitted and set free by Mary Ann Grimes, by Deed of Manumission dated the 13th day of January 1857, and now of record in my office. Said Stephen is about 42 years of age; is 5 feet 5 inches high; has lost a front tooth; and in complexion tolerably black, and is bald.
In Testimony etc. Isaac Nesbitt, Clk   Jany. 17th 1857.

B144b State of Maryland, Washington County, Towit:
I, Isaac Nesbitt, Clerk of the Circuit Court for said County, do hereby certify to all whom it doth or may concern, that the bearer

List of Negro Clothing

1858			$	cts
Jan 21	To Julius Arnold Thread and buttons		0	20
" 30	" Mr. Myers for Charles one Cap — — —		0	50
Mar 23	" Mrs. George for knitting 4 pair of socks		2	25
" 23	" Dr. Finy for Medical services rendered		5	00
dec. 3	" Mrs. Lovatt for Making 4 dresses Mama Susan		2	00
" 3	" Small " Making Morris 1 pair pants		0	62½
" 3	" Small " Making Morris one Red		0	50
" 3	" Small " Making Eli 1 pair pants		0	62½
" 3	" Small " Making Tom 1 pair pants		0	50
" 3	" Small " Making Morris 2 Shirts		0	75
" 3	" Small " Making Eli 2 Shirts		0	75
" 3	" Small " Making Tom 2 Shirts		0	50

Nesbit Diary, Clear Spring, Maryland, Copy in Collection of Marguerite Doleman

Maryland, Washington County, ss:

I, O. H. Williams, clerk of Washington County Court, hereby certify that, to all whom it may concern — that it appears from the records of Washington County Court that the bearer hereof William B. Norris is a freeman, having been manumitted by a certain Andrew Harover, by deed of Manumission, bearing date the day of _____ and duly recorded in Liber A. H. W. N. 2. one of the Land Records of said County. The said William, is a negro, of the age of twenty six years on the sixth day of March next, is five feet seven inches high, and of rather a light complexion.

Test: O. H. Williams, Clk.

December 31st 1814

William B. Norris

hereof, a negro man, named John Williams, has satisfactorily proven to me that he was born free. He is five feet three inches high, has a scar on the left cheekbone, and some two or three marks or scars on his forehead above the right eyebrow; he is thick set, and tolerably black.   In Testimony whereof etc. Isaac Nesbitt, Clk   March 6th, 1857.

B145a   State of Maryland, Washington County, Towit:
I, Isaac Nesbitt, Clerk of the Circuit Court for said County, do hereby certify to all whom it doth or may concern, that the bearer hereof, a negro man, named Horatio Adley has been satisfactorily proven tome, that he was born free. He is five feet five & three quarter inches high, has a scar or mark on the second finger of the left hand, twenty two years of age, a dark mulatto & has curly hair.
In Testimony etc. Isaac Nesbitt, Clk   March 24th 1857.

B145b   State of Maryland, Washington County, Towit:
I, Isaac Nesbitt, Clerk of the Circuit Court for said County, do hereby certify to all whom it doth or may concern, that the bearer hereof, a negro man, named Dennis Lewis, was duly manumitted and set free by Mrs. Eliza Davis, by deed of manumission, dated the 14 day of April 1857, and now of record in my office. Said Dennis is about 28 years of age; is five feet, nine inches high; dark colored, with a mark on the side of each little finger, showing that he had thereon, an odd finger.
In Testimony etc. Isaac Nesbitt, Clk   April 14th 1857

B146a   State of Maryland, Washington County, Towit:
I, Isaac Nesbitt, Clerk of the Circuit Court for said County, do hereby certify to all whom it doth or may concern, that the bearer hereof, Henry Turner, a negro man, was duly manumitted from slavery by John S. Bowles, by Deed of Manumission duly executed and recorded according to law. The said deed having been acknowledge on the 12th day of June, 1857, and recorded the day of the date hereof. The said Henry is 5 feet 5 inches high, with a small scar on the forehead, is about 34 years of age, and of a very black complexion.
In Testimony whereof etc. Isaac Nesbitt, Clk   June 20, 1857.

African American Manumissions

B146b State of Maryland, Washington County, Towit:
I, Isaac Nesbitt, Clerk of the Circuit Court for said County, do hereby certify to all whom it doth or may concern, that the bearer hereof, a negro man, named Hercules Turner, was duly manumitted from slavery by John S. Bowles, by Deed of Manumission executed and acknowledged the 12th day of June, 1857, and recorded on the day of the date hereof, according to law. The said Hercules is 5 feet 5 1/4 inches high, has a scar over each eye, and has bad or decayed front teeth; - complexion very black; aged about 38 years. In Testimony whereof & C Isaac Nesbitt, Clk   June 20th, 1857.

B147a State of Maryland, Washington County, Towit:
I, Isaac Nesbitt, Clerk of the Circuit Court for said County, do hereby certify to all whom it doth or may concern, that the bearer hereof, a colored woman named Charity Ellen Caution, is a free woman, having been duly manumitted by deed dated October 17, 1835, by Samuel Lake, her father, and recorded in Liber R.R. folio 264. The said Charity Ellen was born the 16th day of June, 1818; is 5 feet 2 inches high; has the mark of a felon on the thumb of the right hand. She has the following children: Joshua, born April 7, 1844; Mary Martha, born March 20, 1846; John Lake, born February 11th, 1850; Catharine, born October 12th, 1852; and Louisa Ellen, born 13th day of December, 1856.
In Testimony whereof etc. Isaac Nesbitt, Clk   June 25th, 1857.

B147b State of Maryland, Washington County, Towit:
I, Isaac Nesbitt, Clerk of the Circuit Court for said County, do hereby certify to all whom it doth or may concern, that the bearer hereof, a colored woman, named Susan Trueman, is a free woman, - she having been duly manumitted by her father, Samuel Lake, by deed duly executed, acknowledged, and recorded in Liber RR, folio 264, on the 17th day of October, 1835. The said Susan was born the 8th August, 1828, and is 5 feet 2 1/4 inches high, of a yellow complexion, without any visible marks. She has the following children: Isabella aged about 7 years; John Matthew, aged about 6 years; Mary Elizabeth, aged about 5 years; Samuel Lake, aged about 2 years; and Joseph Lake aged about one year.
In Testimony whereof etc. Isaac Nesbitt, Clk
June 25th, 1857.

of Washington County, Maryland

B148a State of Maryland, Washington County, Towit:
I, Isaac Nesbitt, Clerk of the Circuit Court for said County, do hereby certify to all whom it doth or may concern, that the bearer hereof, a colored girl, named Louisa Lake was born free, - she being the daughter of Mary Lake, manumitted by Samuel Lake, by Deed of Manumission duly made and executed the 17th day of October, 1835, and recorded in Liber RR, folio 264, one of the Land Records of said county. The said Louisa was born the 24th day of July, 1838; is five feet three & 1/2 inches high; of a yellowish complexion, and of likely personal appearance.
       In Testimony whereof etc.   I saac Nesbitt, Clk   June 25th, 1857

B148b State of Maryland, Washington County, Towit:
I, Isaac Nesbitt, Clerk of the Circuit Court for said County, do hereby certify to all whom it doth or may concern, that the bearer hereof, a negro woman, named Sally Brown, was duly manumitted from slavery by William Dellinger and Christiana Dellinger, by deed of manumission, executed and acknowledge the 3d day of June 1857, and recorded in Liber I.N. No. 12, on the 28th July 1857. The said Sally is 5 feet 1 1/2 inches high, dark complexion and about 44 years of age.
In Testimony whereof etc. Isaac Nesbitt, Clk   Sept. 2nd. 1857.

B149a State of Maryland, Washington County, Towit:
I, Isaac Nesbitt, Clerk of the Circuit Court for said County, do hereby certify to all whom it doth or may concern, that the bearer hereof, Nancy Watts, was duly manumitted and set free by the late Col. William H. Fitzhugh, by Deed of Manumission bearing date the 10th day of March, 1842, and recorded in Liber ZZ, folio 42, one of the Land Records of said county. The said Nancy Watts is now about thirty seven years of age; is five feet one and a half inches high; has a small scar in her right eyebrow; and of a bright yellow complexion.
In Testimony whereof etc. Isaac Nesbitt, Clk   December 29th, 1857.

B149b State of Maryland, Washington County, Towit:
I, Isaac Nesbitt, Clerk of the Circuit Court for said County, do hereby certify to all whom it doth or may concern, that the bearer hereof, Lucy Lynch, a negro woman, was duly manumitted by J.[?] Campbell White, by deed of Manumission properly

African American Manumissions

executed, acknowledged, and this day recorded in my office. The said Lucy Lynch is now about 32 or 33 years of age; five feet, two & a half inches high; with no perceptible marks, and of a yellowish complexion.
In Testimony whereof etc. Isaac Nesbitt, Clk   February 10th, 1858,

B149c State of Maryland, Washington County, Towit:
I hereby certify to all whom it doth or may concern, that the bearer hereof, Isaac Nesbitt, Clerk of the Circuit Court for said County, do hereby certify to all whom it doth or may concern, that it hath been satisfactorily proven to me, that the bearer hereof, a negro man, named John Duckett, was born free, and is therefore entitled to this his certificate of Freedom. The said John Duckett is five feet, eight & an half inches high, dark complexion & has one scar on the palm of the right hand; near the little finger; and is about 27 years of age.
In Testimony whereof etc. Isaac Nesbitt, Clk   [no date]

B150a State of Maryland, Washington County, Towit:
I, Isaac Nesbitt, Clerk of the Circuit Court for said County, do hereby certify to all whom it doth or may concern, that the bearer hereof, a negro man, named Peter Taylor, was duly manumitted from slavery, by Henry Firey, by deed of Manumission, executed and acknowledge on the 23 day of April 1858 and recorded in Liber I.N. No.[blank] folios [blank]. The said Peter Taylor is about 5 feet. 5 1/4 inches high, Scar on the nose near left eye, caused by a burn, and 2 warts on 1st finger, dark complexion, aged 24 years.
In Testimony whereof etc. Isaac Nesbitt, Clk   April 27th. 1858
    ["Not made out" written in pencil]

B150b State of Maryland, Washington County, Towit:
I, Isaac Nesbitt, Clerk of the Circuit Court, for said County, do hereby certify, to all whom it doth or may concern, that it hath been satisfactorily proven tome, by competent testimony; that the bearer, a negro man named Bartley Holmes, was born free; and is therefore entitled to this his Certificate of Freedom. The said Bartley Holmes is 5 feet, 8 inches high, has a scar on the left arm by the elbow, he is 21 years of age, dark complexion.
In Testimony whereof etc.   Isaac Nesbitt, Clk
April 29. 1858

of Washington County, Maryland

B150c State of Maryland, Washington County, Towit:
I, Isaac Nesbitt, Clerk of the Circuit Court, for said County, do hereby certify, to all whom it doth or may concern, that it hath been satisfactorily proven to me, by competent testimony; that the bearer, a negro man named Martin Holmes, was born free; and is therefore entitled to this his Certificate of Freedom. The said Martin Holmes is 5 feet, 10 inches high; has a scar above the right eye, and one on the instep on the left leg, he is 25 years of age, of a dark complexion.
In Testimony whereof etc.   Isaac Nesbitt, Clk
April 29th. 1858.

B151a State of Maryland, Washington County, Towit:
I, Isaac Nesbitt, Clerk of Washington County Court, do hereby certify that it appears from the records of my office, that the bearer hereof, a negro man, named Arthur Washington was manumitted by Nathaniel Summers, on the 1st day of October, 1845, to serve ten years from that date, as by Deed of Manumission duly acknowledged and recorded in Liber I.N. No. 1 folios 363 & 364, will more fully appear. The aid Arthur is now in the 40th year of his age; is 5 feet 8 inches high; has a small scar near the end of the right eye-brow; also one on the left cheek bone; and one on the right leg above the ankle caused by a cut. His complexion nearly that of copper.
In Testimony whereof I hereunto subscribe my name etc. Isaac Nesbitt, Clk   May 10th, 1858.

B151b State of Maryland, Washington County, Towit:
I, Isaac Nesbitt, Clerk of the Circuit Court in any[?] for said County, do hereby certify to all whom it doth or may concern, that it hath been satisfactorily proven to me, upon the testimony of James Morgan Esquire, that the bearer, a negro woman named Eliza Holmes, was born free, and is therefore entitled to this her Certificate of Freedom. The said Eliza Holmes is 5 feet, 1 1/2 inches high, has a scar on her right wrist, she is 29 years of age, of a light complexion.
In Testimony whereof etc. Isaac Nesbitt, Clk   May 17th 1858.

B152a State of Maryland, Washington County, Towit:
I, Isaac Nesbitt, Clerk of the Circuit Court, for said County, do hereby certify, to all whom it doth or may concern, that it hath been satisfactorily proven to me by competent testimony, that

African American Manumissions

the bearer, a negro girl named Maria Chase, is entitled to this her Certificate of Freedom. The said Maria Chase is four feet, eight inches high; has a scar on her right wrist, of a light complexion, and is 23 years of age.
In Testimony whereof etc.c Isaac Nesbitt, Clk   May 24th, 1858

B152b State of Maryland, Washington County, Towit:
I, Isaac Nesbitt, Clerk of the Circuit Court for said County, do hereby certify to all whom it doth or may concern, that it hath been satisfactorily proven to me, that the bearer hereof, by competent testimony, that the bearer, a negro girl named Sarah Moseley, is entitled to this her Certificate of Freedom. The said Sarah Mosley, is 31 years of age, 5 feet 3 1/2 inches high, has a dark complexion.
In Testimony whereof etc. Isaac Nesbitt, Clk   May 31st, 1858.

B152c State of Maryland, Washington County, Towit:
I, Isaac Nesbitt, Clerk of the Circuit Court for said County, do hereby certify to all whom it doth or may concern, that it hath been satisfactorily proven to me, , by competent testimony, that the bearer hereof a, negro girl, named Amanda/Adamie [? - Adanda or Adamie], was born free, and entitled to this here Certificate of freedom. She is now 28 years of age; five feet four inches in height; has a small scar on her left cheek, and one on her throat, and her right ear is marked by a burn; her complexion a bright copper color; of a good form and likely.
In Testimony whereof I hereunto subscribe my name etc. Isaac Nesbitt, Clk   May 31st, 1858.

B153a State of Maryland, Washington County, Towit:
I, Isaac Nesbitt, Clerk of the Circuit Court for Washington County, do hereby certify that the bearer hereof , a negro man named Samuel Brooks, is free, he having been sold by a certain Jacob Bayer to Jacob T. Towson in the year 1826, to serve until the 1st April 1844; as will appear by reference to Liber H.H. folios 941 & 942, one of the Land Records Books, of Washington County. Also upon the Testimony of W. William Towson, that he is entitled to his free papers. The said Samuel is 43 years of age, 5 feet 7 1/2 inches high; has a scar on the right leg, below the knee; also a scar on the left thigh, and of a dark complexion.

of Washington County, Maryland

In Testimony whereof, I hereunto subscribe my name etc. Isaac Nesbitt, Clk   August 3d. 1858.

B153b   State of Maryland, Washington County, Towit:
I, Isaac Nesbitt, Clerk of the Circuit Court for said County, do hereby certify to all whom it doth or may concern, that it hath been satisfactorily proven to me, , by competent testimony, that the bearer hereof, a negro girl named Ann Sophia Martin formerly Ann Sophia Carey, was born free, and entitled to this her certificate of freedom. She is now 23 years of age; five feet two and a half inches in height; has a scar on the right arm, near the elbow, her complexion a bright copper color.
In Testimony whereof, I hereunto subscribe my name etc. Isaac Nesbitt, Clk   August 6th, 1858.

B154a   State of Maryland, Washington County, Towit:
I, Isaac Nesbitt, Clerk of the Circuit Court for said County, do hereby certify, to all whom it may or doth concern, that it appears from the Records of my office, that the bearer hereof, a negro man named Henry Brooks is free; he having been sold by a certain Jacob Bayer to Jacob T. Towson Esq. in the year 1826, to serve until the 1st. April 1846; as will appear by reference to Liber H.H. folios 941 & 942, one of the Land Records of Washington County. Also upon the testimony of W. William T. Towson, that he is entitled to his free papers. The said Henry Brooks is 41 years of age, 5 feet 10 inches in height; has a scar on his left foot, and one above the left eye; and of a dark complexion.
In Testimony whereof, I hereunto subscribe my name, etc. Isaac Nesbitt, Clk   August 7th, 1858.

B154b   State of Maryland, Washington County, Towit:
I, Isaac Nesbitt, Clerk of the Circuit Court for said County, do hereby certify, to all whom it may or doth concern, that it appears from the Records of my office, that the bearer hereof, a negro man named Thomas Mills was manumitted by Mrs. Mary Schnebly on the 1st day of June 1858; and Deed of Manumission recorded in Liber I.N. No. 13, folios 197 & 198. The said Thomas is now in his 27th year of his age, is 5 feet 4 inches high, has a scar on his right shoulder; also one on the right side of his head, a small scar near his left ear, and one on the inside of his left leg. His complexion of a copper color.

African American Manumissions

In Testimony whereof, I hereunto subscribe my named etc. Isaac Nesbitt, Clk   August 17. 1858

B155a   State of Maryland, Washington County, Towit:
I, Isaac Nesbitt, Clerk of the Circuit Court for said County, do hereby certify, to all whom it may or doth concern, that it appears from the Records of my office, that the bearer hereof a negro man named John Gant was manumitted by Mrs. Catharin Shindel on the 27th May 1856 to serve until the 1st April 1858, Recorded in Liber I.N. No. 12 folios 83 & 84, one of the Land Records of Washington County. The said John Gant is 5 feet 6 inches in height, in his 31st year of age; has scars on both knees; lost the 1st joint of his left thumb; of a pleasant countenance, not of a very dark complexion.
In Testimony whereof, I hereunto subscribe my name, etc. Isaac Nesbitt, Clk   August 17th. 1858

B155b   State of Maryland, Washington County, Towit:
I, Isaac Nesbitt, Clerk of the Circuit Court for said County, do hereby certify to all whom it doth or may concern, that it hath been satisfactorily proven to me, upon the testimony of Jacob Powles Esquire, that the bearer, a negro woman named Louisa Ellen Henry was born free; and is therefore entitled to this her Certificate of Freedom. The said Louisa Ellen Henry is five feet, 2 1/2 inches in height, has a Mole on her Chin, and one under her left ear. She is 30 years of age, and of a dark complexion, and her child Ann Rebecca, three years old.
In Testimony whereof, I hereunto subscribe my name, etc. Isaac Nesbitt, Clk   September 7th. 1858

B156a   State of Maryland, Washington County, Towit:
I, Isaac Nesbitt, Clerk of the Circuit Court for Washington County, do hereby certify, to all whom it may or doth concern, that the bearer hereof, a negro man, named James Dover, was manumitted and set free by the late Nathaniel Summers, of said county, by Deed of Manumission duly executed, and now of record in my office, in Liber I.N. No. 9, folios 145 and 146, one of the Land Records of said County. The said James Dover is now about 50 years of age; is 5 feet 9 1/4 inches high; of a brown or copper color; has a small scar on his nose; and is of slender form.
In Testimony whereof I hereunto etc. Isaac Nesbitt, Clk Novem. 16, 1858.

B156b State of Maryland, Washington County, Towit:
I, Isaac Nesbitt, Clerk of the Circuit Court for Washington County, do hereby certify, to all whom it may or doth concern, that the bearer hereof, a negro man, named William Gasper, was manumitted and set free by Joseph S.[?] Moore, of said county by Deed of Manumission duly executed, and now of record in my office, in Liber I.N. No. 13, folio 197, one of the Land Records of said County. The said William Gasper, is now about 40 years of age, is 5 feet 4 1/2 inches high, of a brown or copper color; has a small scar on the right hand, and one on his forehead.
In Testimony whereof, I hereunto etc. Isaac Nesbitt, Clk
November 27th. 1858.

B157a State of Maryland, Washington County, Towit:
I, Isaac Nesbitt, Clerk of the Circuit Court in and for the county of Washington, do hereby certify to all whom these presents doth or may concern, that ["the bearer hereof" crossed out] it hath been satisfactorily proven to me that the bearer hereof, a mulatto woman, named Caroline Hall, is free, and entitled to her certificate as such. She is now about 37 years of age, 5 feet 3 3/4 inches high, and a bright mulatto. She has the following children, all born free, towit: Thomas, aged about 21 years; Mary Ellen aged about 18 years; Sarah Catharine aged about 17 years; Margaret Jane, aged about 15 years; Caroline Virginia aged about 14 years; and Ardenia Alice, aged about 9 years.
In Testimony whereof etc. Isaac Nesbitt, Clk   November 29th, 1858.

B157b State of Maryland, Washington County, Towit:
I, Isaac Nesbitt, clerk of the Circuit Court for Washington County, in the State of Maryland, do hereby certify, to all whom it doth or may concern, that the bearer hereof, a negro man, named Laurence Taylor, was manumitted and set free by Mrs. Elizabeth Kershner, of said County by Deed of Manumission, duly executed and now of record in my office, in Liber I.N. No. 11 folio 167, one of the Land Records of said County. The said Laurence Taylor, is now about 44 years of age, is 5 feet, 9 inches high, has a small scar on the right hand, near the second finger; complexion not very dark.
In Testimony whereof, I hereunto etc. Isaac Nesbitt, Clk
December 16th. 1858.

African American Manumissions

B157c   State of Maryland, Washington County, Towit:
I, Isaac Nesbitt, Clerk of the Circuit Court, in and for the County of Washington, do hereby certify, to all whom these presents doth or may concern, that it hath been satisfactorily proven to me that the bearer hereof, a mulatto man named Thomas Hall, is free and entitled to his certificate as such. He is now about 21 years of age; 5 feet 8 3/4 inches high, and a bright mulatto.
In Testimony whereof etc. Isaac Nesbitt, Clk   [no date]

B158a   State of Maryland, Washington County, Towit:
I, Isaac Nesbitt, Clerk of the Circuit Court for Washington County, do hereby certify to all whom it doth or may concern, that it hath been satisfactorily proven to me, upon competent testimony, that the bearer hereof, a colored woman, named Mary Dorsey, is a free woman, and entitled to here certificate as such. She was born on the 10th day of February, 1800, and is now nearly 59 years of age: She is 5 feet 4 3/4 inches high, of a light copper complexion, without any perceptible marks upon her person. She is the mother of the following children, all of whom were born free, viz: Mary Theodosia Dorsey, born July 23, 1834; Evelina Dorsey, born December 14th, 1837; Margaret Eliza Jane Dorsey, born October 12th, 1839; and all of whom were born in said County.
In Testimony whereof I hereunto etc. Isaac Nesbitt, Clk
        December 24th, 1858.

B158b   State of Maryland, Washington County, Towit:
I, Isaac Nesbitt, Clerk of the Circuit Court for Washington County, do hereby certify to all whom it doth or may concern, that the bearer hereof, a colored girl, named Margaret Eliza Jane Dorsey, who applies for a certificate of her freedom, hath satisfied me upon competent testimony, that she was born free. She was 19 years of age on the 12th day of October, 1858; is 5 feet 4 inches high; slender form; and of a light complexion.
In Testimony whereof etc.   December 24th, 1858.

B159a   State of Maryland, Washington County, Towit:
I, Isaac Nesbitt, Clerk of the Circuit Court for Washington County, do hereby certify, to all whom it doth or may concern, that it hath been satisfactorily proven to me, upon competent testimony of Doct. Otho J. Smith & Theodore Burkhr[?], that the

It has been proven to my satisfaction that Sarah Ann Belghomin and Henry Belghomin are the Children of Henry & Amelia Belghomin, the said Amelia Belghomin being a free woman of color manumitted by Thomas Prather of this County before the birth of said Children — the said Sarah Ann was born on the 12th of March 1818 and Henry Ginghli on the 15th of July 1819 in this County —

Jany 7. 1830

R Ridgewith Op. Clk

Washington County

Received this 25th May 1812 of Barton Carico Six hundred and thirty dollars for four Negroes To Wit One Negroe man aged 36 years One negroe woman about 29 years old One boy about 4 years old one Girl 2 years old, The mans name Nace the womans name Miney the boys name Nace the Girl Suckey, Which Negroes I warrant Sound and warrant and defend from any claim or claims by any person or persons whatever, and Slaves for life

Barton Carico

Witness
James Prather

March 28th 1817 Received of Johnathan Nesbitt the sum of four Hundred Dollars as a Deposit for the Use of Nathaniel Nesbitt accidents to be at the Rique of S.d Nathaniel
Given Under my hand

Jn.o Nesbitt

29th on more Rec.d Ten Dollars

Slave Bill of Sale
Copy in Collection of Marguerite Doleman

of Washington County, Maryland

bearer hereof, a colored girl named Lethea Ellen Thompson, is a free girl, and entitled to her certificate as such. She was 22 years of age on the 1st July 1858, is 5 feet high; slender form; both eyes affected, both hands also, from fits, forefinger of right hand hurt by having a felon, small dent on the forehead, of a dark complexion. Her child Ann L. Dorsey 4 months old.
In Testimony whereof, I hereunto etc. Isaac Nesbitt, Clk
December 29. 1858

B159b State of Maryland, Washington County, Towit:
I, Isaac Nesbitt, Clerk of the Circuit Court for Washington County, do hereby certify, to all whom it doth or may concern, that it hath been satisfactorily proven to me, upon competent testimony of Thomas Harbine Esquire that the bearer hereof, a colored man named Henry Sanders, was born free, and entitled to his Certificate as such. He will be 34 years of age the 27th day of May 1859, is 5 feet 2 1/2 inches high, 2 marks on the right jaw and scars on the left wrist, of a dark complexion and a good countenance.
In Testimony whereof, I hereunto etc. Isaac Nesbitt, Clk March 11th. 1859.

B159c State of Maryland, Washington County, Towit:
I, Isaac Nesbitt, Clerk of the Circuit Court for Washington County, do hereby certify, to all whom it doth or may concern, that it hath been satisfactorily proven to me, upon the testimony of Thomas Crampton, that the bearer hereof, a colored woman named Babara Reeder, ["was born free and" crossed out] is entitled to her freedom by Deed of Manumission given by Philip Reeder on the 4th March 1837 & recorded in Liber YY folio 584, one of the Land Records of Washington County. She is 37 years of age, is 5 feet 8 1/2 inches high, a very bright mulatto, & a pleasant countenance. Her daughter Hellen Reeder, 16 years of age.
Isaac Nesbitt, Clk   March 18th. 1859.
[Barbara Reeder in margin]

B160a State of Maryland, Washington County, Towit:
I, Isaac Nesbitt, Clerk of the Circuit Court for Washington County, do hereby certify, to all whom it doth or may concern, that it hath been satisfactorily proven to me, upon the testimony of Casper W. Wever Esq., that the bearer hereof, a colored man

African American Manumissions

named John Henry Ogleton is a free man, and entitled to his Certificate of freedom. He was born on the 17th day of September 1818, and is now nearly 41 years of age. He is 5 feet 11 inches high, a bright mulatto; has a scar on the top of the head, the 3d. finger on the right hand crooked, has a good countenance.
In Testimony whereof, I hereunto etc. Isaac Nesbitt, Clk   March 21st. 1859

B160b   State of Maryland, Washington County, Towit:
I, Isaac Nesbitt, Clerk of the Circuit Court for said County, do hereby certify, to all whom it doth or may concern, that the bearer hereof a negro man, named Stephen Stansbury, was duly manumitted by Joseph M. Middlekauff, by Deed of Manumission bearing date the 6th day of April, 1859, and regularly executed and recorded among the Land Records of my office, according to law. The said Stephen Stansbury is now about thirty five years of age, five feet ten and a half inches high, has a slight scar and lump on the forehead, over the left eye; complexion tolerably black.
In Testimony whereof I hereunto subscribe my name etc. Isaac Nesbitt, Clk   April 15th, 1859.

B160c   State of Maryland, Washington County, Towit:
I, Isaac Nesbitt, Clerk of the Circuit Court for Washington County, do hereby certify, to all whom it doth or may concern, that it hath been satisfactorily proven to me, that the bearer hereof; a negro man, named Benjamin Saunders, was born free; and who now applies for his certificate of Freedom. The said Benjamin Saunders is now in the 33d year of his age, and is five feet six inches high; has a scar over the left eye running through the eyebrow; and another scar at the corner of the same eye; complexion tolerably black.
In Testimony whereof etc. Isaac Nesbitt, Clk   April 16, 1859.

B161a   State of Maryland, Washington County, Towit:
I, Isaac Nesbitt, Clerk of the Circuit Court for Washington County, do hereby certify, to all whom it doth or may concern, that it hath been satisfactorily proven to me, upon competent testimony, that the bearer hereof Catharine Hatton, wife of Jacob Hatton, who now applies for a certificate of her freedom, was born free. She is now in the 26th year of her age; is four feet

of Washington County, Maryland

eleven and a half inches high, and has a scar on the left arm near the elbow; complexion a dark brown or light copper color. She has two children: one named William Albert who will be 2 years old in July next, the other an infant 4 months old.
In Testimony whereof I hereunto etc. Isaac Nesbitt, Clk   April 18, 1859.

B161b   State of Maryland, Washington County, Towit:
I, Isaac Nesbitt, clerk of the Circuit Court in and for said County, do hereby certify to all whom it doth or may concern that it has been satisfactorily proven to me, upon competent testimony, that the bearer hereof, a colored woman, named Nancy Saunders, who now applies for her certificate of freedom, was born free, and is entitled to the same. She is now in the 20th year of her age; and is five feet two inches high; has a scar on the ball of her thumb on the right hand, and is of a dark brown color.
In Testimony whereof I hereunto subscribe my name etc. Isaac Nesbitt, Clk   April 18th, 1859.

B162a   State of Maryland, Washington County, Towit:
I, Isaac Nesbitt, Clerk of the Circuit Court for Washington County, do hereby certify, to all whom it doth or may concern, that it hath been satisfactorily proven to me, that the bearer hereof, a negro man, named Benjamin Washington, who applies for a certificate of his Freedom, was duly manumitted by Nathaniel Summers, on the 6th day of April, 1847, to take effect at the end of twelve years therefrom, as appears form a deed of manumission, duly acknowledged and recorded among the Land Records of my office. The said Benjamin is now 37 years of age; five feet seven inches high; has a small scar in the right eye brow; is well formed, and of a dark yellow or copper complexion.
In Testimony whereof I hereunto etc. Isaac Nesbitt, Clk   May 12th, 1859.

B162b   State of Maryland, Washington County, Towit:
I, Isaac Nesbitt, Clerk of the Circuit Court for Washington County, do hereby certify, to all whom it doth or may concern, that it hath been satisfactorily proven to me, that the bearer hereof, a negro man named James Brown, who applies for a certificate of his Freedom, was duly manumitted by Mrs. Mary A. Shafer on the 25. day of April 1859, duly acknowledged and

African American Manumissions

recorded in Liber I.N. No. 13, folios [blank] The said James Brown is now in his 40th year, five feet, five & an half inches high, has a scar on the 2d. finger and one on the right knee, is well formed, and of a dark complexion.
In Testimony whereof, I hereunto etc. Isaac Nesbitt, Clk [no date]

B163a State of Maryland, Washington County, Towit:
I, Isaac Nesbitt, Clerk of the Circuit Court for Washington County, do hereby certify, to all whom it doth or may concern, that it hath been satisfactorily proven to me, that the bearer hereof, a negro man, named Samuel Curtis, who applies for a certificate of his freedom, was manumitted on the 20th day of March, 1859, by Mary Ann McKinley, as it appears by a Deed of Manumission duly made and executed, and now of record in the office of said Court. The said Samuel Curtis is five feet seven inches high; has a scar on the forehead, and the mark of a burn above the right ear; complexion tolerably black; age not given, but has the appearance of being about 45 years.
In Testimony whereof etc. Isaac Nesbitt, Clk   May 25th, 1859.

B163b State of Maryland, Washington County, Towit:
I, Isaac Nesbitt, Clerk of the Circuit Court for Washington County, do hereby certify, to all whom it doth or may concern, that it hath been satisfactorily proven to me, upon the testimony of Mrs. Sarah Price, that the bearer a mulatto woman named Elizabeth Herbert, was born free, and entitled to her Certificate of Freedom. She is 5 feet 3 3/4 inches high, [blank] years of age of a light copper complexion, without any perceptible marks upon her person. She is the mother of the following children, all of whom were born free, viz; Charles Herbert aged 13 years Sophia Herbert aged 11 years - Mary Jane Herbert, 9 years, Caroline Virginia, 5 years of age; all of whom were born in said County.
In Testimony whereof etc. Isaac Nesbitt, Clk
July 27th. 1859

B164a State of Maryland, Washington County, Towit:
I, Isaac Nesbitt, Clerk of the Circuit Court for Washington County, do hereby certify, to all whom it doth or may concern, that it hath been satisfactorily proven to me, that the bearer hereof, a negro woman named Nancy Campbell, who applies for a Certificate of her Freedom, was duly manumitted by Andrew

of Washington County, Maryland

Miller, on the 14 day of June 1859, duly acknowledged and recorded in Liber I.N. No. 14, folio 130. The said Nancy Campbell is now in her 42 year, 5 feet 1 1/2 inches high, of a dark complexion, without any perceptible marks upon her person.   In Testimony whereof etc. Isaac Nesbitt, Clk
      August 2nd, 1859

B164b   State of Maryland, Washington County, Towit:
I, Isaac Nesbitt, Clerk of the Circuit Court for Washington County, do hereby certify, to all whom it doth or may concern, that it hath been satisfactorily proven to me, that the bearer hereof, a negro girl, named Martha Ann White, who now applies for a certificate of her Freedom, was born free, - her mother having been duly manumitted by John W./V.[?] Swearingen, on the 11th day of October, 1836. The said Martha Ann was born on the 4th day of July, 1837; she is 5 feet one inch high, nearly; has a mole below the right corner of the mouth, and one on the right cheek bone; her complexion a dark copper, and of good person.
In Testimony whereof etc. Isaac Nesbitt, Clk   August   16th, 1859.

B165a   State of Maryland, Washington County, Towit:
I, Isaac Nesbitt, Clerk of the Circuit Court for Washington County, do hereby certify, to all whom it doth or may concern, that it hath been satisfactorily proven to me, by Thomas Boteler Esquire, that the bearer hereof, a negro man, named Levi Hall, who now applies for a certificate of his Freedom, was born free, he is 5 feet 4 inches high, 38 years of age, has a scar on first finger of left hand, one above the left eye, one on the upper lip, and one on the top of his head, of a light complexion.
In Testimony whereof, etc. Isaac Nesbitt, Clk [no date]

B165b   State of Maryland, Washington County, Towit:
I, Isaac Nesbitt, Clerk of the Circuit Court for Washington County, do hereby certify to all whom it doth or may concern, that it hath been satisfactorily shown to me by record and other evidence, that the bearer hereof, a negro man named William Henry; who applies for a certificate of his freedom, is entitled to the same; having been born of free parents on the 16th day of October 1836, and having duly served an apprenticeship to the business of a farmer. The said William Henry is 5 feet 5 inches

high; has a scar on the left hand, and a small one on the forehead above the right eye; complexion tolerably black.
In Testimony whereof etc. Isaac Nesbitt, Clk   August   31st, 1859.

B166a   State of Maryland, Washington County, Towit:
I, Isaac Nesbitt, Clerk of the Circuit Court for Washington County, do hereby certify, to all whom it doth or may concern, that it hath been satisfactorily proven to me, by H. B. Rohrback, that the bearer hereof, a negro boy, named Washington Adley, who now applies for a certificate of his Freedom, was born free. He is 5 feet 6 3/4 inches high, 24 years of age; has two scars on his left arm, and a scar on his little finger, on left hand, his complexion, a dark copper, and of good person. In   Testimony whereof etc. Isaac Nesbitt, Clk   September 26th 1859.

166b   State of Maryland, Washington County, Towit:
I, Isaac Nesbitt, Clerk of the Circuit Court for Washington County, do hereby certify, to all whom it doth or may concern, that it hath been satisfactorily proven to me, on oath, by Elizabeth Hale, that the bearer hereof, a negro woman, named Hester Turner, formerly Hester Chase, who now applies for Certificate of her Freedom; was born free, and is entitled to her certificate. She is about 35 years of age, has a scar, on the right arm, above the wrist and a small speck on the right eye. She is 5 feet 2 1/2 inches high of a dark copper complexion. Also her two children, Richard Allen & Melcha Bond.
In Testimony whereof etc. Isaac Nesbitt, Clk   September 21st, 1859.

B167a   State of Maryland, Washington County, Towit:
I, Isaac Nesbitt, Clerk of the Circuit Court for Washington County, do hereby certify, to all whom it doth or may concern, that it hath been satisfactorily proven to me, by John Kretzer Esquire, that the bearer hereof, a negro woman, named Eve Ann Garner, who now applies for a Certificate of his Freedom, was born free. She is 5 feet 1 1/2 inches high, 31 years of age, has two Scars, one on the 1st and 2d. fingers, of her left hand, and a mole on the left Cheek, of a bright complexion and of good person.
In Testimony whereof etc. Isaac Nesbitt, Clk   October   4th. 1859.

of Washington County, Maryland

B167b State of Maryland, Washington County, Towit:
I, Isaac Nesbitt, Clerk of the Circuit Court for Washington County, do hereby certify, to all whom it doth or may concern, that it hath been satisfactorily proven to me, that the bearer hereof, a mulatto woman, named Jane Miles, (formerly know as Jane Howard,) is a free woman, as it hath been satisfactorily shown to me. The said Jane is 5 feet 5 3/4 inches high, is about forty two years of age, and has several large scars on the right side of her neck. It also appears that she has six children not heretofore recorded, whose names and ages are respectively as follows: Laura Louisa Howard, now aged 16 years; Allbertus Miles, now aged 12 years; Elie Miles, aged 10 years; Alice Jane Miles, aged 7 years; Joseph Lewis Miles, aged 5 years; and Jesse Miles, aged 15 months.
In Testimony whereof I hereunto subscribe etc. Isaac Nesbitt, Clk   October 17th, 1859.
Note   The above named woman is the same recorded on page 37 together with two of her children not included in the above.

B168a State of Maryland, Washington County, Towit:
I, Isaac Nesbitt, Clerk of the Circuit Court for Washington County, do hereby certify, to all whom it doth or may concern, that it hath been satisfactorily proven to me, by Dr. Elijah Bishop, that the bearer hereof, a negro woman named Mary Able, who now applies for a Certificate of her Freedom; was set free by Miss Ann Hoye late of Allegany County deceased. The said Mary Able is 5 feet 5 3/4 inches high, is about 31 years of age, has a scar on the right arm, her complexion, of a dark copper colour.   In Testimony whereof etc. Isaac Nesbitt, Clk
November 21st. 1859.

B168b State of Maryland, Washington County, Towit:
I, Isaac Nesbitt, Clerk of the Circuit Court for Washington County, do hereby certify, to all whom it doth or may concern, that it hath been satisfactorily proven to me, by Miss Eliza Schnebly, that the bearer hereof, a negro Girl named Susan Dorsey, who now applies for a Certificate of her Freedom; was born free. The aid Susan Dorsey is about 21 years of age; 5 feet 4 1/4 inches high, has a scar on the left cheek, complexion tolerably black.
In Testimony whereof etc.   Isaac Nesbitt, Clk
Nov. 23rd. 1859.

African American Manumissions

B168c State of Maryland, Washington County, Towit:
I, Isaac Nesbitt, Clerk of the Circuit Court for Washington County, do hereby certify, to all whom it doth or may concern, that it hath been satisfactorily proven to me, on the testimony of Elisha Miles, that the bearer hereof, a negro man, named Moses Gray, who now applies for a Certificate of his Freedom; was born free. The said Moses Gray will be 22 years of age on the 29th December 1859. He is 6 feet, 4 inches high, has a scar near the left eye, & one on the 3rd finger of the left hand; his complexion, a dark copper colour.
In Testimony whereof, etc. Isaac Nesbitt, Clk   November 29th 1859

B169a State of Maryland, Washington County, Towit:
I, Isaac Nesbitt, Clerk of the Circuit Court for Washington County, do hereby certify, to all whom it doth or may concern, that it hath been satisfactorily proven to me, that the bearer hereof, a negro man named Henry Long, who now applies for a Certificate of his Freedom was born free. The said Henry Long is about 6 feet high, is about 27 years of age, has no scars perceivable, of a dark complexion.
In Testimony whereof etc. Isaac Nesbitt, Clk   [no date]

B169b State of Maryland, Washington County, Towit:
I, Isaac Nesbitt, Clerk of the Circuit Court for Washington County, do hereby certify, to all whom it doth or may concern, that it hath been satisfactorily proven to me, that the bearer hereof, a negro woman, named Louisa Hawkins, was duly manumitted by the late Nathaniel Summers, of said County, by deed bearing date the 6th day of April, 1847, and which is duly recorded among the Land Records of said county. The said Louisa is 5 feet 4 1/2 inches high, and is now 35 years of age; is of a dark copper color, without any perceptible marks. She has 3 children: One named Sarah Ellen, born February 11th, 1848; one named Georgianna, born April 4th, 1851; and one named Milligan, born in the month of October 1853.
In Testimony whereof etc. Isaac Nesbitt, Clk
April 16th, 1860.

B169c State of Maryland, Washington County, Towit:
I, Isaac Nesbitt, Clerk of the Circuit Court for Washington County, do hereby certify, to all whom it doth or may concern,

Slave Rental Paper, Western Maryland Room, Washington County Free Library

RUNAWAYS.

WAS committed to the jail of Washington county, Md. as runaways, on the 8th August instant, two negro men who call themselves JAS. RANDLE & WILLIAM HARRIS. James is about 5 feet 9 or 10 inches high, about 30 or 32 years of age, proportionably made, of a bright copper colour, has lost all his front teeth; had on when committed, a pair of grey mixt cassinett pantaloons, do. vest, black cloth coat, black fur hat and coarse shoes.— William is about 22 or 23 years of age, about 5 feet 8 or 9 inches high, of a bright copper colour, free and good countenance; had on which committed, a pair of blue mixt cassinett pantaloons, blue cloth vest, drab domestic cloth coat, coarse shoes, and old black fur hat. The said negroes say they belong to Mr. John Cana[...] town and Battle [...] The owner of [...] come and prov[...] take them awa[...] charged accordi[...]
CHRIST[...]
August 20.
The Editors [...]
Charlestown [...]
[...] of 1 [...]

Hagerstown Newspapers

A Runaway Negro.

In the custody of the Sheriff of Washington County, viz.

A NEGRO man who calls himself Robin Major, about forty years of age, five feet four inches high, of a yellowish complexion, a little bow legged, has two scars, one on his forehead over his left eye, and the other on the big toe of his left foot, and his back much marked with the whip.—Had on when committed a little wool hat, kendal cotton coat, and jacket, coating overalls (all much worn) and a country made linen shirt.—Says he belongs to Ralph Worgley, Middlesex County, state of Virginia.

REZIN DAVIS, Sheriff.

Hagerstown, August 17, 1796.

of Washington County, Maryland

that it hath been satisfactorily proven to me, that the bearer hereof, a negro woman, named Ann Eliza White was duly manumitted by the late John V. Swearingen of said County, by deed bearing date the 11th October 1836 & recorded in Liber S.S, folios 335 & 336, one of the Land Records of said County. The said Ann Eliza White is 5 feet 1 3/4 inches high and is now 30 years of age; with a Scar above the left eye, of a bright mulatto colour.
In Testimony whereof etc. Isaac Nesbitt, Clk   April 20th 1860.

B170a   State of Maryland, Washington County, Towit:
I, Isaac Nesbitt, Clerk of the Circuit Court for Washington County, do hereby certify, to all whom it doth or may concern, that it hath been satisfactorily proven to me, that the bearer hereof, a negro man named David Lyles, was duly manumitted by Thomas H. Crampton Esquire of said County, by Deed bearing date the 29th day of May, 1860, and which is duly recorded among the Land Records of said County. The said David Lyles is 5 feet, 8 inches high, and is now 39 years of age; and of a dark color, has a mark on the second finger of his left hand.
In Testimony whereof etc. Isaac Nesbitt, Clk   May 29th. 1860

B170b   State of Maryland, Washington County, Towit:
I, Isaac Nesbitt, Clerk of the Circuit Court for Washington County, do hereby certify, to all whom it doth or may concern, that it hath been satisfactorily proven to me, that the bearer hereof a negro woman named Mary Anderson, was duly manumitted by Miss Milcah Grimes of said County, by Deed bearing date the 24. day of May 1860, and which is duly recorded among the Land Records of said County. The said Mary Anderson is 5 feet 1 inch high, and is now 38 years of age; no marks perceptible, of a dark complexion.
In Testimony whereof etc. Isaac Nesbitt, Clk   May 29th. 1860

B170c   State of Maryland, Washington County, Towit:
I, Isaac Nesbitt, Clerk of the Circuit Court for Washington County, do hereby certify, to all whom it doth or may concern, that it hath been satisfactorily proven to me, that the bearer hereof a negro woman named Isabella Small, was duly manumitted by Miss Mary Jane Watson Watson [sic] of said County, by Deed bearing date the 30th day of May 1860, and

African American Manumissions

which is duly recorded among the Land Records of said County. The said Isabella is 5 feet 3 inches high, 38 years of age, has a large Scar on her right arm, and one on her right wrist, of a dark complexion.
In Testimony whereof etc. Isaac Nesbitt, Clk   May 31st, 1860

B171a   State of Maryland, Washington County, Towit:
I, Isaac Nesbitt, Clerk of the Circuit Court for Washington County, do hereby certify, to all whom it doth or may concern, that it hath been satisfactorily proven to me, that the bearer hereof, a negro man named Lloyd Pearce, who now applies for a Certificate of his Freedom; was born free, satisfactorily proven to me, by Mrs. Melivia O. Dall, and is entitled to his freedom. The said Lloyd Pearce was born 15th September 1835, and is now in his 25 year of age. He is 5 feet 2 1/2 inches high has a scar on the right knee, of a dark complexion.
In Testimony whereof etc. Isaac Nesbitt, Clk   June 2nd, 1860.

B171b   State of Maryland, Washington County, Towit:
I, Isaac Nesbitt, Clerk of the Circuit Court for Washington County, do hereby certify, to all whom it doth or may concern, that it hath been satisfactorily proven to me that a negro man named Samuel Pearce, who now applies for a Certificate of his Freedom; was born free, satisfactorily proven to me, by Mrs. Meliora O. Dall, and is entitled to his freedom. The said Samuel Pearce was born August 4th. 1839, and is now near 21 years of age. He is 5 feet 4 3/4 inches, a dark mulatto has a pleasant countenance.
In Testimony whereof etc. Isaac Nesbitt, Clk   [no date]

B171c   State of Maryland, Washington County, Towit:
I, Isaac Nesbitt, Clerk of the Circuit Court for Washington County, do hereby certify, to all whom it doth or may concern, that it hath been satisfactorily proven to me, on oath, by competent testimony, that the bearer hereof, a negro woman, named Catharine Ellen Walker, (formerly Gross,) was born free, and is entitled to here certificate of Freedom. She is now 24 years of age; 5 feet 2 1/2 inches high; has a small mole on the right cheek bone, with no other perceivable marks, - complexion a dark brown, approaching black, but good countenance.
In Testimony whereof etc. Isaac Nesbitt, Clk   June 5th, 1860.

of Washington County, Maryland

B172a   State of Maryland, Washington County, Towit:
I, Isaac Nesbitt, Clerk of the Circuit Court for Washington County, do hereby certify, to all whom it doth or may concern, that it hath been satisfactorily proven to me, that the bearer hereof, a negro woman named Rebecca Young, was duly manumitted by Stephen Putterbaugh of said County, by Deed bearing date the 5th day of March 1860, and which is duly recorded in Liber I.N. No. 14 folios 545 & 546, one of the Land Records of Washington County. The said Rebecca Young is 5 feet 1 inch high, 33 years of age, has 2 scars on her right hand and on the left cheek near the ear and of a dark complexion.
In Testimony whereof etc. Isaac Nesbitt, Clk   June 5th. 1860

B172b   State of Maryland, Washington County, Towit:
I, Isaac Nesbitt, Clerk of the Circuit Court for Washington County, do hereby certify, to all whom it doth or may concern, that it hath been satisfactorily proven to me, that the bearer hereof, a negro woman named Louisa Emmerson, formerly Louisa Handy[?], was duly manumitted by Daniel Sprigg Esq. formerly of this County, now residing in Baltimore City, by Deed bearing date the 3d day of March 1828, and which is duly recorded in Liber K.K. folios 324 & 325, one of the Land Records of Washington County. The said Louisa will be 31 years of age on the 3d. day of October 1860. She is 5 feet 1/2 inch high, has no perceptible marks; of a pleasant countenance, complexion a dark brown.
In Testimony etc. Isaac Nesbitt, Clk   June 6th. 1860

B173a   State of Maryland, Washington County, Towit:
I, Isaac Nesbitt, Clerk of the Circuit Court for Washington County, do hereby certify to all whom it doth or may concern, that it appears from the Records of said Court that the bearer hereof, a negro man, named John Henry Lewis, by the Judgment of said Court on the 23d day of November, 1857, was declared free and discharged from all manner of servitude or slavery to any and every person or persons whatsoever. The said John Henry Lewis is now in the 39th year of his age; is 5 feet 9 inches high; has a scar on the right wrist; high cheek bones, and of a black complexion.
In Testimony whereof etc. Isaac Nesbitt, Clk   June 15, 1860.

African American Manumissions

B173b State of Maryland, Washington County, Towit:
I, Isaac Nesbitt, Clerk of the Circuit Court for Washington County, do hereby certify, to all whom it doth or may concern, that it hath been satisfactorily proven to me, that the bearer hereof, a negro girl named Margaret Elizabeth Williams, was duly manumitted by John and Benjamin Ingram of said County by Deed bearing date the 29th day of May 1860, and recorded in Liber I.N. No 14, folio 644, one of the Land Records of Washington County. The said Margaret Elizabeth Williams will be 21 years of age on the 30th day of September next, she is 4 feet 10 inches high, has a mole on the Chin and two moles on the left Cheek, and one on the right hand, near the thumb, of a light copper color.
In Testimony etc. Isaac Nesbitt, Clk   June 23d, 1860

B174a State of Maryland, Washington County, Towit:
I, Isaac Nesbitt, Clerk of the Circuit Court for Washington County, do hereby certify, to all whom it doth or may concern, that it hath been satisfactorily proven to me, by Samuel Zeller, that the bearer hereof, a negro man named George Keel, who now applies for a certificate of his Freedom, was born free. He is 30 years of age, 5 feet 4 1/2 inches high, has a small scar on the left hand near the wrist, also a scar on the left side of his chin. Complexion dark of a good countenance.
In Testimony whereof etc. Isaac Nesbitt, Clk   June 26th, 1860

B174b State of Maryland, Washington County, Towit:
I, Isaac Nesbitt, Clerk of the Circuit Court for Washington County, do hereby certify, to all whom it doth or may concern, that it hath been satisfactorily proven to me, by competent testimony, that the bearer hereof, a negro woman, named Hetty Stewart, who now applies for her certificate of freedom, was born free. She is now thirty-two years of age, is 5 feet 1 1/4 inches high, without any perceivable marks upon her person; Complexion quite black. She is now the mother of two children, - one named John Thomas, aged about 4 years, the other named Isaac Cornelius, aged 18 months.
In Testimony whereof I hereunto subscribe my name, and affix the seal of said Court this 17th day of July, 1860. Isaac Nesbitt, Clk   [no date]

of Washington County, Maryland

B175a State of Maryland, Washington County, Towit:
I, Isaac Nesbitt, Clerk of the Circuit Court for Washington County, do hereby certify; to all whom it doth or may concern, that it hath been satisfactorily proven to me, by James H. Grove Esquire, that the bearer hereof, a negro man named Joseph Stansberry, who now applies for a certificate of his Freedom, was born free. He is 27 years of age, has a scar on the left eye, and a mark on the right arm. He is five feet, 9 inches high, of a bright color & pleasant countenance.
In Testimony whereof etc. Isaac Nesbitt, Clk   August 17th 1860.
[Margin reads "Joseph Stansbury"]

B175b State of Maryland, Washington County, Towit:
I, Isaac Nesbitt, Clerk of the Circuit Court for Washington County, do hereby certify, to all whom it doth or may concern, that it hath been satisfactorily proven to me by James H. Grove Esquire, that the bearer hereof, a negro man named John Lee, who now applies for a certificate of his Freedom, was born free. He is now twenty four years of age, is 5 feet 11 1/2 inches high; has a scar on the inside of the right leg, caused by a burn, mark on each arm by Indian Ink, of a bright color & pleasant countenance.
In Testimony whereof, I hereunto subscribe my named, and affix the seal of sad Court this 1st day of August A.D. 1860 Isaac Nesbitt, Clk

B176a State of Maryland, Washington County, Towit:
I, Isaac Nesbitt, Clerk of the circuit Court for Washington County, do hereby certify, to all whom it doth or may concern, that it hath been satisfactorily proven to me, that the bearer hereof, a mulatto man named William Russell, who now applies for a Certificate of his freedom, was born free. He is 40 years of age, 5 feet 6 1/2 inches high; has a scar on the right eye, and one on the middle finger of the left hand, two moles on the left cheek, near the nose of a bright complexion and good countenance. He has 5 Children: one named William L. Russell aged 15 years & 6 months, Richard H. Russell aged 13 years, Mary Elizabeth 3 years old and Cecilia Ann one year old the 11th July 1860 all of a bright mulatto color.
In Testimony whereof etc. Isaac Nesbitt, Clk   September 5th 1860

African American Manumissions

[there are only 4 children named in the record even though it says 5 children]

B176b   State of Maryland, Washington County, Towit:
I, Isaac Nesbitt, Clerk of the circuit Court for Washington County, do hereby certify to all whom it doth or may concern, that it has been satisfactorily proven to me that the bearer hereof, Thomas Green Parker, a mulatto, who applies for his certificate of Freedom, is entitled to the same - having been born free. The said Thomas is now in the 28th year of his age; is five feet one inch high, and has a scar on the back of his right hand; has straight hair, and complexion nearly white.
In Testimony etc.   Isaac Nesbitt, Clk   October 2d, 1860.

B176c   State of Maryland, Washington County, Towit:
I, Isaac Nesbitt, Clerk of the Circuit Court for Washington County, do hereby certify to all whom it doth or may concern, that the bearer hereof, a negro man named Charles Solomon, being a native of said said [sic] county, and raised therein, was duly manumitted by Elizabeth Solomon, by deed, on the 26th day of March, in the year 1852, and recorded among the land Records of said county. The said Charles is now about thirty-seven years of age; is 5 feet 11 inches high; has a small pock mark on his forehead, above the right eye; his left wrist is slightly twisted from an injury received when a boy; his upper teeth are much decayed; and his complexion a dark brown, or chocolate color, and rather slender in person.
In Testimony whereof I hereunto subscribe my name etc. Isaac Nesbitt, Clk   November 21st, 1860.

B177a   State of Maryland, Washington County, Towit:
I, Isaac Nesbitt, Clerk of the circuit Court for Washington County, do hereby certify, to all whom it doth or may concern, that it hath been satisfacorily [sic] proven to me, that the bearer hereof, a colored man, named Paris Sopers who now applies for a certificate of his freedom, was born free. He is 21 years of age, 5 feet 7 3/4 inches high; has a small scar on the left thumb; and one on the back of the right hand; has a narrow head; & forehead projects; he is of a dark color, & pleasant countenance.
In Testimony whereof etc.   Isaac Nesbitt, Clk [no date]

KNOW ALL MEN BY THESE PRESENTS:

That I _____ of Washington County in the State of Maryland, for and in consideration of the sum of seven hundred and fifty dollars current money, to me in hand paid by Henry Freaner, of Washington County, and State aforesaid, the receipt whereof, I solemnly acknowledge, having parted, bargained, sold, and delivered, and by these presents do part, bargain, sell and deliver, unto the said Henry Freaner, my negro William aged about twenty ↓ years, and a slave for life, which said slave named William as aforesaid; I will warrant sound and sane, and a slave for life, and will also warrant and defend him to the said Henry Freaner, his Executors, Administrators, and Assigns, against me, my Executors, and Administrators, and against the claim or claims, of any or all persons whatever. In witness whereof, I the said Geo. Thomson Mason have hereunto set my hand, and affixed my seal, this twenty fifth day of August ; One Thousand, Eight Hundred and Thirty-eight.

Geo. Thomson Mason {Seal}

Signed, sealed, and delivered in the presence of

J. Rausler

MARYLAND, Washington County, sct.

On this twenty ninth day of August 1838, before me the subscriber, a Justice of the Peace in and for said County, personally appeared Geo. T. Mason and acknowledged the within Bill of Sale, or instrument of writing to be his act and deed, according to the purport, and intent and meaning thereof, and the acts of Assembly in such cases made and provided. Acknowledged before

J. Rausler

→⚜ Slave Bill of Sale, Collection of Doug Bast, Boonsboro, Maryland ⚜←

For Sale.

Three very valuable young Negro Men, the oldest not more than twenty-four years of age, all able good plantation hands. One of them is active and useful in a mill, having worked in one for about two years. Enquire of the Printer.

March 28, 1799.

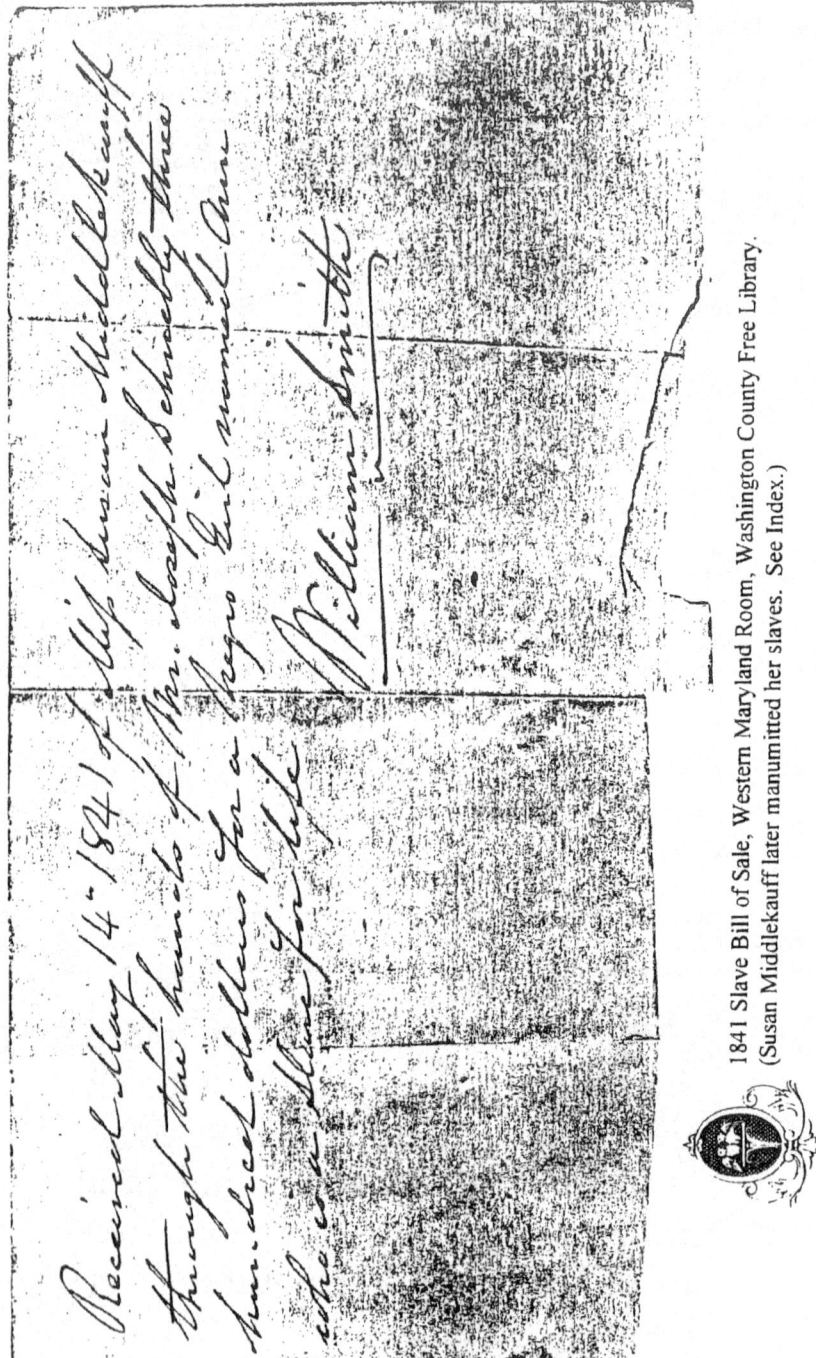

Received May 14th 1841 of Miss Susan Middlekauff through the hands of Mr. Joseph Schnebly three hundred dollars for a Negro Girl named Ann she one slave for life

William Smith

1841 Slave Bill of Sale, Western Maryland Room, Washington County Free Library. (Susan Middlekauff later manumitted her slaves. See Index.)

of Washington County, Maryland

B177b   State of Maryland, Washington County, Towit:
I, Isaac Nesbitt, Clerk of the circuit Court for Washington County, do hereby certify to all whom it doth or may concern that the bearer hereof, a Mulatto Girl, named Mary Ann Eliza Snyder, who now applies for her certificate of Freedom, was born free, as from the records of my office is manifest. She was born in Washington county, Maryland, and is now in the 20th year of her age, is five feet two & 3/4 inches high, and stout built, with no perceivable marks, and of a bright complexion.
In Testimony whereof etc. Isaac Nesbitt, Clk
April 13th, 1861.

B177c   State of Maryland, Washington County, Towit:
I, Isaac Nesbitt, Clerk of the Circuit Court for Washington County, do hereby certify to all whom it doth or may concern, that the bearer hereof, a negro man, named Theophilus Green, who now makes application for his certificate of freedom, was duly manumitted, as it appears from the records of my office, by a certain Jacob Funk, (of John,) on the 25th day of March, in the year 1856. The said Theophilus is now about 40 years of age; is 5 feet 4 inches high; has a large scar over the left eye; and his complexion quite black.
In Testimony whereof I hereunto subscribe my name, and affix the seal of the said Circuit Court this 2 day of November, in the year 1861. Isaac Nesbitt, Clk [no date]

B178a   State of Maryland, Washington County, Towit:
I, Isaac Nesbitt Clerk of the circuit Court for Washington County, do hereby certify, to all whom it doth or may concern, that the bearer hereof, a negro woman named Maria Hall, who now makes application for her certificate of freedom, was duly manumitted, as it appears from the records of my Office, by a certain I. Clay Sperrow, of Cherokee County, in The State of Texes, on the 11th May A.D. 1854. The said Maria Hall is now about 31 years of age; is 4 feet 8 inches high, and of a bright complexion.   In Testimony whereof, I hereunto subscribe my named, and affix the Seal of the said Circuit Court this 20th day of December 1861 Isaac Nesbitt, Clk

B178b   State of Maryland, Washington County, Towit:
I, Isaac Nesbitt, Clerk of the Circuit Court for Washington County, do hereby certify, to all whom it doth or may concern,

African American Manumissions

that the bearer, a negro man named Samuel Chesley, who now makes application for his Certificate of Freedom, was duly manumitted, as it appears from the records of my Office, by Miss Sarah Gaither of Washington County, on the 29th day of May A.D. 1860. The said Samuel Chesley is now about 31 years of age. She is 5 feet, 4 inches high, has two marks, one on the upper lip, & the other on the nose, of dark complexion stout built.
In Testimony whereof, & . Isaac Nesbitt, Clk   April 8th 1862.

B179a   State of Maryland, Washington County, Towit:
I, Isaac Nesbitt, Clerk of the Circuit Court for Washington County, do hereby certify, to all whom it doth or may concern, that the bearer hereof, a mulatto girl named Ellen Robinson who makes application for her certificate of freedom; was born free, and hath all her life resided in said County. She is now about 21 years of age; 5 feet 4 3/4 inches high; of delicate form; light colored eyes; without any perceptible marks; and of a bright ["color" crossed out] complexion.
In Testimony whereof I hereunto subscribe my name and affix the seal of the Circuit Court for said County, this 19th day of April, 1862. Isaac Nesbitt, Clk

B179b   State of Maryland, Washington County, Towit:
I, Isaac Nesbitt, Clerk of the Circuit Court for Washington County, do hereby certify, to all whom it doth or may concern, that the bearer hereof, a negro man, who makes application for his certificate of freedom, named Alexander Pearce, was duly manumitted, as it appears from the records of my Office, by David Long, of Washington County, on the 25th day of September 1849. The said Alexander Pearce, is now about 25 years of age; He is five feet, seven inches high, has two moles; one below the nose, the other on the chin, of dark complexion, stout built.
In Testimony whereof, etc. Isaac Nesbitt, Clk   December 23d. 1862.

B179c   State of Maryland, Washington County, Towit:
I, Isaac Nesbitt, Clerk of the Circuit Court for Washington County, do hereby Certify, to all whom it doth or may concern, that the bearer hereof, a negro man, who makes application for his Certificate of freedom, named James Sewell, was duly manumitted, as it appears from the records of my Office, by

of Washington County, Maryland

Sarah South, of Washington County, on the 29th day of May 1860. The said James Sewell, is now about 44 years of age. He is 5 feet 10 1/4 inches high, has a small scar above the left eye of dark complexion, stout built.
In Testimony whereof, etc. Isaac Nesbitt, Clk   [no date]

B180a   Pasted on Inside Back Cover:
This is to certify that I know Elizabeth Herbert to be a free woman - and that her children herein named were born free -
    Charles Herbert - aged 13 yrs.
    Sophia Herbert - 11 yrs.
    Mary Jane Herbert - 9 yrs.
    Caroline Virginia - 5 yrs.

                  Sarah A. Price
Hagerstown
July 26th 1859

B180b   Pasted on Inside Back Cover:
This is to certify that the bearer of this (Louisa) has served her time and she is now at Liberty to enjoy the benefit of Manumission executed by Nathaniel Summers dec. which takes effect this day
April 12th 1860   Mary Summers for [?] Son

[Written in pencil] #363 No 1 607 No. 2 - 446 Apl 6. 1847"

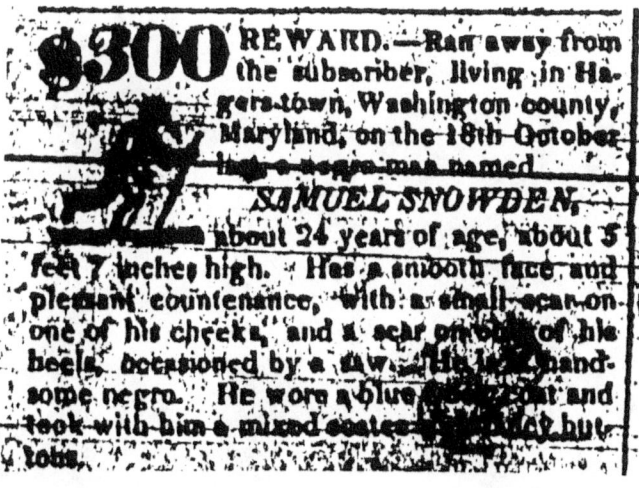

Index

*The numbers beside each name refer to entry numbers and not to page numbers.
The names listed in the Appendices are not indexed.*

Able, Daniel, B18b
Able, Lewis P.F., B5b
Able, Mary, B168a
Adam Tim, A24b
Adamie, B152c
Adams, Charles, A51b
Adamson, Charles, B30c
Adley, Charles, A94a
Adley, Corban, B115c
Adley, Henrietta, B73b
Adley, Hilliary, B118a
Adley, Horatio, B145a
Adley, James, A94a
Adley, John Henry, B73b
Adley, Sarah Ann, B73b
Adley, Washington, B166a
Alfred, A90b, B87a, B87b
Allegany Co., Maryland,
   A35b, A42b, A67c,
   B168a, B37d
Allen, Richard, B166b
Amanda, B116c, B152c
Ambush, Polly, B91a
Ambush, Yorick, B90c
Anderson, Brister, A100b
Anderson, Joshua, B94b
Anderson, Juliet, B12a, B13b, B20b
Anderson, Mary, B170b
Anderson, Stephen, B144a
Angle, David, A53b
Ann Arundel Co.,
   Maryland, A53b, A102b,
   A106a,
Ann Eliza, B88b
Ann Maria, A69b
Ann Rebecca, B155b
Annapolis, Maryland,
   A18b, A64b, A86b, B54b,
   A38a, A19a

Antietam [Iron] Works,
   A9a, A35a, A10a, A38a,
   A38b.
Ardenia Alice, B157a
Arms, Jacob, B140b
Arms, John Henry, B120a
Army, A24a
Ash, John, A63a
Ashberry, John, A53a, A69a
Backstone, George, A26b
Backstone, Tabathey, A26b
Baines, Col. Richard, A43b
Baker, Richard, B25b
Ballard, Somerset, B43b
Baltimore County,
   Maryland, A11b, B78a,
   B78b, B125a
Baltimore, Maryland,
   A104a, A54b, A26c,
   B139b, B172b
Barnes, Catharine, B74a
Barnes, Charles, B28b, B30a
Barnes, Daniel, B96c
Barnes, Eleanora, A99a
Barnes, Elisabeth, A98b
Barnes, Henrietta, B46a
Barnes, James, B28a
Barnes, Letty, B13a
Barnes, Philip, B37c
Barnes, Richard, A22b, A23a,
   B14b, B68c, B69b, B70b, B70c,
   B71a, B71b, B74a
Barnes, Samuel, B20a
Barnett, Sarah, B29a, B29d
Barns, Henry, B6a
Barns, Richard, A18b
Bateler, Thomas, B52c
Bayer, Jacob, B153a, B154a
Bayley, George, B85c

Beall, Eleanor, A72a
Beall, Prissy, B20c, B37d, B38a
Beall, Samuel B., B20c, B37d, B38a
Bean, Samuel, B60b
Beard, George B50a
Beathy, Edward W., B68b
Bedford County, Pennsylvania, A44a, A71a
Bell, Eliza Jane, B125a
Bell, Eliza, B20b
Bell, Hillery, B12a
Bell, Isabella, B125a
Bell, John William, B83a
Bell, Lucretia, B125a
Bell, Mary, B125a
Bell, William D., A104a
Bell, William, B13b
Belt, Thomas, A46a
Belthower, Henry Joseph, A1a
Beltzhour, Henry, A1a, B28c
Beltzhower, Amelia, A1a
Beltzhower, Melcher, A23a
Beltzhower, Sarah Ann, A1a
Ben, A43b
Benjamin Edward, B114b
Berkeley County, West Virginia, A60a, A61a
Bets, David, A45a
Bett, Mrs., A46a
Bett, Thomas, A46a
Biles, John, A21b
Bishop, Dr. Elijah, B168a
Blake, Cecelia, B100b
Blake, Charlotte, B132c
Blake, James Robert, B121c
Blake, Jane N., B76b
Blake, Joseph, B139b
Blake, Louisa, B121c
Blakes, Lucy, B72b, B72c, B73a
Blanchard, Peter, A26c
Blanchard, Rachel, A28a
Blue, Harriet, B40a
Bond, Melcha, B166b
Bonhom, Thomas, B82b
Boonsboro, Maryland, A72b, A105b
Booth, Betsey, A25b
Booth, David, A19a
Booth, Eleanor, A90a, B39c
Booth, James, A22a
Booth, Maria, B39c
Booth, Rachel, A19a, A22a, A25b, A90a
Bosley, John, A11b
Bostick, Vachel, A38a
Boteler, Hezekiah, A58b
Boteler, Thomas, A36a, B165a, B83a
Bowles, John S., B146a, B146b
Boyd, David, A39a
Boyer, Joseph Young, B134a
Braggonien, George, A50b
Branchman, Jacob, A43b
Brashear, Van S., B25b, B26d
Brasher, Maria, B24b
Brashier, Van S., B24a
Breathed, Edward, A3a
Brien, Charles, A18a, A46a
Brien, Fanny, A46a
Brien, John, A10a
Brisco, Esther, B137c
Brisco, Matthias Hanson, B137c
Briscoe, Henry, B78a
Briscoe, John, B78b
Briscoe, Joseph, B4b
Briscoe, Samuel H., B78a, B78b, B78c
Briscoe, Terry Cooper, B78c
Briscoe, Thomas, B111a
Brister, Joseph, A39b
Brister, Rachel, A39b
Brooks, Henry, B154a
Brooks, John W., B30b
Brooks, Nace, A107a
Brooks, Samuel, B153a
Brooks, Stephen, B56b
Broscius, Jacob, A21b
Brown, Ann, B38b
Brown, George, B29b
Brown, James, B162b, B33d
Brown, Jane, A87b
Brown, John, B70a, B95a
Brown, Josiah, A87b
Brown, Louisa, B31d
Brown, Lucy, B27a, B38b, B42b

Brown, Martha Linnette, B42b
Brown, Sally, B148b
Brown, Susan, B95b
Brown, William T., B9b
Brown, William, B102b
Brumbaugh, Samuel, B134c
Brumley, Rachel, A66b
Bryam, Lucy, B66b
Bryan, Frederick, B118c
Bryan, John, A1d
Bull, Doctor, A24a
Burkhart[?], Theodore, B159a
Butler, Cecelia, A1c
Butler, Henry J., B108b
Butler, James, A10a
Butler, Jenny, A31a
Butler, John, A35a, B85a
Butler, Leonard, B85b
Butler, Letty, A14b
Butler, Rebecca, B17b
Butler, Robert, A68b
Butler, Sarah, A1c, A68a, A68b
Butley, Letty, A95b
Butley, William, A95b
Butter, Sophia, A103a
Caff, Caleb, A12a
Cain, Aaren, A32b
Cain, Isaiah Hughes, B1b
Caleb, A12a
Callihan, William, A71a
Calvert County, Maryland, A59b, A83b
Campbell, Ann Eliza, B88b
Campbell, Catharine, B121b
Campbell, Mary Isabella, B88b
Campbell, Nancy, B164a
Campbell, Susanna, B88b
Campbell, Thomas Franklin, B88b
Campbell, William, A67a, B121b
Cane, Isaac, B98a
Carey, Ann Sophia, B153b
Carlisle, Charlotte, A12b
Carlisle, Jean, A12b
Carlisle, William, A12b
Carn, Catharine Jane, B133b
Carn, Columbus, B133b
Carn, Ellen Lavinia, B133b

Carn, Louisa, B133b
Carn, Margaret Rebecca, B133b
Carn, Mary Louisa, B133b
Caroline Virginia, B157a, B180a
Carroll, Charles, A44a
Carroll, James, A41a
Carson, James O., B41a
Caru, Catharine Jane, B133b
Caru, Columbus, B133b
Caru, Ellen Lavinia, B133b
Caru, Louisa, B133b
Caru, Margaret Rebecca, B133b
Caru, Mary Louisa, B133b
Catharine Jenifer, B80b
Catharine, A13a, A50b, A51a, B147a
Caution, Catharine, B147a
Caution, Charity Ellen, B147a
Caution, Elisha, B55b
Caution, John Lake, B147a
Caution, Joshua, B147a
Caution, Louisa Ellen, B147a
Caution, Mary Martha, B147a
Cecilia Ann, B176a
Chaplain, Joseph, A57b
Charity, B27c
Charles County, Maryland, A3b, A4a, A49b, A75a, B72b, B72c
Charles Edward, B89a
Charles Town, Virginia, A94a
Charles, B65b
Chase, Charity, A67b
Chase, Chloe, B126c
Chase, Esther, A84a, B23b
Chase, Hester, B166b
Chase, John, A84a
Chase, Kitty, B23b
Chase, Letty, A54b
Chase, Lewis, A104a
Chase, Maria, B152a
Chase, Melcha Bond, B166b
Chase, Richard Allen, B166b
Chase, Solomon, A45a
Cherokee County, Texas, B178a
Chesley Jacob, B75a
Chesley, Charlotte, B132c
Chesley, Oliver, A75a

Chesley, Samuel, B178b
Chew, Elijah, B49a
Chew, Samuel L., A21a,
 A25a, A29a, A9b
Chloe, A20b
Christopher, B89a
Clagett, Dr. Zachariah,
 A33b, A55b, A51b, A51c,
 B121a, B124a, A31b
Clagett, John Beall, A83b
Clagett, Samuel, B80b, B80c,
 B81a, B81b, B98b, B99a,
 B99b
Claggett, Dr. Horatis, A52a
Claggett, Milton M., B135b
Claggett, Posthumous,
 A31b, A33b, A34a, A41b,
 A49a, A51c, A52a, A55b
Clare, A70a
Clark, Lives, A74a
Clarke, Molly, A10b
Clasg, P, A45b
Clemens, Hezekiah, A68a
Clemens, Jane, A68a
Clements, Charity, B65b
Clements, Charles, B65b
Clements, Eliza, B65b
Clements, George Henry, B65b
Clements, Hezekiah, A14a
Clements, Mary, B65b
Clements, Susannah Emma
 Ramsey, B65b
Clements, Thomas, B65a
Cline, James Cheston, B44b
Colbert, Catharine, B123c
Colbert, Jeremiah, B122b
Colbert, Mary, B135a
Cole, Frances, B47a
Cole, Isaac, A81a
Cole, Joseph H., B134c
Cole, Nancy, A66a
Cole, Sarah, A88a
Collins, Lloyd, A99b
Collins, Harry, A6a
Collins, Margaret, B114b
Collins, Moses, A63a
Collins, Noah, B9b
Collins, William, B114b

Compton, Eliza, B71a
Compton, Rebecca, B70b,
 B70c, B71a
Compton, William S., A58a
Concy, Priscilla, B60a
Conn, Bartley, B111b
Cook, John, B97b
Cook, William, B9a
Coon, Nancy, A67a
Cooney, Mary, B66a
Cooper, Henry, B83c
Cooper, Nancy, B75b
Cooper, Samuel Benjamin, B84b
Cooper, Sarah, B77a
Cooper, Terry, B78c
Cooper, William Camfield, B77c
Cosey, Jane, B107a
Craig, Henry, B61a
Craig, Samuel, B128a
Cramer, William, B141a
Crampton, Elie, A62b, A73a
Crampton, John E., A62b
Crampton, Thomas H., B170a
Crampton, Thomas, A73a, B159c
Crawford, Catharine, A34b
Crawford, Diana, A34b
Crawford, Dinah, A34b
Crawford, Edward, A34b
Crawford, Elizabeth, A34b
Crawford, Frances, A34b
Crawford, Isaac, A34b, B59a, B59a
Crawford, James, A34b, B59a
Crawford, Jesse, B59a
Crawford, Maria, B59a
Crawford, Mary, A34b, B59a
Creek, Fanny, A29a
Creek, Hannah, A64a
Creek, Mary, A88b
Creek, Peggy, A21a
Creek, Robert, A15b, A25a
Creek, Sophia, A21a, A88b
Creek, Williams, A21a
Crew, Mahala, B137b
Cromwell, Henry Elie, A16a
Cromwell, Jenny, A16a
Crowl, Joseph, B125a
Cuff, Caleb, A12a
Curtis, Harry, A17a

Curtis, Maria, B32a
Curtis, Samuel, B163a
Cushwa, Ann E., B105a
Cynthia Ellen, B89a
Cyrus, Nathaniel, B26a
Dall, Meliora, B171b
Dall, Melivia O., B171a
Darby, Charles A., B45b
Darky Jones, A30b
Datcher, Maria, A95a
David Henry, B117a
David Norman, A82b
Davis, Catharine Jane, B133b
Davis, Catharine, B74a
Davis, Columbus, B133b
Davis, Eliza, B145b
Davis, Ellen Lavinia, B133b
Davis, Josiah, B82b
Davis, Louisa, B133b
Davis, Margaret Rebecca, B133b
Davis, Mary Louisa, B133b
Dayly, Samuel, A43a
Delaware, A40b
Delia, A86b
Dellinger, Christiana, B148b
Dellinger, Jacob, B139a
Dellinger, Mrs., B109a
Dellinger, William, B109a, B109b, B148b
Demby, Jim, A2a
Dennison, Hugh, A44a
Dickerson, Mary, B141c
Dickinson, Joseph, A61c
Digges, Nelly, A44a
Diggs, Jacob, A47a
Diggs, Maria, B115b
Diggs, Nace, B11a
Diggs, Thomas, B36b
Dillehunt, Mary, B1d
Ding, James, B68a
Ditto, Abraham, A85a
Ditto, James B., A85a
Dixon, Pruelender, B16a
Domanak, Jeremiah, B1c
Dorcas, B48b
Dorey, Doct. Frederick, A40a
Dorsey, Ann L., B159a
Dorsey, Catharine, B32b

Dorsey, Dr. Clagett, B142b
Dorsey, Dr. Frederick, A78b, B19c, B9b
Dorsey, Evelina, B1a, B158a
Dorsey, George, B83b
Dorsey, Margaret Eliza Jane, B1a, B158a, B158b
Dorsey, Margaret, B36b
Dorsey, Mary Theodosia, B158a
Dorsey, Mary Theodosin, B1a
Dorsey, Mary, B1a, B158a
Dorsey, Rosa Ann, B89b
Dorsey, Susan Ellen, B97b
Dorsey, Susan, B168b
Douglas, Mahala, B49c
Dover, James, B156a
Dragoonier, George, A13a, A50b
Ducket, Alfred, B52c
Ducket, Sophia, A46b
Duckett, Jane, B105b
Duckett, John Henry, B135b
Duckett, John, B149c
Duckett, Sophia, A48b
Duckett, Thomas B., B101a
Duckett, Thomas, A36b, B25c
Duckett, Williams, B25c
Duffin, George, B27d
Duke, Andrew, A59b
Duncan, William, A77a
Dunham, Mary Ann, B72c
Dunmore, Levina, B104a
Dunmore, Sheckey, A57a
Dunmore, William, B39d
Dunn, Thomas S., A70a
Dunward, Mary, B113a
Dutler, Richard, A26a
Eastern Shore, Maryland, A1d, A28b, A61c, A66b
Eaty, Jack, A67c
Eavey, Christian, B38d
Eavey, Isaac D., B38d
Edward, B87b
Edwards, Benjamin, A80a
Edwards, Elizabeth, A79a
Edwards, John T., B92c
Edwards, Mahala, A79a
Edwards, Thomas, A66b, B73b
Eelwise, John, A60a

Eichelberger, Theobald, A15a
Eleanor, A89a
Eliza Ellen, B79b
Eliza Jane, B125a
Eliza, B65b
Elizabeth Town, Maryland, A6a, A9b
Elliot, Elie Williams, A29a
Emmerson, Louisa, B172b
Emmitsburg, A60b
Eversole, Christian, B19a
Fanny, B1d
Fansler, Michael, A12a
Farmer, Hannah, B34c
Fechtig, Christian, A63b
Feeby, Mary Ann, B115b
Feidt, George, B136b
Firey, Henry, B70a, B150a
Firey, Jacob, B96c
Fitzhugh, Col. William, A57a, A61c
Fitzhugh, William H., B39a, B64c, B149a
Fleming, James, B7b
Fletcher, John, B141b
Fletcher, Lewis, B53a
Foaman, Thomas M., A9b
Forrest, Ned, B14a
Foster, Sarah, A1d
Fowler, R., B87a
Fox, Daniel, B26a
Frances, Grace, A64b
Franklin County, Pennsylvania, A70a, A74a
Frederick County, Maryland, A60b, A78a, B7b
Frederick, Maryland, A39a
Fredericke, A69b
French, A26c
Friend, Eleanor, B65b
Funk, Jacob, B177b
Funk, John, B177b
Gabby, William, A69b, B34c
Gaither, Henrietta, B138a
Gaither, Julianna, B141b, B141c
Gaither, Sarah, B141b, B141c, B178b
Galloway, Jarrett, B10b

Galloway, Regis, B56a
Galloway, Sivilla, B38a
Gant, John, B155a
Garner, Eve Ann, B167a
Garner, Mahala, B116a
Garner, Sarah, B116b
Gasper, Henrietta, B62c
Gasper, William, B156b
Gates, Charles, B74b
Gates, Elizabeth, B72b
Gates, Jack, A67c
Gates, Rachael, B123b
Gates, Richard, B74c
Gearhart, Catharine, A76b
Geary, Richard, A37b
Gehr, Daniel, A14b
George Henry, B65b
George Town, Maryland A19a, A67c, A68b
George, A53a
Georgianna, B169b
German language, A8b, A10b, A12a, A39b, A42b, B4b
Goens, Jennie, B130c
Goens, John Henry, B142b
Going, Madison, B135c
Goings, Henry, B59b
Goings, Madison, B140a
Goings, Margaret, B130b
Goins, Barbara, B73a
Graham, Henson, B17a
Graham, Milly, B92c
Gray, David, B47b
Gray, George, A5a
Gray, Moses, B168c
Green, Benjamin Edward, B114b
Green, Charity, A96b
Green, Henry, B23a
Green, Jane, A96b
Green, Jesse, A52b
Green, Joseph Hanson, B114b
Green, Mary, A88a
Green, Theophilus, B177b
Grimes, Joseph, A81b
Grimes, Mary Ann, B144a
Grimes, Milcah, B170b
Groce, John, A84b

Gross, Benjamin, A76a
Gross, Catharine Ellen, B171c
Gross, Chargo, A73b
Gross, Henrietta, B31c
Gross, Lewis, A65b
Grove, James, H., B175a, B175b
Grub, Betsy, A35a
Gruber, James, B114a
Gruber, John, B69a
Gruber, Lavinia Susan, B44b
Gruber, Robert Henry, B67b
Gunderman, Charles L.D., A98a
Gunderman, Jane A., A98a
Gurnin, Mary, B34a
Guting, Jacob, A93a
Hagerstown, Maryland,
  A6a, A7a, A9b, A18b,
  A20b, A22b, A25a, A26c,
  A30b, A37a, A38a, A46a,
  A48b, A60b, A64a, A67a,
  A78b, B41a
Hagan, Francis, B7b
Hagan, Margaret, B7b
Hager, Jonathan, A37a
Hains, Adam, B1c
Hale, Elizabeth, B166b
Hall, Ardenia Alice, B157a
Hall, Caroline Virginia, B157a
Hall, Caroline, B157a
Hall, Isaiah, A102a
Hall, Levi, B106b, B165a
Hall, Margaret Jane, B157a
Hall, Maria, B178a
Hall, Mary Ellen, B157a
Hall, Sarah Catharine, B157a
Hall, Thomas, A101a,
  B157a, B157c
Hamilton, Lydia, A91b
Hammer, Susan, B32c
Handy, Louisa, B172b
Handy, Lucinda, B42c
Handy, Nelly, B42c
Hanson, George, A69a
Hanson, Matthias, B137c
Hanson, William, B86c
Harbine, Thomas, B159b
Harper, Mary Ellen, B128a
Harpers Ferry, WV, A61b

Harriett, B7b
Harris, Simon, A8b
Harris, Thomas, A4b
Harrison, George, B80a, B132b
Harrison, Richard, A85a, B132b
Harrison, Samuel, A65a, A86a
Harrison, Sarah, B106c
Harry, George I., B94b
Harry, George S., B46c
Harry, Jacob I., B94b
Harry, John, A9b
Harry, Susan, B94b
Hattan, David, B44c
Hattan, Margaret, B44c
Hattan, Mary Ann, B44c
Hatten, Mary, A97a
Hatton, Catharine, A13a,
  A50b, A51a, B161a
Hatton, David, A50b
Hatton, Infant, B161a
Hatton, Jacob, A51a, B161a
Hatton, Jane, A89b
Hatton, Richard, A13a
Hatton, William Albert, B161a
Hawkins, Georgianna, B169b
Hawkins, Louisa, B169b
Hawkins, Milligan, B169b
Hawkins, Sarah Ellen, B169b
Hay, George, A90b
Hedrick, Margaret, B47c
Heister, Genl. Daniel, A42b
Heister, Mrs., A42b
Henderson, Richard, A10a, A35a
Henny, B40c
Henrietta, B73b
Henry Elie, A16a
Henry, Ann Rebecca, B155b
Henry, B116c
Henry, Isaiah, B117c
Henry, John Robert, B134b
Henry, Jsaiah, B117c
Henry, Louisa Ellen, B155b
Henry, William, B165b
Henson, Ann Maria, B138a
Henson, Michael, B17a
Herbert, Caroline Virginia,
  B163b, B180a
Herbert, Charles, B163b, B180a

Herbert, Elizabeth, B163b, B180a
Herbert, Mary Jane, B163b, B180a
Herbert, Sophia, B163b, B180a
Herletin, Charles, A62a
Hershey, John, B131a
Hess, Abraham Valentine, B19a
Hess, David, A65a, A86a
Hess, William, B47c
Hete, Samuel, A50a
Hicks, Jacob, A83b
Hiester, Gen. Daniel, A4b, A8b
Hill, Henry, B86b
Hill, Richard, B94a
Hinton, Polly, A75b
Hitt, Samuel M., B42a, B110a
Holland, Henry, A19a
Holliday, Richard T., B136a
Holmes, Bartley, A38b, B150b
Holmes, Eliza, B151b
Holmes, Martin, B150c
Holmes, Mary, B42a
Homas, Jacob, A36a
Hopewell, David, A49a
Hopewell, Elijah, A34a
Hopewell, Notley, B21b
Hopewell, Peter, A51c
Howard, Abraham, B143c
Howard, Alfred, B37d
Howard, James Henry, B37d
Howard, Jane, B37d, B167b
Howard, Laura Louisa, B167b
Hoye, Ann, B168a
Huflich, Peter, A48a
Hughes Forge, A13b, A26b
Hughes, Col, Daniel, A26b, A38a, A40b, A61c
Hughes, Esther, A61c
Hughes, Fanny, B1d
Hughes, H. Courtenay, B18b
Hughes, Isabella, B18b
Hughes, Letitia, B18b
Hughes, Rebecca, B18b
Hughes, Samuel, Jr., A29a
Hughes, Susan, A38a, A61c, B18b
Hunt, Job, A39a
Huyett, Martha, B141b, B141c
Hyland, John A., A30b
Hyland, John R., B19b, B34b

Imes, Susanna, A20a
Ingram, Benjamin, B84c, B173b
Ingram, John, B129b, B173b
Irwin, John, A30a
Isaac Cornelius, B174b
Isabella, B125a, B147b
Isaiah Henry, B117c
Jackson, Fanny, A29a
Jackson, Isabella, B136b
Jackson, Jacob, A11b
Jackson, Mount Joy William, B15b
Jacob, A80a
Jacques Furnace, A13a, A50b, A51a
James Henry, B79b
James, A58a
James, Letitia, B75c
James, Maria, A13b
James, Matilda, B50b
James, Solomon, B50a, B86c
James, Sophia, B35c
James, Tabitha, A13b
James, Thomas, B82a
Jane, A87b, B116c
Jefferson County, West Virginia, A61b
Jeffreys, Jacob, B140b
Jenkens, Mary G., B37b
Jenkins, Ann C., B52a
Jenkins, Ellen, A80b
Jenkins, Frisby T., B141a
Jenkins, Henry Brown, B79a
Jenkins, James, B27b
Jenkins, Susan Ann, B44a
Jenny, A23a
Jeremiah, A69b
Jerry, A12b
Jjams, Jack, A53b
John Dorsey, B117a
John Henry, B73b
John Lake, B147a
John Matthew, B147b
John Thomas, B174b
John, B116c
Johns, Leonard H., B60a
Johnson, Arthur, B41a
Johnson, Delia, B118c
Johnson, Fanny, B57b

Johnson, Harry, A6b
Johnson, Robert, A65b, B89c
Johnson, Sarah, B18a
Johnson, Tobias, A65b,
    B21b, B136b
Johnston, Charlotte, A65b
Johnston, Greenbury, A77a
Johnston, Mary Jane, A107b
Johnston, Mary, A84b
Johnston, Queenbery, A65b
Johnston, Robert, A77a
Johnston, Susan, A72a, A108a
Jones, Adelia, B89a
Jones, Ann Matilda, B99a
Jones, Charles Edward, B89a
Jones, Christopher, B89a
Jones, Cynthia Ellen, B89a
Jones, Darky, A30b
Jones, Elias, B2a
Jones, Enoch, A30a
Jones, Hanson, A60a
Jones, Henrietta, B98b
Jones, Henson, B68a
Jones, John Dawson, B99b
Jones, Lucinda, B133a
Jones, Mary Sophia, B89a
Jones, Nancy, B79b
Jones, Rachael, B33a
Jones, Robert, B77b
Jones, Samuel W., B68b, B107a
Jones, Sarah, B77a
Jones, Sophia, B76c
Jones, Thomas, B93a
Jonson, Nathan, B23c
Jordon, Cecelia Elizabeth, A108b
Joseph Hanson, B114b
Joseph Lake, B147b
Joseph, B87a
Joshua, B147a
Josiah, B117a
Jsaiah Henry, B117c
Kane, Frances, B104b
Kane, Isaac, B29a, B29d, B40c
Kane, Thomas, B67a
Kapp, Michael, A25a
Keedy, David H., B113a
Keefer, Isaac, A35a
Keel, George, B174a

Keishner, George, A10b
Keller, Aaron, B36a
Keller, Ann Rosane, B36a
Keller, Elizabeth, B36a
Keller, Rebecca, B36a
Keller, Solomon, B36a
Keller, Susan, B36a, B62b
Keller, Thomas, B37a
Kelly, Nathan, B32c
Kennedy, James H., B25a
Kennedy, Thomas, A1d
Kent County, Maryland,
    A2a, A7b, A8a, A9a, A9b,
    A15a, A21a, A25a, , A29a
Keppler, Wm. M.K., B100b
Kershner, Elizabeth, B157b
Kettle, John, B3b
Key, Jesse, A82a
Key, Valise, B96a
Keyser, John, B46b
Kieff, Michael, A15a
Kizen, Samuel, A105a
Kreek, George, A9b
Kretzer, John, B167a
Lair, Moses, B31a
Lake, Catharine, B147a
Lake, Charity, B4a
Lake, Elizabeth I., B122a
Lake, Gitty, B122a
Lake, Isabella, B147b
Lake, John Lake, B147a
Lake, John Matthew, B147b
Lake, Joseph Lake, B147b
Lake, Joshua, B147a
Lake, Louisa Ellen, B147a
Lake, Louisa, B148a
Lake, Mary Elender, B122a
Lake, Mary Elizabeth, B147b
Lake, Mary Martha, B147a
Lake, Mary, B148a
Lake, Moses, B4a
Lake, Samuel Lake, B147b
Lake, Samuel, B6c, B122a,
    B147a, B147b, B148a
Lake, Thomas E., B122a
Lake, Thomas, B122a
Lake, Wesley, B122a
Lake, William Campbell, B121b

Lane, Jane, A83a
Langbridge, John, A87a
Lantz, Christian, A18a, A32b
Laura, B87a
Laurence, Upton, B27a
Lawrence, Elizabeth, B87b, B93a, B112b
Lear, Ann Eliza, B31b
Lear, Catharine, A61a
Lear, Charles, A61a, A61b
Lear, Darnella, A61a, A61b
Lear, Dorcas, B11b
Lear, Esther, A61a, A61b
Lear, Juliet, A61a, A61b, B40b
Lear, William Van, B8a
Leasure, Susan, B126a
Lee Town, Virginia, A61a
Lee, Catharine, B58a
Lee, Jackson, B100a
Lee, John, B175b
Lee, Joshua, B58a
Lee, Levi, A33b
Lee, Mazy, A41b
Lee, Robert, B103b
Lee, Sealy, B58a
Lee, William, B58a, B119c
Leonard, Henry A., A107b
Lewis Calvin, B117a
Lewis, A50a
Lewis, Dennis, B145b
Lewis, Frances Ann, B72a
Lewis, John Henry, B173a
Lewis, Major Henry, A27a
Light, Peter, A27a
Lindsay, Abraham, B37a
Little, Charles, B12b
Long, David, B179b
Long, Henry, B58a, B169a
Long, Isaac, A58a
Long, Jesse, A62a
Long, Joseph, B86b
Loudon County, Virginia, A77b
Louisa Ellen, B147a
Louisa, B87a, B180b
Lucretia, B125a
Lucy, A39a, B121c
Lyles, David, B170a
Lyles, Elizabeth Ann, B117b

Lynch, Harriett, B30c
Lynch, John, A53a, A69a
Lynch, Lucy, B149b
Lynch, Lymus, B105a
Lynch, Susan, B62c
Magruder, James A. B102a., B143c
Manjelic, B87a
Mann, John H., B95a
Mann, Warford, B95a
Margaret Jane, B157a
Margaret, A59b
Maria, A72b
Marian, A45b
Marion Co. Ohio, A81a
Marke, Nancy, A10b
Marshall, Emily, B131b
Marshall, John, A77b
Marshall, Mark, B132a
Martin, Ann Sophia, B153b
Martin, Henry, B34a
Martin, Jefferson, B97a
Martin, Joseph Jr., B66a
Martin, Joseph, A61c, B9a
Martin, Lewis R., B85c
Mary Ann, B87b
Mary Catharine, B143b
Mary Elizabeth, B147b, B176a
Mary Ellen, B27c, B87a, B157a
Mary Isabella, B88b
Mary Louisa, B121a
Mary Martha, B147a
Mary Sophia, B89a
Mary, A106b, B65b
Maryland, A14a, A52b, A79a
   Allegany Co., A35b,
     A42b, A67c, B168a, B37d
   Annapolis, A18b, A64b,
     A86b, A54b, A38a, A19a
   Baltimore County, A11b,
     B78a, B78b, B125a
   Baltimore, A104a, A54b,
     A26c, B139b, B172b
   Boonsboro, A72b, A105b
   Calvert County, A59b, A83b
   Charles County, A3b, A4a,
     A49b, A75a, B72b, B72c
   Eastern Shore, A1d, A28b,
     A61c, A66b

Frederick County, A60b,
A78a, B7b
Frederick, A39a
George Town, A19a,
A67c, A68b
Hagerstown, A6a, A7a,
A9b, A18b, A20b, A22b,
A25a, A26c, A30b, A37a,
A38a, A46a, A48b, A60b,
A64a, A67a, A78b, B41a
Kent County, A2a, A7b,
A8a, A9a, A9b, A15a,
A21a, A25a, , A29a
Montgomery County,
A14a, A52b, A79a
Pleasant Valley, A31b,
A33b, A34a, A36a, A36b,
A41b, A49a, A51a, A51c, A58b
Prince Georges County,
A3a, A18a
Queen Annes County, A8a
Sharpsburg, A57b, A81b
St. Mary's County, A1c,
A17a, A18a, A21b, A22b,
A23a, A47a, A51b, A58a,
A62a, A68a, A76a, A85a, A94b
Williamsport, A27a, A30a,
A66a, A67c, A68b, A88a,
A103a, B41a
Mason, A23a, A28a, A43b,
A56a, A74a
Mason, Jeremiah, B2b
Mason, John T. A18b, A20b,
A22b, B100a, B103b, B119c
Mason, Samuel, B115a
Mason, V.W., B92a
Mason, Virginia W., B92b
Mason, Virginia, B90c, B91a
Mathews, Edward, B112b
Matthews, Alfred, B87b
Matthews, Ann Rebecca, B42d
Matthews, Edward, B87b
Matthews, Emma, B42d
Matthews, Frank, B42d
Matthews, Maria, B87b
Matthews, Mary Ann, B87b
Matthews, Samuel S., B87b
Matthews, Sarah Ellen, B103a

Matthews, Susan Rebecca, B87b
May, Thomas, A40b
Mayberry, B116c
McCardell, Willoughby S.G., B90b
McClaughlin, John, B56a
McCoy, Archibald, B39b
McCubbins, Charity, B20c
McDade, Charles, A14a
McGirty, Robert, A59b
McKinley, Henry, A35b
McKinley, Mary Ann, B163a
McMahan, Richard, A62a
McNamee, John, A39b
McPherson & Brien, A9a,
A35a, A38a, A38b
McPherson, John, A10a
Melcha Bond, B166b
Mercersburg, Pennsylvania,
B41a
Meredith, Elizabeth, B89c
Merrich, Joseph J., A61c
Middlecauff, Christian, A47a
Middlecauff, Mrs. Mary, A20a
Middlekauff, B126c
Middlekauff, Joseph M., B160b
Middlekauff, Samuel, B40a,
B58b, B80a
Middlekauff, Susan, B57a
Miles, Alice Jane, B167b
Miles, Allbertus, B167b
Miles, Elie, B167b
Miles, Elisha, B168c
Miles, Henry, B49b
Miles, Jane, B167b
Miles, Jesse, B167b
Miles, Joseph Lewis, B167b
Miles, Loyd, B71c
Miller, Andrew, B164a
Miller, Catharine, A64b
Miller, Daniel P., B60b
Miller, Daniel, A74a
Miller, E., B110a
Miller, Elizabeth, B35d
Miller, Jacob, A32a, A57a, B39d
Miller, James, B58b
Miller, John, A4a
Miller, Rachel, A27a
Miller, Samuel, B57a

Miller, Tobias, A57a
Milligan, B169b
Millings, Charles, A24a
Mills, Lewis, B108a
Mills, Thomas, B154b
Milly, A11a
Mingo, Betsey, B76a
Minor, Rebecca, B70b, B70c, B71a
Mitchell, Alexandrice, B18c
Mitchell, Henry, B63b
Moles, Eleanor, A78b
Moles, Joseph, B19c
Moles, Nelly, B19c
Moles, Sophia, B35a
Moles, Zachariah, A78b
Mong, Joseph P., B109b
Montgomery County, Maryland, A14a, A52b, A79a
Montgomery, Vincent, A21b
Moody, Barbara, B73a
Moody, Elizabeth, B72b
Moody, Henry, B54a
Moody, John, A30a, B79c
Moody, Lucy, B72b, B72c, B73a
Moody, Mary Ann, B72c
Moody, Mary, B55a
Moody, Nancy, A43a
Moody, William, B54b
Moore, Alexander, A41a
Moore, James H., A44b
Moore, Joseph, B156b
Morgan, James, B151b
Moseley, Sarah, B152b
Motter, Jacob B., B29b
Motts, Diana Dorothy Jane, A92a
Motts, Ellen, A91a
Motts, Job, A57b
Motts, Nilly, A57b
Motts, Robert, A92b
Motts, Thomas C., A91a
Moudy, Eve, B121c, B132c
Muary, Nathan, A60b
Mulien, Samuel, A33a
Mumma, Samuel, B142a
Murray, William, B22a
Myers, Elizabeth, B34b
Myers, Jacob, A59a
Myers, John, A106b

Myers, Jonathan J., B19b
Myers, Mary, B34b
Nace, A58b
Nancy, A96a
Neal, James, B83c, B84a, B84b
Neale, James, A62a
Neall, Aquila, A49b
Neilson, Tone, A37a
Nelly, A37b, A40a, B19c
New Jersey, A4b
Newcomer, Andrew, B51b
Newcomer, Joel, B137c
Newcomer, Peter, A26a, A52b
Newson, Abraham, A81a
Newson, John, A81a
Night, Marian, A45b
Night, Sarah, A45b
Nikirk, David, B94a
Nimmy, Eleanor, A89a
Nimmy, Harriet, B131a
Nimmy, Samuel, B10a
Norman, David, A82b
Norris, Dorcas, B48b
Norris, William R., B51b
Oden, Benjamin, A59a
Ogleton, John Henry, B160a
Ohio, A81a
   Marion Co., A81a
Oliver, John, A43b
Orndorff, Jacob, A37a
Oswald, Benjamin, B3b
Oswald, John, B35c, B75c, B82a, B50b
Ott, Adam, A7a
Paca, Frances, B136a
Paca, Stephen, B136a
Parker, Caroline, A59a
Parker, Nancy, A59a
Parker, Thomas Green, B176b
Pattengall, Isaac, B126a
Pearce, Alexander, B179b
Pearce, Lloyd, B171a
Pearce, Samuel, B171b
Pennsylvania, A4b, A23a, A41a, A44a, A70a, A71a, A74a, B41a
   Bedford County, A44a, A71a
   Franklin County, A70a, A74a

Mercersburg, B41a
Philadelphia, A34b
Pittsburgh, A23a
Somerset County, A11b, A16a
Pennsylvania Incorporated
Society for promoting
the abolition of slavery, A40b
Peter, A7a
Peters, Caesar, B57c
Peters, Letty, B41a
Peterson, Nancy, B125b
Prince Georges County,
Maryland, A24b, A30a,
A40a, A43a, A46b, A48b,
A59a, A63a, A77a, A82a
Phebe, A55a
Phenix, Catharine, B114c
Phenix, Mary, B101b
Philadelphia, Pennsylvania, A34b
Philpot, Richard, A4a
Pindell, Doctor, A24b
Pindell, Henny, B40c
Pindell, Mary, B21a
Pindell, Priscilla, B40c
Pindell, Richard, A18a
Pindle, Richard, B98a
Pittsburgh, Pennsylvania, A23a
Pleasant Valley, Maryland,
A31b, A33b, A34a, A36a,
A36b, A41b, A49a, A51b,
A51c, A58b
Plummer, Betsy, A35b
Point, Catharine, B32b
Porter, Anthony, B2b
Porter, George, B115a
Porterfield, Hannah, B125b
Powell, Upton, B79c
Powles, Jacob, B155b
Prather, James, B37d
Prather, Louisa, A78a
Prather, Rebecca, A11a
Prather, Sarah, A67c
Prather, Thomas, A1a,
A42a, A79b, B7a
Price, Col. Josiah, A54a, A55a,
A56a
Price, Sarah Ann, B104b, B107b
Price, Sarah, B163b

Price, William, B28d
Prince Georges County,
Maryland, A3a, A18a
Prince, A9a
Proctor, Edward, B126b
Proctor, Thomas Asbury, B126b
Putterbaugh, Stephen, B172a
Pye, Jeremiah, B127a
Pye, Jonathan Hager, B127b
Pye, Samuel, B90a
Queen Anns County, MD, A8a
Rachel, A19a, A22a, A25b, A39b
Ragan, Richard, A18b
Randall, Jane, B9b
Randall, Vachell W., B9b
Ransey, Susannah Emma, B65b
Rawlings, Col., A28b
Rebel, A72b
Reeder, Alexander, B56b
Reeder, Barbara, B159c
Reeder, Benjamin, B119a
Reeder, Charles, B119b
Reeder, Eliza Ellen, B79b
Reeder, Hannah, B29c
Reeder, Helen, B159c
Reeder, James Henry, B79b
Reeder, Maria, B38c
Reeder, Nancy, B79b
Reeder, Philip, B5a, B29c, B38c,
B57b, B63a, B119a, B124b,
B130a, B159c, B199b
Reeder, Sarah, B63a
Reel, John, B46b, B96b
Reilly, Moses, B28e
Rench, Susan E., B135c, B140a
Rench, Susan, B130c
Revolutionary War, A8a
Reynolds, John, B46c
Reynolds, Mary E., B67a
Reynolds, Wm., A71a
Rice, Charles, A62a, B41a
Richard Allen, B166b
Richard Henderson & Co., A10a
Richard, Negro, A3a
Richardson, Maria, B45b
Richmond, Virginia, A90b
Ridenour, Catharine, B129a
Ridenour, Dorothy, A75b

Ridenour, John, A75b, A85b
Ridout, John, A54b
Ridout, Louisa, B48a
Ridout, Mary, B48a
Ridout, Rachael Ann, B48a
Ridout, Susanna, A16a
Ridout, William Henry, B41a
Riley, William, B43a
Ringgold, Genl., A34b
Ringgold, Maria Antoinette, A90b
Ringgold, Mrs. Mary, A2a
Ringgold, Samuel, A2a, A34b, B59a
Robert, A42a
Robertson, Alexander, A87a
Robertson, Elizabeth, B33b
Robinson, Agnes, B69c
Robinson, Ellen, B179a
Robinson, Samuel, B28d
Robinson, Sarah, A76b
Rochester, Nathaniel, A6a, A19a, A21a
Rohrback, H.B., B166a
Rohrer, Jacob, A26b
Rollings, Emanuel, B61b
Rosier, Mary, B26d
Rosier, Van Maria, B26d
Ross, Elizabeth, B48c
Ross, George, A9b
Ross, Gertrude, B7a
Ross, John, A79b
Ross, Joseph, A79b, B7a
Ross, Phoeba, A79b, B7a
Rossier, Henry, B24a
Rowland, Isaac B., B137b
Rowland, Jonathan, B59b
Rozier, Harriet, B102a
Rozier, John, B90b
Russell, Cecilia Ann, B176a
Russell, Cesar, A40b
Russell, Elizabeth, B26c
Russell, Jacob, A49a
Russell, Mary Elizabeth, B176a
Russell, Mary, B26c
Russell, Richard H., B176a
Russell, Thomas, A28b
Russell, William L., B176a
Russell, William, B26c, B176a

Sammons, Benjamin, B128b
Sammons, David B., B128b
Samuel Lake, B147b
Samuel S., B87b
Sanders, Henry, B159b
Sanders, Thomas, B93b
Sansbury, Frank, B39b
Sarah Catharine, B157a
Sarah Elizabeth, B117a
Sarah Ellen, B169b
Sarah, A66a
Saucer, Sarah, B8a
Saunders, Benjamin, B160c
Saunders, Nancy, B161b
Schnebly, Danial, B31a, A94b
Schnebly, Eliza, B89b, B168b
Schnebly, Mary, B108a, B154b
Scott, Perry, B8b
Seala, A22b
See, John, A52a
Sewall, Otho, B26b
Sewell, James, B179c
Shafer, John Jr., B91b
Shafer, Mary A., B162b
Shaffner, Charles, A76a
Shahlot, Jacob, A15a
Sharer, Catharine, B51a, B53b, B58c, B114c
Sharpsburg, Maryland, A57b, A81b
Shearer, Catharine, B143a
Shindel, Catharin, B155a
Sholl, Jacob, A15a
Shorter, Dolly, A3b
Shorter, Eliza, B92b
Shorter, Jim, B92a
Shorter, Joseph, A62a
Shorter, Margaret, B70c
Shorter, William, B84a
Shorter, Williams, B53a
Shrigg, Genl. Thomas, A32b
Sile, Patrick, A49b
Simms, Catharine, B121a
Simms, Maria, B64c
Simms, Mary Louisa, B121a
Simon, A69b
Sims, Maria, B64c
Siren, Mrs., A32a

Siren, William, A32a
Slifer, Eliza Ellen, B81b
Small, Isabella, B170c
Smith, Ann Maria, B107b
Smith, Charles, B45a
Smith, Dr. Otho, B159a
Smith, George, A22b
Smith, Harriet, B102a
Smith, Jerry, A12b
Smith, Michael P., B54a, B54b, B55a
Smith, Mrs. Margaret, A43a
Smith, Richard, A106a
Smith, Robert, A50a
Smoot, George C., A4a
Smothers, Jeremiah, A78a
Snider, John, A95a
Snively, Eveline, B70b
Snowden, John, A56a
Snyder, Betsy, B14b, B68c, B69b, B71b
Snyder, Frederick, B49a
Snyder, George, B61a
Snyder, Henrietta, B64b
Snyder, John, B118a
Snyder, Margaret, B68c
Snyder, Martha, B71b
Snyder, Mary Ann Eliza, B64b, B177b
Snyder, Mary Jane, B69b
Snyder, Mathias, B14b
Snyder, Otho, A100a
Snyder, Roger, A53a
Solomon, Charles, B176c
Solomon, Elizabeth, B176c
Somerset County, Pennsylvania, A11b, A16a
Sopers, Paris, B177a
Sophus, Peter, B129a
South, Sarah, B179c
Spalden, Jane, B35b
Speilman, Jacob, B115c
Sperrow, I. Clay, B178a
Sprigg, Daniel, B172b
St. Lucia, A26c
St. Mary's County, Maryland, A1c, A17a, A18b, A21b, A22b, A23a, A47a, A51b, A58a, A62a, A68a, A76a, A85a, A94b
Stake, Elie, B90b
Stansberry, Joseph, B175a
Stansbury, Stephen, B160b
Startzman, Martin, B113b
Stemple, John, B114a
Stephen, B24b
Stephens, Peter, B113b
Stewart, Catharine, A31b
Stewart, Comfort, B86a
Stewart, Edward, A31b
Stewart, Hetty, A94b, B174b
Stewart, Isaac Cornelius, B174b
Stewart, John Thomas, B174b
Stewart, John, B110a
Stewart, Samuel Overton, B51c
Stonebraker, John, A48a
Stonebraker, Joseph, A75a
Strite, Col. John, A44b
Strite, Daniel, A44b
Strite, Emely, A44b
Strite, Otho W., A71a
Stuart, Benjamin, B22b
Stube, Mr., A71a
Summers, Arnold, B91b
Summers, Mary, B180b
Summers, Nathaniel, B95b, B151a, B156a, B162a, B169b, B180b
Summers, Patience, A48a
Summers, Paul, B47b
Summers, Richard, A3a
Susan Rebecca, B87b
Susan, A60b
Susanna, B88b
Susannah Emma, B65b
Swan, Alexander, A42b
Swan, Nancy, A42b
Swartzwalder, Isaac, A86b
Swearingen, John V., B169c
Swearingen, John, B164b
Swingley, B71b
Tabathey, A26b
Tabbs, Dr., A76a
Tabbs, Moses, A76a
Tarber, Esther, A48b
Tarvin, Ann, B72b, B72c, B73a
Tatterson, Sandy, B46c

Taylor, Erasmus, B64a
Taylor, Judah, A63b
Taylor, Laurence, B157b
Taylor, Peter, B150a
Tenant, James, B132a, B131b
Texas, Cherokee Co., B178a
Theodocia, A54a
Thomas Franklin, B88b
Thomas Gohean, B117a
Thomas, B157a
Thomas, Daniel, A82a, B115c
Thomas, Emory, A72b
Thomas, Ludwick, A91b
Thomas, Maria, A46b
Thompson, Ann, B123a
Thompson, John William, B138b
Thompson, John, A70a
Thompson, Lethea Ellen, B159a
Thompson, Sophia, B76c
Tiernan, Patrick, A103b
Tilghman, Col. Frisby,
    A80b, B44a, B79a
Tilghman, Frisby, B52a
Tilghman, Frisby, Jr., A106a
Tim, Adam, A24b
Tollinger, Peter, A60b
Tookman, Joseph, A67c
Towson, Jacob T., B153a, B154a
Towson, W. William, B153a, 154a
Towson, Williams, A107a
Troup, Sally, B102b
Trueman, Isabella, B147b
Trueman, John Matthew, B147b
Trueman, Joseph Lake, B147b
Trueman, Mary Elizabeth, B147b
Trueman, Samuel Lake, B147b
Trueman, Susan, B147b
Truman, Peter, B50c
Turner, Edmund H., B83b
Turner, Henry, B146a
Turner, Hercules, B146b
Turner, Hester, B166b
Turner, Jacob, B52b, B129c
Turner, William, B52b, B129c
Twine, Levi, B120b
Vachel, A38a
Van Ear, Marie, B96b
Van Lear, John Jr., B57c, B65a

Van Lear, Mary, B57c
Van Lear, William, B8a
Varner, Anthony, B64a
Vermont, Windsor, A24a
Verner, Hannah, A55b, B124a
Verner, James Edward, B124a
Vernor, Hannah, B121a
Virginia, A21b, A24a, A27a,
    A35b, A77b
    Charles Town, A94a
    Jefferson County, A61b
    Lee Town, A61a
    Loudon County, A77b
    Richmond, A90b
Wager, Mr., A61b
Wagoner, Eliza Jane, B1b
Wagoner, Frances, B136a
Wagoner, George, B88a
Wagoner, Henry, B25a
Wagoner, John, A83a, B45c
Wagoner, Sarah, B106c
Wagoner, Sophia, B6b
Wagoner, Thomas Calvin, B1b
Walker, Catharine Ellen, B171c
War of 1812, A24a
War, Revolutionary, A8a
Washington, DC, A28a, A22a,
    A25b, A42b
Washington, Alfred, B87a
Washington, Arthur, B151a
Washington, Benjamin, B162a
Washington, Catharine, B143b
Washington, Elie, A73a
Washington, George, A62b
Washington, Jacob, B61c
Washington, James, B62a
Washington, John H., B32d
Washington, Joseph, B87a
Washington, Joshua, B112a
Washington, Laura, B87a
Washington, Louisa, B87a
Washington, Manjelic, B87a
Washington, Mary Ann, B87a
Washington, Mary Catharine,
    B143b
Washington, Mary Ellen, B87a
Washington, Rosanna, B110b
Washington, Rozetta, B80c

Watkins, Thomas, B133b
Watson, Mary Jane, B170c
Watts, Charles, B39a
Watts, David Henry, B117a
Watts, John Dorsey, B117a
Watts, Josiah, B117a
Watts, Lewis Calvin, B117a
Watts, Matilda, B177a
Watts, Michael, B109a
Watts, Nancy, B149a
Watts, Sarah Elizabeth, B117a
Watts, Sarah, B109b
Watts, Sealy, B58a
Watts, Thomas Gohean, B117a
Waugh, Archibald M., A20b
Webb, George, A103b
Weis, William, A86b
Welch, Catharine, A102b
Welcome, Jacob, A80a
Wellmore, William, B125a
West Indies, A26c
West Virginia
    Berkeley County, A60a, A61a
    Charles Town, A94a
    Harpers Ferry, A61b
    Lee Town, A61a
    Jefferson County, A61b
Wever, Caspar W., B11b,
    B31a, B31b, B40b, B160a
Wever, Caspar, A61a, A61b
White, Ann Eliza, B169c
White, Campbell, B149b
White, John, B139a
White, Martha Ann, B164b
White, Rev. John Campbell, B139b
Whiting, Sarah, B106a
Wicks, Terry, B38d
Williamsport, Maryland,
    A27a, A30a, A66a, A67c,
    A68b, A88a, A103a, B41a
William Henry, A70a, B165b
William Lee, B119c
Williams, Aaron, B53b
Williams, Amanda, B116c
Williams, Edward E., A28b
Williams, Edward G., A28b
Williams, Eliza, B1b
Williams, Elizabeth, B116c

Williams, Harriett, B15a
Williams, Henry, B55b, B81c,
    B116c
Williams, Jane, B116c
Williams, John, B116c, B144b
Williams, Margaret Elizab., B173b
Williams, Mary F., B84c
Williams, Mayberry, B116c
Williams, Nathan, B58c
Williams, Samuel, B121b, B129b,
    B143a, B51a
Williams., A62a
Williamson, Henry, B43c
Wilson, David, A8a
Wilson, Isaac, A93a
Wilson, May, A44b
Wilson, Nancy, A44b
Wilson, Robert, A27a, A30a
Windsor, Vermont, A24a
Wingert, Philip, A42b
Winkley, Mary Ellen, B124b
Winkley, Mary, B5a, B124b
Winkly, Milly, B130a
Winnie, B74a
Winters, Daniel, B93b
Winters, Polly, A105b
Wise, Elizabeth, A96a
Wise, Nancy, A96a
Witmer, Benjamin, B101b
Witmer, Henry, A24b
Wolf, John, A77b
Woltz, Elie, B113b
Worthy, Frank, B3a
Wright, Lewis, B16b
Yates, Charles, A94a
Yoe, Benjamin, B11a, B57b
Young, Dr. Samuel, A73b
Young, Elias, A85b
Young, Ellen, B81a
Young, James, A7b, A33a
Young, Lucy, B142a
Young, Rachel, A15a, A64a
Young, Rebecca, B172a
Young, Samuel, A7b, A15a, B41a
Young, Sarah, A66a
Younker, Mary Jane, B118b
Zellar, Jacob, A100b
Zeller, Samuel, B120b, B174a